Peace is Everything

World View of Muslims
in the Senegambia

INTERNATIONAL MUSEUM OF CULTURES

Publication Number 28

C. Henry Bradley
Series Editor

William R. Merrifield
*General Editor
Academic Publications Coordinator*

Peace is Everything

World View of Muslims in the Senegambia

David E. Maranz

International Museum of Cultures
Dallas, Texas
1993

Copyright ©1993 by the Summer Institute of Linguistics, Inc.
Library of Congress Catalog Card No. 92–83905
ISSN: 0–0895–9897
ISBN: 0–88312–816–0

Printed in the United States of America
All Rights Reserved

No part of this publication may be reproduced, stored in a retrieval system, or transmitted in any form or by any means—electronic, mechanical, photocopy, recording or otherwise—without the express permission of the Summer Institute of Linguistics, Inc., with the exception of brief excerpts in magazine articles or reviews.

Copies of this and other publications of the International Museum of Cultures may be obtained from:

International Museum of Cultures
7500 West Camp Wisdom Road
Dallas, Texas 75236

Jàmm ci la lépp xejj

"Everything is contained in Peace"

—Wolof proverb

The cover drawing is by Michael Harrar.

Peace is symbolized by the palaver tree.
In the shade of this tree elders meet for friendship
and village business. Their highest purpose
is to serve as justices of the peace.

To my mother,
who whetted my appetite
for knowledge

Contents

Preface xiii
Acknowledgments xv

1 Introduction 1
   Statement of the Problem 1
   Purpose and Hypothesis of the Study 3
   Methodology 4
      Data Collection 4
      Analysis 6

2 Background 9
   The Senegambia and Its Peoples 9
      Social Context 9
      Current and Historical Background 15
      Religious Background 18
      Implantation of Islam 20
   The Study of Islam 25
      Background 25
      Approach to Islam in This Study 28
   A Selective Review of World View Study 30
   An Eight-level Model of World View 35
      Definitions of World View 35
      Cultural Behavior 39
      World View Assumptions or Deep Levels 39

	Themal Propositions	49
	Thematic Range	54
	Metathemes and Ethnoscience	55
	Culture versus World View	59
3	Metatheme 1: Personal, Transcendent Peace	61
	Theme 1: Alliances Needed	62
	Supernatural Beings	63
	Souls of the Dead	64
	Human Intermediaries	64
	Saints	75
	Subtheme 1-A: Peace, in Accordance with Laws	76
	Subtheme 1-B: Man's Role to Initiate Action	78
	Subtheme 1-C: Masters of the Seen and Unseen	95
	Theme 2: Peace is a Consequence of Harmony	99
	Subtheme 2-A: Interior Radiance of Peace	101
	Subtheme 2-B: Consequences of a Breach	106
	Theme 3: Harmony with Established Laws	109
	The Laws That Govern the Exterior Life	111
	The Laws That Govern the Interior Life	112
	Subtheme 3-A: Fullness of the Soul	113
	Subtheme 3-B: Experience of Personal Peace	119
	Theme 4: Spiritual and Material Blessing	125
	Socioeconomic Dynamics	125
	National Economics	128
	Minimizing Risk	129
	Living for Appearances	130
	Consequences	130
	Concept of Prosperity	131
	Theme 5: Laws of Cosmic Balance	134
4	Metatheme 2: Peace Achieved by Means of Power	139
	Introduction to Peace, Happiness, and Success	139
	Peace through Assertion versus Peace through Submission	140
	Description of Peace, Happiness, and Success	143
	Explanation, Prescription, and Control of Destiny	145
	Theme 1: Understanding and Controlling Events of Life	146
	Explanation and Prescription	146
	Knowing the Future	152

Explanation and Preconditions	153
Elements of Explanation	155
Elements of Prevenient Action	156
Theme 2: Knowledge of Future Destiny	159
Elements of Control: Self-increasing and Other-decreasing	160
Theme 3: Protection through Esoteric Power	163
Charmed Elements: Amulets and Talismans	164
The Prosperity Genie	166
Esoteric Control over People	168
Imposition of Will over Others	171
Success in Social Competition	171
The Transfer of Evil	172
Recapitulation of Explanation, Prescription, and Control	178
Complementary Distribution of Practitioners	178
Religious Symbiosis	189
5 Pilgrimage to Touba, the Sacred City of Senegal	193
World View in Real Life	193
Pilgrimage in Sufi Islam	195
Pilgrimage in the Senegambia	199
Amadou Bamba, the Saint	203
The Magal, or Pilgrimage	210
Introduction	210
Theoretical Framework and Thesis	210
Description of the Magal	211
The Matrix	215
Analysis of the Magal as Ritual and Symbol	220
Some Observations about the Magal	221
The Magal and Senegambian World View	221
Metatheme 1	222
Metatheme 2	223
Metatheme 3	225
Metatheme 4	226
Metatheme 5	227
Metatheme 6	230
Metatheme 7	231
Metatheme 8	233
Conclusions	236

Appendix 1 Pronunciation Guide for Wolof 239
Appendix 2 Glossary of Senegambian Words 241
Appendix 3 Senegambian World View Propositions 249
Appendix 4 Resumé of Senegambian World View 257
Appendix 5 Ontological Absolutes 259
Appendix 6 Selected Senegambian Taboos 261
References 265
Index 285

Preface

Living in a foreign culture can be by turns fascinating and frustrating. Much of the fascination comes from those things that are different yet understandable. Food often fits into this category. In Senegal the dish *yaasa* is an example. It is a fish or meat dish with a lemon, onion, and spice sauce—simple, delicious, and understandable. But not all is easily understandable, for some of the most visible elements do not seem to fit together or make sense. For example, how is one to understand the many mosques, or the diviner and her customers who almost habitually block the entrance to the post office, or the little picture badges worn by many people? How do the seemingly disparate elements of daily life fit together? Or *do* they? How does the culture work?

This study began with such fascinations and frustrations. Having the opportunity to live and travel within the Senegambian region[1] for several years, I was able to enjoy the fascinations while systematically attempting to reduce the frustrations by gaining an anthropological understanding of how the culture worked.

My first purpose was to achieve as comprehensive an understanding of the culture as possible. The second purpose was to attempt to describe the results so that others, less fortunate than I, might also be fascinated by a rich, complex, and hospitable region of Africa.

---

[1]For a definition of the area contained in the Senegambian region, see the first paragraph of chapter two.

Acknowledgments

Several organizations and many individuals contributed to this study. First of all, I acknowledge the constant support of my interest in increasing my knowledge and understanding of Senegambian culture provided by the international administration of the Summer Institute of Linguistics (SIL). The encouragement of Africa Area Director, Dr. Frank Robbins, was of critical importance to my undertaking a study program of which this volume is a part. Without the overall SIL support and the freedom provided me, this study would not have been possible.

The government of Senegal freely provided the legal status needed by a foreign researcher to work in the country. From 1982 to 1984, the Secretariat for Scientific and Technical Research graciously provided me with authorizations which were always happily supported by regional and local officials. Their welcome to my numerous research trips greatly facilitated my efforts. From 1984 to 1990 my work, as well as that of all SIL personnel, was carried out under a protocol signed with the Ministry of Social Services and the Ministry of National Education. Mr. Frédéric Badiane, Director of the Department of Literacy and Basic Education, kindly and promptly supplied me with any needed authorizations and with his encouragement. I give him special thanks.

Of the many Senegambians who answered countless questions and patiently explained and then reexplained their cultural viewpoints to my foreign ears, I owe special recognition to Mr. Oumar Diallo. He served as my part-time research assistant from 1984 to 1987, and full-time for almost two years during the 1988-1990 period. His profound understanding of Senegambian culture and Senegambian Islam and his ability to articulate complex concepts made him an especially valuable associate, as well as friend.

Many other Senegalese provided hospitality, openness about their culture and deeply held beliefs, and even interest in many of the fundamental issues of life I was trying to understand. Their never-failing help and patience made my work enjoyable. I trust that the analyses, which are strictly my own, accurately reflect what they so patiently tried to help me understand.

I owe my mentor and committee a large note of appreciation. These are: Earl E. Grant, James O. Buswell III, James P. Dretke, and C. Henry Bradley. They provided great freedom which allowed me to proceed wherever my interests and the data took me. I hope they will find that this has brought positive dividends.

Thanks are expressed to Corinne Armstrong for her sharp editorial scrutiny of the entire manuscript. My sister, Mrs. Bonnie Grindstaff, brought her professional editorial expertise and fine-tooth comb to the long editorial task; I am extremely grateful. Dr. Henry Bradley, Editor of the International Museum of Cultures Publications, not only ably looked after the final editing but throughout the research and writing provided me with invaluable suggestions and encouragement. Without these contributions, this writing project could not have been carried to term.

I need to underline that the support of my wife, Louise, and my children has been constant and very sustained, as this project covered a period of several years. My wife's support and encouragement have been the key ingredients that have finally seen the project to completion.

1
Introduction

Statement of the Problem

Muslim peoples and their religion, Islam, have long been the subject of much scholarly research and writing. These works typically have focused on one of three major facts of Muslim society: (1) orthodox Islam, (2) Sufi Islam, or (3) Islam as a folk religion. Examples could be cited ad infinitum, but only a few are mentioned here.

H. A. R. Gibb (1975) and Fazlur Rahman (1979) are examples of critically recognized, widely read studies of orthodox Islam written from a classical point of view. They describe Islam principally as a set of established beliefs and practices that are followed by Muslim peoples everywhere.

Sufi Islam is a subset of Islam and is spread throughout most of the Muslim world. Sufi Muslims practice orthodoxy plus various particular forms of Sufi mysticism. Many studies have focused on this expression of Islam that centers on divinely gifted men and their brotherhoods of followers. See Arberry (1950) and Lings (1971).

Scholars of Orthodox and Sufi Islam alike tend to minimize regional and local varieties of the Muslim faith, especially the widespread and pervasive nonorthodox practices found all across the Muslim world. Such practices may be mentioned or even briefly described, but they are presented as exceptional, or even as deplorable, aberrations.

The scholars who have examined Islam as a folk religion can be divided into two subgroups. First are anthropologists, folklorists, and specialists in folk religion. These specialists tend to produce broad, general studies with the Muslim elements described as part of the religious aspects of the cultures or else as specialized treatments of religious phenomena.[2] The second subgroup is comprised of Christian missiologists who study Muslim society and religion with the goal of determining implications for the enterprise of Christian mission.[3]

Yet a fourth, synthetic, approach is followed by many Africanists and Arabists.[4] In these studies, societies and religions are treated in their broad contexts, but examples are taken from a whole region or even from all of Islamdom; general patterns may be clarified in their syntheses but at the expense of a detailed understanding of Muslim society and praxis as found in any one place. This critique also applies to most missiological studies. Zwemer and Musk alike provide many examples of the practices of folk Muslims over a wide area (Zwemer of the whole Muslim world and Musk largely of the Middle East), but these examples have limited value in helping the reader understand how a particular Muslim society functions as a complete religious system.

Hence, a major aim of this essay is to examine one Muslim society and its beliefs without preconceived ideas or definitions as to what is Islamic, or proper, or deplorable. The major goal is to gain an understanding of this Muslim society and belief as a system, attempting to identify the strands of which it is composed and how these strands are integrated into one whole. Through this analysis it is expected that the relationships, interdependencies, and complementarities between the subsystems (the strands) will be clarified. Thus, Islam will be revealed a posteriori for what it means in the local context whether or not that accords with a priori definitions that could be imported and applied from classical studies.

An anthropological world view approach is followed, as that is thought to provide the means of arriving at an understanding of the assumptions and the structures upon which the whole culture—including beliefs and practices—is based, whether secular-neutral, Islamic, Sufi, or traditional.

---

[2]Examples are Schaffer and Cooper (1980) and Stenning (1959).

[3]Early missiological works include those of Zwemer (1920, 1939). A modern treatment is provided by Musk (1989).

[4]Examples are Monteil (1980) and Trimingham (1959b).

Introduction

Purpose and Hypothesis of the Study

The purpose of the study is to examine a whole, living Muslim society, without a priori definitions as to what constitutes a Muslim belief system, and how it functions in the lives of ordinary people.

This purpose leads naturally to the main hypothesis: In Senegambian Muslim society, orthodox Islam, Sufi Islam, and African traditional religion constitute one coherent religious system rather than three separate or parallel systems.

To what extent and in what ways the system is one will be clarified in the essay. But, even if it is shown to be a unitary system, a further question needs to be addressed: what kind of system? This can be clarified with two analogies. Both ropes and rivers are systems, but of different kinds. A rope of three strands, for example, is not so unified that its strands cannot be separately identified. In contrast, a river with three sources feeding into it becomes so unified that the sources completely lose their separate identities. Islam in the Senegambia will be seen to be more analogous to the rope, with its strands bound together as one yet not completely inseparable from the whole. The three-stranded rope is made up of Islam, Sufi Islam, and African traditional religion. Each strand is visible and definable, yet together they are clearly parts of one whole social and religious system. At the deepest level there is only one world view, not three.

In chapter two, Senegambian peoples and history are reviewed, including the implantation of Islam in the region. Classical, orthodox, and anthropological approaches to Islam and Islamic society are contrasted.

The anthropological study of world view is reviewed, focusing on the works of Redfield, Opler, and Kearney. Then, since the previous approaches to the analysis of world view are found to be inadequate for the purposes of this essay, a new model is developed, modifying and extending the concepts developed in previous work. The new model is called the EIGHT-LEVEL MODEL.

Previous world view studies have tended to focus on one or a few of the main themes of a culture. The eight-level model takes the whole breadth of a culture into consideration. Previous studies have recognized that world view deals with assumptions, but have not systematically sought to formulate them as a complete, coherent set. And few, if any, studies have sought to describe and analyze a whole cultural system on the basis of its world view.

World view is a complex matter, and this essay makes no claim of being the last word on the subject. It is presented, however, as a tool that may be usefully applied to the analysis of any culture, certainly not just those that are Muslim.

In the eight-level model, the concept of metathemes is developed. In chapter three, the first metatheme is described and analyzed. It deals with the quest for personal transcendent peace and includes what are labeled THEMES and SUBTHEMES which operate at lower levels of abstraction.

The description and analysis of metatheme two is the subject of chapter four. This metatheme is an extension of metatheme one but focuses on peace that can be achieved by means of the appropriation of esoteric power.

The last chapter of the essay shows how Senegambian world view operates and is seen in the events of real life. The major event that is treated in detail is the Magal, the annual pilgrimage to the city of Touba in central Senegal. Two anthropological analyses are provided. The first follows a symbolic approach. It is then contrasted with a world view approach based on the eight-level model.

A concluding section ties together the major threads of the essay.

Methodology

Data Collection

The fieldwork for the essay was carried out from early 1982 to 1987, for three months in early 1989, and from February 1990 to mid-1991. During the 1982 to 1987 period, fieldwork alternated with administrative responsibilities. My administrative work, however, included cross-cultural language research projects and took me to all parts of the Senegambia. It involved contacts with a wide range of peoples, from high government officials to rural villagers. Hence, it was largely related to the subject matter of the essay.

The initial fieldwork was carried out among the Serer of central Senegal during the 1982 to 1983 period when I made repeated research trips to Diakhao, a historically and culturally important village. In the 1983 to 1984 period my research trips took me to the area of the Palor people, some thirty miles east of Dakar. Palor is one of the Cangin languages (Grimes 1988:300). Virtually all adult Palor are bilingual in Wolof.

Introduction

The most intensive research was carried out during the 1989 to 1991 periods. During most of this time my main residence was in Dakar. The principal exception was five months in early 1991 when my wife and I lived in a small Wolof village about thirty-five miles northeast of Dakar.

A number of Senegalese men in their twenties and thirties provided intensive long-term assistance, directly as knowledgeable informants and as researchers themselves, frequently traveling around the suburbs of the city where Senegambian peoples are constantly on the move to and from all the urban and rural areas of the region. They also traveled to villages in the near hinterland, within a few hours' travel from the city. On these excursions they interviewed many people, usually eliciting and recording open-ended answers to questions we had worked out together. Some of the questions were derived from two questionnaires which related to immediate and life values. On numerous occasions an associate and I made research trips together.

A further comment on the questionnaires is needed. I had intended to administer them to a significant population sample, but found resistance in two directions. One, Senegambians preferred to give answers to serious matters in a group atmosphere of discussion and consensus, rather than in a situation demanding an individual response. Two, my assistants strongly resisted using the questionnaires with strangers as it seemed to them the questions were intrusive and personal, going beyond the bounds of polite discourse.

In spite of these problems, the effort of developing the questionnaires was worthwhile as it involved ascertaining and discussing the important concerns, values, and even beliefs of members of the culture. The questionnaires were administered to some twenty people of varied ethnic origins, educational backgrounds, and ages. The sample was too small and heterogeneous to provide the basis for a valid statistical analysis; hence, responses have not been explicitly included in the study.

All my associates spoke at least three languages; one spoke seven. One had worked for many years at the University of Dakar as a researcher for several social scientists. Most of my work was carried on in French, as my Wolof was never developed to the point of carrying on monolingually in that language. Hence, I always used either bilingual (French plus another Senegalese language) informants and/or had an assistant translate and transcribe recorded interviews and texts. Most were then entered into a computer and cross-indexed for relatively easy access to all of the material.

The data obtained were primarily from the Diola, Lebou, Saafi, Serer, Tukolor, and Wolof ethnic groups.

Men were the source of almost all of my information, although there were a few interviews with women healers, and some data were reviewed with women. I have already stated that all my research associates were men. Hence, on the whole, the essay represents men's viewpoints. To what extent those of Senegambian women might differ I cannot say, although I never found indications that women's culture was different in significant ways. This is an admitted gap in the study, and one that should be filled in the future.

Besides the primary data, I had many excellent secondary sources available. The researcher working in Senegal has a great advantage over those working in many other parts of Africa. Many Senegalese, European (primarily French) and American anthropologists, historians, linguists, geographers, and other specialists have studied and published much material based on Senegambian data. Many of their works are cited in the study. Two departments of the University of Dakar, the Institut Fondamental de l'Afrique Noire (IFAN) and the Centre de Linguistique Appliquée de Dakar (CLAD) have published many invaluable works over the decades. The Nouvelles Editions Africaines, a publishing house based in Dakar and Abidjan, and other smaller publishing houses also have made accessible many fine volumes on subjects of special Senegambian and regional interest.

Analysis

The analysis of the large quantity of personally collected data plus that of the many secondary sources was carried out principally with the assistance of Mr. Oumar Diallo. Mr. Diallo was found to have a wide and deep knowledge of the culture and, in particular, of people's religious beliefs and practices. He is the epitome of the cultural thinker as described by anthropologist Paul Radin (1957). In addition to his natural gifts, Mr. Diallo has an indispensable family background. His family is descended from old *toorobbe* stock, which provided leadership for all the major West African jihads of the 18th and 19th centuries (Clarke 1982:82). His father was a *muqàddam* of the Tijani Sufi order. His mother's kin are well-known in the Senegal river valley for their esoteric knowledge. Hence, from an early age Mr. Diallo was steeped in Islamic, Sufi, political, and traditional subjects.

Introduction

The reader may well question, when reading chapters three and four, how the author arrived at his formulations of the sixty-three themes and the ten ontological absolutes. The process consisted of several steps. A list was made of the widest possible types of cultural behavior from all domains of life including religious phenomena, economics, social relations and organization, geography, history, politics, and education. Then an iterative process was begun to determine which behaviors could be related to other behaviors. That is, all these behaviors were grouped together from a SENEGAMBIAN point of view, avoiding their classification according to a Western scheme of being religious, economic, political, or whatever. This was done by having Senegalese decide which behaviors and other cultural elements had different kinds of relationships in common. From these analyses, further questions were asked, especially why certain things went together and why other things did not. Thus, the process began to reveal the reasons behind the behaviors, the folk and existential assumptions, and the deeper levels of the culture. These concepts and terms are discussed in the relevant sections of the essay.

The process was deductive, iterative, and intuitive. Lists of behaviors were made and categorized, then re-sorted, and the process begun again until patterns emerged, and until the process seemed to have reached its limits with what I call "level eight," or the deep level assumptions of the culture. Although this analysis was largely carried out by Mr. Diallo and me, we both consulted other Senegambians to test our ideas and tentative results. The formulations of the themes and ontological absolutes were reviewed to a greater or lesser extent with more than twenty Senegambians from several ethnic groups, educational backgrounds, age groups, and other variable factors. Without exception, I believe, the reactions to the concepts expressed in the themes were quite positive. The final formulations incorporate many changes suggested by these reviewers.

One of the problems in testing world view formulations expressed as an extended series of propositions, as done in this essay, is that it is atypical of the cognitive processes used in Senegambian culture. In terms being used in the field of cross-cultural cognitive studies, my world view formulation is extremely linear.[5] It describes ultimate reality as a series of statements that are claimed to represent reality as conceptualized in Senegambian culture. The Bowens, among others who have studied cognitive styles, have found that West Africans in general think globally rather than linearly. This has nothing to do with mental abilities or intelligence;

---

[5]See Dorothy Bowen (1981) and Earle Bowen (1981).

it is merely a cultural and/or personal preference in conceiving and thinking about reality. But it does relate to the question of testing a long series of concepts with people who seem to prefer to deal with their ideas and beliefs as whole packages, rather than serially in dissected pieces. It is not within the scope of this essay to pursue this subject; it is presented as a cross-cultural epistemological question that needs further research.

The analysis was begun with the goal of revealing the DEEP LEVELS, the organizing basic assumptions of the culture. It is difficult to reconstruct the process in detail as it involved numerous sharp turns, dead ends, and retracing of steps. Hence, it is low in precise replicability. At first glance this may seem to limit the usefulness of the study. I think not, however, as the real value lies in its formulation of Senegambian world view. This is contained in the themes (on three levels) and the ontological absolutes. With these, a high degree of replicability is possible. These world view propositions are totally amenable to comparison with those that could be formulated under different analyses. Thus, the analysis is replicable at the deep levels. This level of testing of validity is much more significant than a mere replication of the particular analytical process that was employed in the study.

2
Background

The Senegambia and Its Peoples

Social Context

The Senegambia is a general, rather than a precisely defined, geographical unit. Peter Clarke (1982:32) defines it as "that area of West Africa which is today covered by the Republics of Senegal, Gambia, Guinea Bissau and the coastal and central area of Guinea (Conakry)." A common, minimum, definition includes simply Senegal and The Gambia (Murdock 1959:265). The latter country is an artificial construction of the colonial era. It is entirely enclaved within Senegal except for a short coastline. Since the 1960s, these have been two independent countries but only one geographical area. In this study the more extensive geographical area is used: Senegal, The Gambia, and their cultural and geographical extensions into Guinea-Bissau and Guinea (Conakry). See figure 1 for a map of this region.

Many historical studies have focused on or included Senegambian peoples and their interaction with Arabic, Islamic, European, and other African civilizations.[6] A considerable number of anthropological studies also have been carried out on Senegambian peoples and cultures, which

---

[6]Examples are Behrman 1970, Clarke 1982, Colvin 1972, Cruise O'Brien 1975 and 1979, Klein 1968, Leary 1970, Magassouba 1985, Mark 1985, and Quinn 1972.

Fig. 1. Map of the Senegambian region of West Africa

Background

have provided an invaluable wealth of scholarship and greatly aided the more specialized approach of the present study.[7]

In this essay the conceptual system, or world view, of the dominant Islamized peoples of the Senegambia is examined. Major goals of the study are described as follows:

> *A broad cross section of African Muslim society is examined from a world view perspective.* A world view approach is taken in an attempt to get beneath the surface features of a particular Islamic society, to which the observer can all too easily attribute stereotypic understandings of Islamic culture and religion.

The generalized, standard Islamic definitions and explanations are inaccurate and misleading if applied directly to many particular Senegambian cultural facts. This problem of ascertaining the real meanings of universal Islamic forms and, in particular, ascertaining the meanings for African Muslims, is succinctly explained by J. Spencer Trimingham (1980:55): "In the Islam of Africa as in African religion, whilst ritual and practice are fixed, the content and meaning of the ritual remains vague."

Barbara Tedlock (1983:238), in her study of Catholic-Indian religion in Guatemala, articulates a very similar problem, and the remedy:

> In order to see and describe with new eyes the meaning of what was occurring in the religious life of this community during that period [1975–79], I found it necessary to suspend what Husserl called the "natural attitude" and set aside, or "bracket," the raw data of immediate sense experience—for example, the observation of persons burning copal incense at a mountaintop altar dedicated to a saint. For... naive empiricism leads only too quickly to "common sense" explanations for these actions. In this case the easy way out is to conclude that these people are either Catholics, but "folk" Catholics, or else that they are part of a grand syncretistic Christo-pagan religion that has an existence all its own. This kind of explanation for social action avoids the difficult question of the *intentionality of the action, the question of its meaning, for the actors.* [italics mine]

---

[7]These include Ames 1953, Cottingham 1969, Dilley 1984, Diop 1965, 1981, and 1985, Gamble 1957, Girard 1984, Gravrand 1983, Irvine 1973, Mercier and Balandier 1952, Nolan 1986, Pollet and Winter 1971, Schaffer and Cooper 1980, Simmons 1971, Thomas 1959, Trincaz 1981, and Wane 1969.

The present study is aimed directly at these questions of intentionality of cultural action and its meaning for the members of this Muslim society. World view is by definition the study of cultural assumptions. Such an approach should enable us to come to an understanding of the principles that lie beneath behavior.

A second goal is to examine the data to see if Senegambian culture evidences a dominant theme. The concept of a dominant theme, or organizing principle, is common to the anthropological literature. One of the best known and most discussed is George Foster's "image of limited good." Foster (1965:296) describes this concept as "the dominant theme in the cognitive orientation of classic peasant societies." He then delineates its explanatory power:

> The model of cognitive orientation that seems to me best to account for peasant behavior is the "Image of Limited Good." By "Image of Limited Good" I mean that broad areas of peasant behavior are patterned in such fashion as to suggest that peasants view their social, economic, and natural universes—their total environment—as one in which all of the desired things in life such as land, wealth, health, friendship and love, manliness and honor, respect and status, power and influence, security and safety, *exist in finite quantity* and *are always in short supply*, as far as the peasant is concerned.

A comprehensive model of world view is developed, building especially on the work of Robert Redfield 1941, 1952a, and 1952b; Michael Kearney 1975 and 1984; and Morris Opler 1945, 1959, and 1968. The goal is to achieve greater comprehensiveness and explanatory power than has seemed possible with world view models to date.

Most of the research data collected for the study came from the Wolof, Tukolor, and Serer ethnic groups. Besides these large groups, some data were taken from small groups such as the Lebou, Jakhanke, and Saafi. The principal peoples of the Senegambia are shown in figure 2.

A study of the general world view of such populations spread over a large area is justifiable on the basis of: (1) their being relatively closely related linguistically as members of subfamilies of the Niger-Congo linguistic family, with the great majority being members of the West-Atlantic subfamily, (2) a relatively homogeneous regional culture, (3) centuries of close contact and interaction, (4) two large Muslim ethnic groups, the

Background

Wolof and the Tukolor, having for centuries dominated the region culturally, politically, and religiously, and (5) centuries of exposure to and acceptance of Islam (although the Islamization of the Serer and the Diola has been recent).

Ethnic Group	Population	Percentage Muslim	Niger-Congo Subfamily
Wolof	3,000,000	97	West-Atlantic
Tukolor-Peul-Fula[8]	1,600,000	93	West-Atlantic
Serer	1,000,000	82	West-Atlantic
Diola	600,000	54	West-Atlantic
Mandinka[9]	3,900,000	61	Mande
Soninké[9]	2,450,000	47	Mande

Note: Population figures are from the National Census of 1988 (Mademba Ndiaye 1990), percentages of Muslims from Weekes (1984), and linguistic affiliations from Greenberg (1970).

Fig. 2 The larger Islamized ethnic groups of the Senegambia

Africanist Michael Crowder (1962:76–77) describes the homogeneous character of Senegalese society in some detail:

> The French sociologist Mercier has already remarked the fundamental homogeneity of Senegal's main ethnic groups, which "Whatever their cultural differences and whatever their traditional hostility to one another (which has by no means completely disappeared) all had the same type of social and political organisation."
>
> Of the major groups the Wolof and the Lebou are for all intents and purposes indistinguishable, the Lebou being the Wolof-speaking inhabitants of the Cape Verde peninsula. The Serer are also very closely related to the Wolof, being considered as tribal

---

[8]Weeke's percentages of Muslims applies to the whole West African Fulani, numbering over sixteen million. The Tukolor-Peul-Fula peoples are part of this linguistic complex. In Senegal they are very nearly 100 percent Muslim (Johnstone 1986:367).

[9]Only small minorities of the populations of these widely dispersed groups are found in the Senegambia. No attempt has been made to study the culture(s) of the non-Senegambian populations.

cousins. The Toucouleur, Serer and Fula are traditionally connected, it being held that the Toucouleur are the result of an ancient mixing between the Serers, with whom they have a strong joke-relationship, and the Fulas whose language is very close to their own. Thus nearly three-quarters of the population have closer historical and ethnic connexions than exist in any other area of West Africa save Hausaland in Northern Nigeria. With the exception of the Serers, of whom a substantial minority is Christian, these people are almost exclusively Muslim. They also tend today to use Wolof as a lingua franca. Even the Diola, from the Casamance, which is in many ways a minority area of Senegal, especially because it is cut off from the north by the Gambia, have strong traditional connexions with the Serer and assert in effect that they are descended from the same ancestor. This leaves only the Mandingo people out of the pattern and as we shall see they do tend to be a minority group in Senegal.

The recognized historian and ethnographer, Henri Gravrand (1983:18), corroborates the relative uniformity of the cultures in his much-researched conclusion:

> The 17 Senegalese ethnic groups come from 3 families. The 3 families were intimately fused into one people 800–900 years ago ... The origins of the ethnic groups, within the 3 families, are one and the same. They have been fused since the 11th and 12th centuries. Thus, for 8 or 9 centuries, there has been but one Senegalese people, perhaps more united by biology and culture than certain peoples of the West, which is a situation not often found in Africa. The totality of the Senegambian people today is founded on a real anthropological and historical unity, that can be verified as far [south] as The Gambia.[10]

The usage of the concept of TRIBE as an accurate characterization of the similarities and differences in African cultures has frequently been questioned. One recent example is cited. Cultural and religious historian Terence Ranger (1983:248) expresses his doubts about the general concept:

---

[10]The translation from the French, here and throughout the essay, is my own unless otherwise noted.

Almost all recent studies of nineteenth-century precolonial Africa have emphasized that far from there being a single 'tribal' identity, most Africans moved in and out of multiple identities, defining themselves at one moment as subject to this chief, at another moment as a member of that cult, at another moment as part of this clan, and at yet another moment as an initiate in that professional guild. These overlapping networks of association and exchange extended over wide areas. Thus the boundaries of the 'tribal' polity and the hierarchies of authority within them did *not* define conceptual horizons of Africans.

Thus, with Senegambian peoples having common origins, relatively close linguistic affinities, long and familiar associations, and remarkably similar cultures, and given the current questioning of the whole concept of Western-derived definitions of tribal units, I believe the search for an understanding of the general, common conceptual system of the Senegambia is justified. If an American world view can be analyzed, given the diversity and size of its people, the same certainly can justifiably be done for the Senegambia. This does not mean that there are no differences in world view between one ethnic group and another. It will be seen, for example, that the Serer give much more emphasis to the man-nature relationship than do the Wolof, but still certain basic assumptions about man and nature are common to both. It does mean that, in this study the search will be made for a general Senegambian world view, parts of which may be a more pertinent reality for one group than for another but which reflect the realities of all the groups studied.

Current and Historical Background

Life in the Senegambia is difficult for a majority of rural and urban dwellers alike. In the rural areas and small towns, there are chronic problems of drought, and some years there even have been famines. There are periodic plagues of locusts. Population pressures and the resultant overuse of farmland have made it increasingly difficult to maintain the fertility of the soil, yet commercial fertilizer is prohibitively expensive. The land is largely deforested, and the scarcity of firewood and charcoal is a growing problem. Many people believe corruption is rampant, from the top on down, in government, in state-run enterprises, and in the political parties. The prices paid farmers for their cash crops have been low, although the government now is seeking to raise them. The cost of such staples and essentials as cooking oil, rice, cloth, and other basic items keeps rising in spite of government subsidies for some basic foodstuffs. Various kinds of illnesses are common, including malaria, leprosy, and many parasites. Medical care is limited and of poor quality for those who cannot afford private care.

Water is increasingly in short supply. In countless villages, wells go dry weeks or months before the scant annual rains replenish the water table. In other widespread areas, the water table is so depressed from long-term drought and deforestation that salt water from the ocean or brackish water from the lowered-level rivers is increasingly invading wells, even some deep in the interior.

In the cities, which are being flooded by a massive exodus from the hinterlands, it is arguable whether conditions are better or worse. Certainly there is widespread poverty. The numbers of unemployed and underemployed people probably exceed the numbers of those that are employed. The water supply to the cities has not kept up with population growth; the scattered public taps which are the only sources of water in poorly developed urban districts are frequently dry.

On the national level, violent clashes have occurred in recent years between Senegal and Mauritania to the North, with hundreds killed in widespread rioting and with violence on both sides of the border. This has had a profound impact inside and outside the country as Senegal had a reputation for being a stable, peace-loving country. Trouble has also plagued Senegal and its southern neighbor, Guinea-Bissau, over oil discovered in an area which each country considered its territory. Even within Senegal a partly latent, partly open secessionist movement has been fermenting in the southernmost part of the country. Terrorist acts have greatly disturbed local populations and the nation as a whole.

To round out this litany of troubles, the Senegambian Confederation, so loudly hailed at its inauguration (see, for example, Kirtley and Kirtley 1985), has now been nullified by the President of Senegal, who was forced to take the action because of obstacles raised by The Gambia (*Africa Confidential* 1989). This has greatly increased tension between Senegal and The Gambia, the latter being an enclave that impedes communication and logistics between the central heartland and the region that has the greatest agricultural potential in Senegal.

This set of facts may seem unduly negative. That is not the purpose of providing them. Senegambian peoples, their societies, and their governments have many outstanding qualities. What is in specific focus are

Background

problems that people have expressed to me as being concerns to them, their families, and society, and some of the strategies they use in dealing with them. If that overall purpose is not understood, the description may appear unbalanced. Thus, these facts describe a significant part of the context of the Senegambia and thereby give some perspective to the large preoccupation of so many people in the search for help from any quarter, including transempirical, or supernatural, help. The clear presumption is that long-term social and economic conditions will be reflected in world view assumptions.[11]

The economic and national woes briefly summarized above are not the only ones. Social woes also abound in families and in society at large; educational woes, likewise. These problems seem to have had their origins in a turbulent history. Many date back to the precolonial era. Some historians would fix the date of the beginning of present-day woes at the beginning of the widespread turmoil created by slave raiding and the long process of Islamization. Slave raiding was first carried out by or for Arabs and after the early 15th century was dominated by Europeans. The eminent African historian, Basil Davidson (1968:193), summarizes the history in these terms:

> If the economic effects were generally bad, some of the political effects surpassed them. Because the demand for slaves far exceeded the supply of those who actually lived under servile conditions...it was necessary to supply captives. And since African kings and merchants were generally hindered by their own social norms or political expedience from supplying their own people... they could obtain sufficient captives only by warfare or violence. Knowing that without captives they could not hope for European trade, the chiefs...sent...expeditions into the populous inland country. The lords of near-coastal states plundered their tributary peoples for the same purpose. Wars and raids multiplied.

---

[11]The term TRANSEMPIRICAL that is often used in this essay is obviously a culture-bound Western term; certainly to most Senegambians, transempirical forces are looked to for daily help precisely because they have found them to be empirically valid. But the alternative, SUPERNATURAL, has even greater drawbacks as a general term. For instance, what seems perfectly natural to a Senegambian may be considered supernatural to a Westerner. In any case these two terms will be used, along with a third, SUPRAMUNDANE, to refer to beings and forces that are not normally discernible to the senses.

Religious Background

The religious context also has had a tumultuous past. Islamization was brought about largely as the result of jihad of the sword or a reaction against colonial conquest and domination. A lengthy quotation from historian Charlotte Quinn (1972:193) paints a typical picture of events that took place in the Senegambia over a period of hundreds of years:

> Maba, sweeping through the kingdom 'like a comet,' was left without rivals in Salum. Marabouts came in great numbers from both north and south banks of the Gambia, as well as Salum, to join him... Altogether the army was estimated at 11,000 fighting men. Cattle, goods, and supplies were gathered daily from raids in adjoining districts of Salum. A number of towns there were burned ... In March, 1863, several hundred Marabouts crossed the river from Baddibu to Kiang and destroyed several Soninke [pagan] settlements around Tendeba. In April they were followed by Maba himself, bringing with him a large number of warriors. At the time they announced that they intended to carry the jihad to all the river states, to end once and for all the Soninke challenge to their position in Baddibu, to destroy all traditional political structures, and to kill the mansas [kings] and alkalis [rulers] of the Soninke towns... Nevertheless... Maba made no further attempt to consolidate his gains along the Gambia. Fighting continued there for over 30 years under local leadership, but no permanent theocratic structures were created. Although Baddibu remained his base and refuge, Maba's energies were increasingly directed toward the Wolof states, as far north as the Senegal River.

Such crises and sets of crises have been common throughout Senegambian recorded history, beginning in the 11th century. Another social historian, E. LeRoy, writing of the 17th and 18th centuries, could be describing recent decades. He identifies the crises as originating in "the three plagues of the Senegambia: the slave trade, internal warfare and famines" (1982:62).

> The connection between the slave trade, the development of wars between kingdoms and internal raiding, the frequence of famines under difficult climatic conditions... is clearly shown by... P. Curtin, where this author puts into relief... the exportation [of slaves] from the Wolof and Serer coastal kingdoms between 1685

and 1789. This...clearly shows the connection between acts of violence (wars, religious revolutions, coups d'état) and the development...of the exportation of slaves.

Even a superficial reading of the devastating consequences of the wars, famines and slave-trade suggests that there were periods, happily exceptional, where the societies did not even have strength to reproduce themselves. Written accounts of travel...between 1750 and 1760 and between 1780 and 1815...testify to devastated regions and a very real state of misery. In effect, the *ceddo*[12] did not just practice extortion against land holders. In their pillaging they captured young adults and food, even to the extent of not leaving enough for seed for the next planting. Insecurity therefore was a constant factor during the whole period up to the French conquest. [LeRoy 1982:63–65]

These extensive quotations are given to make clear the kind of social environment that has existed in the Senegambia for centuries. Peter Mark (1985) and Francis Leary (1970) describe similar events, conditions, and disruptions for the Casamance region of southern Senegal. Present economic and political contexts are not merely recent phenomena, although many are of a very different, modern nature.

The world view of a people develops over centuries. The basic conceptual assumptions upon which world view is built cannot be quickly or easily changed. So by definition, the deep-level assumptions of a culture must reflect the long-term realities perceived by the people holding the culture. The history, the collective experience, of a people shapes their world view. Whatever the world view of Senegambian peoples, I take as a basic assumption that the widespread, persistent, and traumatic conditions described in these pages have had a profound effect on the world view. In this essay there is only a little opportunity to explore the effects of social history on world view, but some effects are ascribed to it in later sections.

These historical remarks are meant to establish two things. One, that if the world view held by Senegambian peoples seems to see the world as full of immediate problems that need to be overcome, there is ample basis to understand this as being a normal reaction to the reality of their daily lives. Secondly, many of these problems date from centuries back and relate to the collective experience of all the ethnic groups of the region. Hence, they support the thesis that many basic world view assumptions are

---

[12]The caste of warrior-slaves attached to Wolof kings.

shared by all peoples living in it. That these current and historical facts have had a causal relationship to Senegambian world view is not being claimed. The facts are presented to help the reader gain an intuitive grasp of the milieu in which the world view is what it is, however it developed. Our goal is to ascertain the extant world view, not analyze its historical development.

Implantation of Islam

I have divided this history into four periods: (1) peaceful implantation, (2) the jihad period, (3) the colonial period, and (4) postindependence.

Peaceful Implantation. Islam arrived in the area before the year 1041, as the ruler of the kingdom of Takrur, located in the lower regions of the Senegal River, converted to Islam and instituted Shari'a law before his death in that year. This is told by Arabic historian al-Bakri, who wrote that the king had converted the people to Islam. The people of Takrur are those known today as Tukolor, one of the largest ethnic groups of the region. To what extent the people were Muslims, and what kind of Islam they practiced, is impossible to determine. It is difficult even to be dogmatic about the degree to which the Islamization was accomplished peacefully. The history of Islamization in later times, where more data are available, has shown that the historical accounts written by early Arabic-Muslim chroniclers were quite biased, generally overstating the case for Islam (Colvin 1974).

A Portuguese account provides information as of A.D. 1507. The Wolof kings of Jolof were Muslims and they retained numerous marabouts in their courts who had come from North Africa. The marabouts were used in official functions and in making amulets.

To the East, in the kingdom of Mali, whose influence and hegemony extended for many centuries into the Senegambia, Mande-speaking traders, usually called Dyula, took Islam with them all along their extensive trading networks. This started at least by the 13th and 14th centuries and has been a fact in the spread of Islam that has continued to the present time, although the Mali kingdom declined and split into smaller entities and yielded to successor realms.

Two classes or castes of Islamic clerics also developed in the area. One was the Mande-speaking Jakhanke, who originated in what is now the Republic of Mali, but who moved into eastern Senegambia in the late 14th century. They spread over a wide area, establishing strong Muslim communities where Islam had not previously been implanted. They engaged in trade and especially became "identified with a vigorous tradition of Islamic scholarship, education and clerical activity" (Sanneh 1979:1). The Jakhanke did much to spread Islam, by strictly peaceful means, in the eastern Senegambian region.

In contrast, a second caste, the Torodbe of the Tukolor ethnic group, were militant warriors on behalf of Islam. They sought political domination and the spread of Islam, not hesitating to advance their interests by military conquest or holy war. In fact, the Torodbe provided much of the leadership of military jihads all across West Africa, from Senegal to Cameroon, over a period of some two hundred years (Cuoq 1984).

A summary of the position of Islam at the end of the period is given by Clarke (1982:82):

> In the Senegambia, therefore, there was a network of Muslim centres, villages, colleges and schools in the 17th and 18th centuries. The people of the villages looked to the Muslim religious specialists for leadership and guidance, and the colleges and schools produced an educated 'elite', some of whom were critical of and challenged the authority of the rulers of the states in which they lived. According to tradition one of these Muslim colleges, Pir Saniokhor, in Cayor in Senegal, produced the leaders of the Muslim revolt which took place in Futa Toro[13] in 1776.

The Jihad Period. Islamic beliefs and practices had become widespread among the Tukolor-Fulani, the Wolof, and the Mande-speakers. By 1673 a Muslim teacher named Nasir al-Din had broken with the regional tradition of spreading Islam by peaceful means. Al-Din came from the lower Senegal river valley area. He launched a military jihad to bring Islamic revival and unite the people in a true Muslim community. The elements of al-Din's reforms included an anti-slave trade provision (in response to the people's increasing opposition to the Atlantic slave trade), which was, of course, an activity carried out by the Christian Europeans. He preached repentance and the need to obey God's law. He said that the end of time was near and the *Mahdi* would soon come to bring justice and

---

[13]The Futa Toro is the region in the central-lower Senegal River valley that is home to the Tukolor people. It partly overlaps with the ancient region of Tekrur.

the triumph of Islam. A large following resulted, and al-Din gained control of several kingdoms in northern Senegal.

Martin Klein, a specialist in the history of the Senegambia, describes four "processes of social and economic change" that had the greatest effect on political, religious, and economic development of Senegambia during the time of most intensive encounters between it and European nations, that is, between 1650 and 1900. These were: (1) the trans-Atlantic slave trade; (2) the growth of legitimate commerce; (3) the incorporation of African political systems into European spheres of influence, which led to conquest and new political orders; and (4) as expressed by Klein (1972:419):

> The eruption of tensions and conflicts, which had long existed in Senegambian society, in a Muslim revolution led by a series of charismatic religious leaders during the latter part of the (19th) century. The victory of Islam became most clear after the colonial conquest, when traditional elites found themselves either completely displaced or forced to operate as agents of the French.

Klein (1972:421) also notes: "It is easier to describe Senegambia's role in the [slave] trade than to describe the trade's effect on Senegambian society." Thus, although the general historical facts can be outlined, this is only half of the story. What people thought, how they perceived and practiced Islam, what long-term attitudes were engendered, and how world view was affected is very difficult to ascertain.

The early reform movement did not last long, but it was significant for being the first of many reform and military jihad movements that involved Tukolor-related leadership. This and other movements became major factors in the spread of Islam in the Senegambia and throughout West Africa. They originated in:

> societies which they believed discriminated against them and their followers, societies, moreover, which experienced the tensions brought about by the Atlantic and trans-Saharan slave trade, the importation of firearms and ammunition, and the growing competition from European powers for control of trade and commerce . . . [Clarke 1982:80]

The Colonial Period. The French conquest began in 1854. The French had long been present but had been satisfied to maintain coastal settlements and trading posts. The last Wolof king was defeated in 1886 (Cruise D'Brien 1971:11, 31). Prior to the French conquest, Islamization largely had been limited to the royal courts where literate Muslims had served as scribes, historians, interpreters, emissaries, practitioners of magical rites, and makers of talismans. The common people remained largely traditionalist (Lewis 1980; Monteil 1980).

With the coming of the Europeans and the disruption caused by their conquests and brutality and with the collapse of traditional, royal authority, the general population turned to the leadership available to it, i.e., the Muslim clerics or marabouts, as they are known in French and even in English. So Islam became the religion of the people.

Even though the extreme pain, turmoil, and humiliation of European conquest were experienced one hundred years ago, they are still vivid in people's minds and are taught to children in school and commemorated in poetry and song. The people were rescued from a chaotic, demoralized situation by Islam and Islamic leaders and they remain grateful. They still identify with their grandfathers and their choice to follow Islam. These factors are very deeply ingrained and have to be taken into account when examining the conceptual system.

One vignette from this period of encounter with the French closes this section. Maba Diakhou Ba, the Torodbe scholar and warrior from northern Senegal previously referred to, launched a jihad of the sword in 1861. He imposed his authority over eastern and central Senegal. His authority was recognized by the French, who were still struggling to gain control of the region. Maba accepted French claims to control trade, but could not accept their claim to political control of the region. A major part of his opposition to the French stemmed from the fact that "he regarded the French as Christians who were opposed to Muslims." In a letter to French governor Faidherbe in 1864, he stated that "he regarded it as his duty to make war on infidels in an attempt to convert them to Islam" (Clarke 1982:142).

Maba wreaked destruction and pillaging over a wide area for some years, attempting to exert political control and the Islamization of all the populations. When, finally, the French saw him as a threat to their goal of controlling trade and commerce, they launched attacks against him, defeating and killing him in 1867.

With conquest achieved in 1886, the French turned to consolidating their realm. In theory, French policy neither favored nor opposed Islam. What the French wanted was cheap raw materials for industry. They wanted, above all, to make their colony pay for itself and to be a profitable venture. Peter Clarke (1982:190) sums up their colonial policy in these terms:

> What the French colonial administration sought was a controlled, a malleable, a pliable Islam that they could twist and bend to serve their purposes. In order to achieve this Muslims were on occasion given special privileges, donations were given towards the construction of mosques, and passages were paid to Mecca. But where there was any hint of opposition, Muslims were harassed, imprisoned or deported.

The net result was that with the countryside pacified, and with many leading marabouts ready to cooperate with the French, Islam grew in extent and in power as it had never been able to do during the centuries of jihads. The Islamization of the great majority of the people became fact. As most of the Islamic leaders were marabouts, Sufi Islam was the form of Islam that became dominant. See figure 3 for Senegalese membership in Sufi orders at the present time.

Sufi Order	Percentage of Population	Number of Adherents[14]
Tijani	51.5	3,354,041
Mouride	29.0	1,888,683
Qadri	13.5	879,215
Layenne	0.5	32,563
Total Sufi adherents	94.5	6,154,502

Note: The Muslim population of Senegal is 94.0 per cent of the total 1988 population of 6,928,405 (Mademba Ndiaye 1990), or 6,512,701.

Fig. 3. Senegalese adherents of Muslim Sufi orders

The Postindependence Period. Senegal's independent governments have continued the basic French policy towards Muslim leaders and the masses of adherents of the orders they lead, even though they are constitutionally secular. This means that the orders are de facto a part of the political system. The government has little means of effectively reaching or mobilizing the rural masses except through the leading marabouts. As Senegal's

---

[14]These numbers are based on the percentages of adherents of the Sufi orders (IGN 1970) applied to the 1988 census figure for the total population of Senegal.

political system is a multi-party democracy (with the party in power never yet losing an election), the political parties depend heavily on the Islamic orders to deliver the vote and otherwise support government policies and programs. This means that favoritism is shown the orders in multitudinous ways and by many means. Membership in an Islamic brotherhood carries more than religious benefits.

The Study of Islam

Background

Islam is typically studied from a classical point of view. That is, the doctrines and practices of the highly educated, literate class of Muslims, and especially of the jurists, theologians, and philosophers, form the basis of study. Western specialists, traditionally called Orientalists, considered this to be Islam. They studied, taught, and wrote about classical Arabic, the history and development of the Islamic civilization, and the basics of orthodox Muslim belief and practice. The specialist continued with detailed study of what are called the sciences, or disciplines, of Islam, among which are *fiqh*, an Arabic term for the study of Shari'a law; *kalam*, scholastic theology; *tafsir*, commentary on the Qur'an; *tasawwuf*, Islamic mysticism; and many more. The development of these Islamic disciplines, given the countless controversies in Islam, its long history, and its wide geographic spread, renders the classical study of Islam a bewildering exercise in arcane doctrines that relate more to academia than to life.

These comments about the classical approach could be applied to any of the historical disciplines, e.g., philosophy, history, or language, where the subject matter consisted of the thought, beliefs, activities, and speech of elites, while almost totally ignoring those of the great majority of citizens and slaves.[15] This approach can be called the top-down approach to scholarship. This characterization is in no way intended as an indictment of such traditional studies, only as an observation to point out how the purposes of this essay are very different from what has been the traditional approach to the study of Islam.

Examples of works following the classical approach can be separated into two groups, introductory and advanced. Introductory works have

---

[15]If this is not clear, one question should serve to clarify the issue: What do classical studies tell us of the beliefs and life of the majority of Greeks of Aristotle's day?

proliferated since the beginning of the Iranian revolution. Examples are Gibb 1975, Hodgson 1974, Jomier 1989, Lippman 1982, Nasr 1975, Rahman 1979, Watt 1962, and countless others. The more recent works, such as Jomier, do contain short sections on the beliefs of the average Muslim, in addition to their introduction to classical Islam.

Examples of more advanced works would be Coulson 1964, Gardet and Anawati 1948, Goldziher 1981, Khadduri and Liebesny 1955, McCarthy 1953, plus countless other monographs and specialized journals with articles in English, French, German, and of course in Arabic.

Another basis for studying Islam is what could be called the anecdotal approach. It developed in part as a reaction to the classical study of Islam when missionary scholars, working in Islamic lands, found that the beliefs and practices of most of the Muslims they encountered were greatly at variance with what had been learned as Islam in classical studies. Samuel Zwemer was a pioneer of this perception of a nonelite Islam, which he called "popular Islam." He wrote *The Influence of Animism on Islam: An Account of Popular Superstitions* (1920) and *Studies in Popular Islam* (1939). Zwemer also started a learned journal in 1910, *The Moslem World*, in which he and other Islamic scholars published papers that endeavored to present Islam as it was found to be believed, practiced, and lived in the real world, from the esoteric subjects of Muslim scholars to the most grossly syncretistic practices of very superficially Islamized peoples.

Although the works of Zwemer (1920 and 1939), Westermarck (1973 originally 1933), and others more recently, e.g., Musk (1984), represent a major step forward in approaching the beliefs and practices of Muslims from the standpoint of praxis rather than of theory, there has been a great tendency in these circles to extract particular beliefs or practices from their social and religious contexts. This tendency results too often in collections and catalogs of cultural elements that are studied as collections of Islamic phenomena and are presented as the universals of popular Islam. Which elements may comprise a particular local belief system, how such elements relate to each other, what they mean in local contexts, and even the specific meanings they have to their practitioners are rather impossible to determine. The reason such collections of decontextualized cultural elements are relatively meaningless is that they are inherently and inevitably symbolic. A business suit may represent simple office attire to an American, whereas to a citizen of a poor country it may represent the ostentatious dress of a much-resented elite. Identical symbols based on different assumptions represent very different values (Firth 1973:56). As an

Background

example, take the recitation of the Qur'an. Although it is a universal feature of the faith, to people who understand Arabic it represents revealed wisdom and instructions from God. The same recitation for many Muslims who do not understand Arabic may represent more the use of a text believed to be imbued with magical powers than a revealed teaching. Therefore, given the multitude of meanings given worldwide to the universal forms, the study of Islam out of its local contexts may be misleading. Form and ritual are emphasized with little control, or even attention, given to belief and content. This emphasis stems from the fact that in Islam the practices are Allah-ordained while beliefs are a personal matter that will only be judged on the Final Day.

The critiques that were made of anecdotal anthropology can well be applied here. Comments made almost sixty years ago by Ruth Benedict cogently point out several of the shortcomings that are still too often characteristic of the study of Islam. If "Islamic" is substituted for her term "primitive"—peoples, mind, and tribe—the application is surprisingly direct:

> In the past twenty-five years the fact of prime importance in anthropology has without doubt been the accumulation of a few full-length portraits of primitive peoples... The best accounts that were available were not the outcome of any purposeful inquiry on the part of students of custom, but of the lucky chances that had brought together a good observer and a striking culture, the records of Sahagun, for instance, or Codrington in Melanesia.
>
> The vast amount of available anthropological material was frankly ancedotal as in travelers' accounts, or schematically dissected and tabulated as in many ethnologists'. Under the circumstances general anthropological discussion of necessity had recourse, as in Tylor's day, to the comparative method, which is by definition anecdotal and schematic. It sought by collecting great series of observations detached from their context to build up "the" primitive mind, or "the" development of religion, or "the" history of marriage.
>
> Out of the necessities of the same situation there flourished also the schools of strict diffusionists who made a virtue out of the limitations of materials at their disposal and operated solely with detached objects, never with their setting or function in the culture from which they came.
>
> The growing dissatisfaction with these two dominant theoretical approaches of what we may well call the anecdotal period of

ethnology has always been explicit in Boas' insistence upon exhaustive study of any primitive culture, and is today most clearly voiced by Malinowski. His vigor is directed against the diffusionist group rather than against the Frazers and the Westermarcks of the comparative method, but in his own work he insists always that anthropological theory must take into account not detached items but human cultures as organic and functioning wholes. He would have us realize that when a museum collection has been installed from the Niam-Niam or a monograph of like type has been published we still know in reality exactly nothing about them unless we know the way in which the arrangement of the house, the articles of dress, the rules of avoidance or of marriage, the ideas of the supernatural—how each object and culture trait, in other words, is employed in their native life. [Benedict 1932:1]

Note her eloquent plea for the study of elements of culture in their setting or function, and that anthropological theory "must take into account not detached items but human cultures as organic and functioning wholes." She concludes by saying that we "know in reality exactly nothing" about a people unless we know "how each object and culture trait ... is employed in their native life." Anthropologists have long since accepted this position, but in Islamic studies such an approach is still too much the exception.

A number of exemplary holistic anthropological studies of Muslim peoples have appeared in recent years. May their numbers continue to increase.[16]

Approach to Islam in This Study

This brings us to the present study and a discussion of the approach to Islam that will be followed in it.

In his Introduction to the compendium *Islam in Tropical Africa*, I. M. Lewis (1980:2–3) describes the need for the sociological study of Islamized African peoples, as follows:

It is ... a fundamental fact that Islam can be analyzed sociologically only within the social context of the actual life and folk beliefs of

---

[16]Some of the outstanding titles that appertain to Africa and the Muslim heartland are: Ahmed and Hart 1984, Berger 1970, Eickelman 1976, Fakhouri 1972, Geertz 1968, Gilsenan 1973, Greenberg 1946, Loeffler 1988, and el-Zein 1974.

living Muslim communities. What is enshrined in the orthodox literary tradition of Islam and usually taken as this religion's essential character is often very differently represented in the concepts and practices which inform everyday Muslim life. Moreover, the method long established in Islamic Studies of tracing the origins and historical development of beliefs and institutions does not necessarily take one very far in understanding their contemporary significance in any given social context of living Islam.

Thus, in this province of Islamic Studies... the final plea must be for more intensive field research on actual Muslim communities. And, for the social anthropologist and sociologist, there is the added challenge that the study of the interaction between traditional pre-Islamic and Muslim beliefs and institutions offers special opportunities for testing the validity of functional hypotheses... Hence the study of Islam in Africa, particularly where Islam and Christianity are competing for new adherents, presents a field full of potentialities for the social scientist and deserves much more rigorous and concerted attention than it has so far received.

This study addresses a number of Lewis's concerns:

1. Islam is studied "within the social context of the actual life and folk beliefs of living Muslim communities."
2. The "concepts and practices which inform everyday Muslim life" are seen to contrast with the "orthodox literary tradition."
3. The historical Muslim "beliefs and institutions" are seen to have limited "contemporary relevance" to the social context of contemporary Senegambian living Islam.
4. An actual Muslim community has been the focus of intensive field research.
5. A great deal of attention is given to the interaction between pre-Islamic and Muslim beliefs and institutions.
6. The region under study is one where Islam and Christianity are still competing for new adherents, although this issue is not in primary focus in the study.
7. In sum, Lewis's call for greater anthropological attention to such a field is the whole purpose of this scholarly endeavor.

An anthropological world view approach is followed in examining the culture of the Muslim Wolof and related peoples. Such an approach seems especially appropriate, as world view studies deal with

> the total perceived reality, or the "world" itself, as it is apprehended and cognitively organized in culturally specific ways. It thus represents an attempt to describe the perception and experiencing of life by peoples of other cultures. [Kearney 1984:32]

Specifically we provide the following original contributions to Senegambian, Islamic, and anthropological studies:

1. Islam, as practiced in the Senegambia, is examined in its context, and especially its context of African traditional religion (ATR).[17] This is designed to meet Benedict's criteria: to give a full-length portrait of a people, to pursue purposeful inquiry, to make observations in their context and cultural setting, and to take a human, Islamic culture as an organic whole.
2. An eight-level model of world view is developed and applied to Senegambian Islamic culture.
3. Senegambian world view is described and analyzed, focusing on one major theme, transcendent peace.
4. The primary themes of Senegambian world view are examined through the institution of religious pilgrimage, a cultural event that is central to the belief system of most Muslims in the region, namely, the annual pilgrimage to Touba, a city in central Senegal.

A Selective Review of World View Study

World view, as a scholarly concept, seems to have originated in Germany. The term *weltanschuung* 'world view' was much used and developed by the influential, empirical philosopher, Wilhelm Dilthey. He used this term as early as 1911, when he wrote *Typology of World-Views*, although it was not published until 1931 in volume eight of his works (Rickman 1979:43). Dilthey published a volume that dealt with *weltanschuung* in 1921 titled *Weltanschuung und Analyse des Menschen seit Renaissance und Reformation* (Hodges 1968:187).

---

[17]As African traditional religion is a term that will be frequently employed, I will use the common abbreviation, ATR.

Background

Dilthey believed that all complete world views:

> invariably contain the same structure. This structure always takes the form of a system in which questions about the meaning and significance of the world are answered in terms of a conception of the world. From this an ideal, a highest good and supreme principles of conduct are deduced. [Rickman 1976:137]

Dilthey defined world view as "the complex of... beliefs and judgments concerning ultimate questions" (Hodges 1968:186). I accept this as a summary definition of world view, but with an enlargement of the scope of the expression "ultimate questions" of the universe. So Dilthey's definition would be revised to read, world view is the complex of man's beliefs and judgments concerning the ultimate reality of all beings, and all existing matter, and all relationships between beings and between beings and matter.

Dilthey developed a typology of world views. His basic types were:

> naturalism, the idealism of freedom, and objective idealism. Naturalism means that one is impressed chiefly by the impersonal order of nature; idealism of freedom, that one gives priority to the unique status of man as a free agent; and objective idealism, that one conceives of the universe as an organic whole. Schools of art, and religious and philosophical systems, can be classified by their conformity to and expression of one of the three main types of attitude or, as may happen, of any combination of these. [Hodges 1968:186]

It will be clear that Senegambian world view is strongly oriented toward objective idealism.

The first use of the term *weltanschuung* in anthropology that I have been able to find is in Malinowski's classic, *Argonauts of the Western Pacific* (1961). In his concluding analysis of the meaning of the kula institution, he (1961:517) writes:

> What interests me really in the study of the native is his outlook on things, his *Weltanschauung*, the breath of life and reality which he breathes and by which he lives. Every human culture gives its members a definite vision of the world, a definite zest of life. In the roamings over human history, and over the surface of the earth, it is the possibility of seeing life and the world from the various angles, peculiar to each culture, that has always charmed

me most, and inspired me with real desire to penetrate other cultures, to understand other types of life.

This study of the world view of the Senegambian has taken part of its inspiration from these words, attempting, along with Malinowski, to comprehend "the breath of life and reality which he breathes and by which he lives" and his "definite vision of the world."

From Malinowski, the trail leads to Sol Tax who seems to have been the first American anthropologist actually to use the term WORLD VIEW. It is employed in his paper "World View and Social Relations in Guatemala," read at a meeting of the American Anthropological Association in 1940 and published in 1941 (Tax 1941).

World view studies in anthropology can be considered to have begun as a theoretical approach with Robert Redfield and some of his students in the 1940s and 1950s.[18] The term world view was not employed in Redfield's early monograph, *The Folk Culture of Yucatan* (1941), but the concept was developed in it as the people's "view of the world around them... the conception of the world and of life" (1941:114). The main world view developmental section of this monograph was later extracted and retitled "The World View of the Yucatecan Maya" in a volume edited by Philip Bock (1970).

Redfield focused on folk societies and primitive world views which he contrasted with modern world views where science has transformed primitive concepts. A major concern of his was to construct a universal world view, an idea which is reminiscent of Dilthey. Redfield (1953:91) wrote, "If world view is universal, it should be possible to say what is true of all world views." He discussed "human universals," "universal sentiments," and "universal culture patterns" (1953:90–91). He isolated features he considered to be universals. These were the concepts of self, other, classification, nature, God, not-man, space, time, and taboos (R. Redfield in M. P. Redfield 1962:270–273). In his 1953 work, additional terms were used: affective and cognitive aspects of experiences and thoughts, cosmology, order/deviation, and values. With all these terms, his goal was to describe universal culture. It is useful to list these categories here as they serve to point out the seminal, broad nature of Redfield's thinking. His writing was largely discursive rather than schematic; hence, although his work has been influential and much referred to by many anthropologists, it has served

---

[18]Redfield 1941, 1952, 1953; and e.g., Mendelson 1956; Guiteras-Holmes 1961.

Background

only to a limited degree as a defined, systematic approach to the study of cultural phenomena.

The principal author continuing the Redfieldian approach in recent decades has been Michael Kearney (1972, 1975, 1984). In his 1975 article, he reviewed the state-of-the-art anthropological approaches to world view theory. His core treatment of world view was based on Redfield's categories, which he presented as seven universal features: self, other, time, space, classification, relationship, and causality. These constitute "a minimum set of universal cognitive categories which could be taken as necessary dimensions of a functional human world view" (1975:249). Thus, the emphasis was changed somewhat from that of Redfield who was seeking a universal world view, to a search for the universal, essential features, or dimensions, that would constitute the fundamental building blocks of all world views. These are closely related, but quite distinct goals. In Kearney's 1984 work, *World View,* he further developed his concepts of 1975, and their application to anthropological studies. It is the only full-length anthropological treatment of world view theory to appear to date.

Although I consider Kearney's work to constitute a major step forward in the theoretical and practical treatment of world view in anthropology, it seems to me his model is of limited use when applied to whole cultures. In his treatment of world view in his 1972 monograph, he applied his universals to limited and selected cultural areas. The same is true in the case studies of ancient Greece, California Indian, and Mexican peasant societies in the 1984 work. As valuable as it is, the model does not easily lend itself, alone, to a culture-wide study, even when all seven of the universal categories are employed.

Why did Kearney not use, and why have other anthropologists not used, the seven universals to build ethnographies? The answer may be because the seven categories are too restrictive, too narrow in focus to serve well in holistic studies.

A simple analogy may serve to clarify what is meant by "element of narrow cultural focus." In the United States, most houses are built using nails as a major, even essential, element of construction. Nails could be called a construction universal. Although they are such a universal, they could hardly serve as the basis for describing or analyzing houses, house architecture, or other holistic treatments of construction. Yet if someone was interested in contrasting frame construction with masonry construction, the place of nails in the former and that of mortar in the latter, could be instructive.

So Kearney's seven categories, although doubtlessly universal components of culture and more particularly of world views, are elements of narrow focus and of limited value to analyses of a general nature. At the same time, they can be very useful in studies that concentrate on unique features of culture or on particular cross-cultural differences.

An example of this is the classic article by Dorothy Lee, "The Conception of the Self among the Wintu Indians" (1959), in which she explains the concepts held by the Wintu concerning two of Kearney's universals, the self and other, although she certainly does not explicitly employ his terms. The Wintus' concept of the self is very different from ours, almost incomprehensibly different. Lee (1959:132) writes:

> In our own culture, we are clear as to the boundaries of the self. In our commonly held unreflective view, the self is a distinct unit, something we can name and define. We know what is the self and what is not the self, and the distinction between the two is always the same. With the Wintu, the self has no strict bounds, is not named and is not, I believe, recognized as a separate unit.

Lee (1959:132) tells us that the Wintu have unidirectional inclusive categories, "so the individual is particularized transiently, but is not set in opposition" to others. So there is no conflict between self and others, no concept of self versus society, but only of self in society.

Although Lee's essay is not explicitly a world view study, it falls within that category and is used by Kearney as such in his short study of California Indians (1984:147–169). Lee examines assumptions of the basic Wintu conceptual system. As outstanding as her description and analysis are of the two universal categories she examines, her approach does not lend itself to a culture-wide study of world view, even if expanded to all seven world view universals. Granted, she informs us of a key Wintu organizing concept, that of unidirectional inclusive categories, which contrasts with the analogous Western concept of mutually exclusive dualistic oppositions. Still, in terms of holistic ethnography, the seven posited universals are too restricted in scope to serve as the basis for full ethnographic descriptions. In Wintu terms, the universals are, as it were, unidirectional categories; that is, they serve admirably in isolating key concepts but not particularly well in clarifying how the culture works as an integrated whole. What is needed for broad-based ethnography, if world view study is to become a useful paradigm in the Kuhnsian sense (Kuhn 1970), is the development of a new model. That is why the eight-level model of world view is developed in the following pages. It is hoped that this model will serve as a framework for world view analyses that can meaningfully, though obviously not exhaustively, be applied to the study of whole cultures.

An Eight-Level Model of World View

Definitions of World View

World view is the study of "the fundamental ways in which all people everywhere conceptually divide up and categorize the phenomena they perceive" (Kearney 1984:37). Kearney (1984:41) further writes that:

> The world view of a people is their way of looking at reality. It consists of basic assumptions and images that provide a more or less coherent, though not necessarily accurate, way of thinking about the world.

Mendelson (1968:576) has carefully defined world view in his article in the *International Encyclopedia of the Social Sciences*:

> World view is one of a number of concepts in cultural anthropology used in the holistic characterization and comparison of cultures. It deals with the sum of ideas which an individual within a group and/or that group have of the universe in and around them. It attempts to define those ideas from the point of view of the individuals holding them, from inside the culture rather than outside... While emphasizing the cognitive aspect of ideas, beliefs, and attitudes, a world view cannot be clearly separated from its normative and affective aspects. Thus, it tends to be confused with such concepts as ethos (relating to values), modes of thought, national character, and even culture itself.

Although there are scores of definitions in the anthropological literature, appeal is made to just one more, one that points to a dynamic, rather than a static, or fixed, nature of world views:

> A person does not receive a world view, but rather takes or adopts one. A world view is not a datum, a *donné,* but something the individual himself or the culture he shares partly constructs; it is the person's way of organizing from within himself the data of

actuality coming from without and from within. A world view is a world interpretation. [Ong 1969:634]

These definitions point out factors that are relevant to the discussion that follows. World view consists of the basic assumptions that are used by a people to interpret, even define, reality. Thus, our search in this study is for the most fundamental assumptions of Senegambian culture. World view study does not evaluate the accuracy of the assumptions of a society. They cannot be evaluated on the basis of accuracy or truth. An assumption is a fact of the culture. Its accuracy can only be either a function of its presence or its absence, or of the correctness of its formulation. The question of it being a "good" or a "bad" assumption is not a part of world view study. The attention is on the culture's interpretation of the world in which it lives. So, to continue with our example of the business suit used above, although to an American the suit was strictly utilitarian clothing, while to the third world peasant it was the dress of an ostentatious elite, we cannot ascertain an objective accuracy of either culture's definition of our assumptions about business suits. For our purposes, accuracy is limited to obtaining a valid inside, or emic (Pike 1967), formulation of concepts in the culture. Other questions that deal with accuracy and verification, such as internal consistencies of world views, will not be dealt with in this study, but see Kearney (1984:54ff.).

World view is ascertained by means of a holistic study of a cultural universe. Again, using the previously cited example of Wintu culture, a world view needs to focus on a broad segment of the culture, not just on the concept of the self. This does not fault Lee, who did not claim to be giving us an analysis of Wintu world view. It also does not fault what might be called partial world view studies. What is meant is that, in the full sense of the term, world view encompasses the entire universe of a culture. This I call THEMATIC RANGE.

The concept of thematic range is in a sense analogous to the anthropological concept of ETHOS. Both concepts deal with the totality of the culture. Ethos refers to "qualities that pervade the whole culture—like flavor..." (Kroeber 1948:294). It is the distillation of the essential quality or qualities of the whole culture, expressed in one word or phrase. Thematic range deals with the whole culture, but in terms of themes that are formulated in particular world view studies. All cultures are assumed to have a full range of world view themes, from themes concerning the cosmos down to themes concerning the individual. Hence, any particular

Background

world view study may include a limited number of themes from the totality of the culture's full thematic range.

Kearney and Mendelson state that world view study emphasizes the cognitive aspects of culture. Kearney (1984:41) uses the terms "systems of knowledge" and "way of thinking" as synonyms of the term world view. But Mendelson considers that world view cannot be separated from its NORMATIVE and AFFECTIVE components. I strongly agree. Taking cognition as an essentially autonomous variable, it seems to me, is an ethnocentric exercise carried on by representatives of a culture that emphasizes rational, logical, cognitive processes.

Even though there is not opportunity to pursue this avenue of thought (ethnocentricity admitted), I point it out as an important area of world view study that needs to be pursued. Talcott Parsons, Edward Shils, and colleagues, pointed out decades ago that human action (human behavior plus cognition) cannot be explained except on the basis of the interaction between human cognition, affectation, and evaluation (1951). Anthropologist Paul Hiebert (1985:30–49) defines culture and world view as being composed of three basic dimensions, the cognitive, the affective, and the evaluative.

Such inclusion of normative and affective dimensions in the concept of world view represents minority viewpoints. I accept that cognition is central to world view but also consider that cognition cannot validly be considered an independent variable of culture. Models that are limited to the cognitive dimensions of world view cannot be considered to be adequately holistic. This proposition applies to the present study.

Kearney (1984:ix) was of the opinion that no comprehensive model of world view had previously been formulated and that his work constituted "a preliminary attempt that I hope will engender further work." It is in this direction of "further work" toward comprehensiveness that the following eight-level model is offered.

There are four basic components in the eight-level model: (1) cultural phenomena, which are composed of the entire range of behaviors in a culture; (2) the deep-level explanations and assumptions that underlie the cultural behaviors; (3) cultural themes organized on three levels of generality; and (4) the thematic range of themes, whether cosmic, social, or naturalistic (see figure 4).

In contrast, figure 5 provides a second version of the same model, showing the three relational categories: organizing principles, surface level, and deep-level supporting causes, corresponding respectively with the three analytical categories: themes, cultural behavior, and world view assumptions. These elements are shown graphically to better reveal how these building blocks of the model fit together.

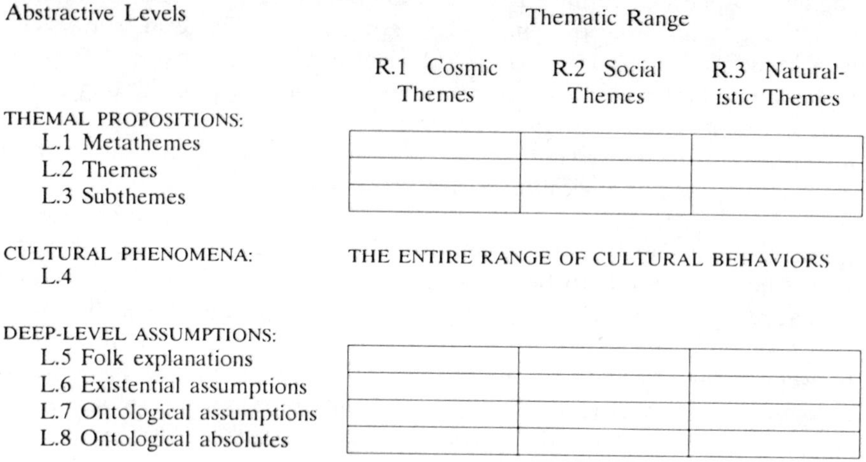

Abstractive Levels   Thematic Range

	R.1 Cosmic Themes	R.2 Social Themes	R.3 Naturalistic Themes
THEMAL PROPOSITIONS:			
L.1 Metathemes			
L.2 Themes			
L.3 Subthemes			

CULTURAL PHENOMENA: THE ENTIRE RANGE OF CULTURAL BEHAVIORS
   L.4

DEEP-LEVEL ASSUMPTIONS:
   L.5 Folk explanations
   L.6 Existential assumptions
   L.7 Ontological assumptions
   L.8 Ontological absolutes

Fig. 4. An eight-level model of world view

Abstractive Levels	Analytical Categories	Relational Categories
Level 1 Level 2 Level 3	Themes	Organizing principles
Level 4	Cultural behavior	Surface level
Level 5 Level 6 Level 7 Level 8	World view assumptions	Deep-level supporting causes

Fig. 5. Major elements of the eight-level model

Cultural Behavior

World view study begins with culture and, empirically, with participant observation of cultural behavior. The term behavior includes visible behavior and mental behavior, or cognition. This is sometimes labeled human ACTION. The study of culture includes material culture as well as immaterial culture, or behavior.

The cover term used for cultural behavior is SURFACE LEVEL culture. This can be thought of as the gamut of cultural subjects as outlined in Murdock's *Outline of Cultural Materials* (1987), which, although it does include categories such as cosmology—number 772,[19] does not deal explicitly with deep-level culture.

World View Assumptions or Deep Levels

One of the bases on which the model is formulated is that world view must be considered on a deep level. This idea is hardly radical but it seeks to make explicit what countless anthropologists have been at least suggesting; yet, as far as I can determine, have not made very explicit and have not explored systematically. Kluckhohn and Kelly (1945:62) report that "Herskovits has said that a culture may be thought of as 'a kind of psychological iceberg of whose totality but a small portion appears above the level of consciousness'." In this study, we are not looking at psychological data, but the analogy of a large part of culture existing below the surface of behavior and conscious thought is applicable to our concept of a culture's deep-levels.

In the anthropological literature, what I am calling the DEEP-LEVEL fraction of culture has had a number of labels applied to it. None of these terms are exactly synonymous, but they do have at least large areas of overlapping meaning. An early formulation was COVERT CULTURE, which is that which is not visible, as contrasted with OVERT CULTURE which is discernible and easily described (Hall 1973:62; Kluckhohn, quoting Linton 1947:217). Other well-known labels were Edward Sapir's "unconscious patterning of behavior" and "deep-seated cultural patterns" (1968:548), and Linton's "core of the culture" (1936:358).

One of the most-used terms is IMPLICIT CULTURE. Clyde Kluckhohn (1944:36) defines it in a way that is helpful to this discussion:

---

[19]This number relates to the coding system of the Human Relations Area Files, as outlined in Murdock 1987.

> Cultures do not manifest themselves solely in observable customs and artifacts. No amount of questioning of any save the most articulate in the most self-conscious cultures will bring out some of the basic attitudes common to the members of the group. This is because these basic assumptions are taken so for granted that they normally do not enter into consciousness. *This part of the cultural map must be inferred by the observer* on the basis of consistencies in thought and action... This is implicit culture. [italics mine]

Kluckhohn (1944:37) then goes on to explain a little of how implicit culture is discovered:

> A factor *implicit in a variety of diverse phenomena may be generalized* as an underlying cultural principle. For example, the Navaho Indians always leave part of the design in a pot, a basket, or a blanket unfinished. When a medicine man instructs an apprentice he always leaves a little bit of the story untold. This "fear of closure" is a recurrent theme in Navaho culture. Its influence may be detected in many contexts that have no explicit connection. [italics mine]

Edward Hall (1976:42) eloquently describes the hidden nature of much of these most significant, even controlling, cultural processes:

> Everything man is and does is modified by learning and is therefore malleable. But once learned, these ways of interacting gradually *sink below the surface of the mind* and, like the admiral of a submerged submarine fleet, control from the depths. The hidden controls are usually experienced as though they were innate simply because they are not only ubiquitous but habitual as well. [italics mine]

The key statements in these quotations have been italicized. The "cultural map must be inferred" by what the observer discerns as consistent patterns of behavior. And factors "implicit in a variety of diverse phenomena may be generalized" as underlying cultural principles. These statements express the essence of the world view study that is carried out in this study. Inferences of implicit culture are made from consistent patterns of behavior in diverse phenomena; these are called world view assumptions. Such assumptions are by definition resident in the deep levels of the culture.

Background

Specifically, the model encompasses four deep-levels with generality increasing with depth, from surface cultural phenomena, L.4, down to ontological absolutes, L.8 (see figure 4). The first deep-level, L.5, is deep only by definition, as it is not much removed from surface behavior. In figure 6 the directions of increasing/decreasing abstractness are shown schematically, with increasing generality up and down from behavior. These abstractions, inferred from behavior, are labeled the ABSTRACTIVE RANGE, or ABSTRACTIVE LEVELS.

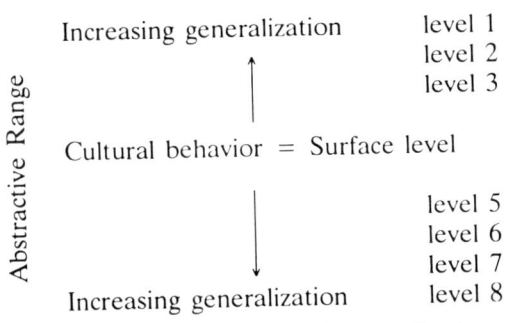

```
                  Increasing generalization      level 1
                              ↑                  level 2
    ⎫                         |                  level 3
    Abstractive Range         |
    ⎬             Cultural behavior = Surface level
    ⎭                         |                  level 5
                              |                  level 6
                              ↓                  level 7
                  Increasing generalization      level 8
```

Fig. 6. Directions of generalization

Folk Explanations. The four posited deep levels are: folk explanations, existential assumptions, ontological assumptions, and ontological absolutes.

As shown in figure 4, the first deep-level, designated level 5 (L.5), is that of folk explanations. If the average man-in-the-street is asked why he does something, or why he believes something, his explanation is called a folk explanation. It is the level of common explanations for cultural behavior. These explanations are specific for specific behaviors, the immediately expressible, conscious purposes that people have, or would provide, to explain their culture.

An example will be taken and followed through on the four deep levels of the model. One of the most common elements of Senegambian culture is the protective amulet. There are scores of terms employed for amulets, corresponding to purposes for their use, physical construction, contents, magical qualities, and the type of religious practitioner that provides them. The most generic term in the Wolof language for this complex of beliefs and corresponding material culture, is *muslaay*.[20] Thus, at the surface level we find *muslaay*. If a Wolof man is asked why he is wearing a *muslaay*, his answer will be a folk explanation, level one. He will probably say either it is to protect him against *cat*, the widely feared evil tongue, or just that it is what his marabout, or Muslim cleric-healer, gave him to carry for protection.

Existential Assumptions. These assumptions are basically the more-or-less nonexpressed purposes that underlie the folk explanations. They are the purposes the ordinary culture bearer would consider to be behind the beliefs and objects of his existence.

Continuing with the example of *muslaay:* If, after learning that the wearer carried the amulet as protection against the evil tongue, he was asked how that protects him, the questioner would receive answers on the level of existential assumptions. Typically, the response would be one or more of the following: (1) My marabout knows about these things, he said it would be effective, and I have confidence in him. (2) The *muslaay* contains a piece of paper on which is written a verse from the Qur'an that my marabout knows has power against the evil tongue. (3) Marabouts have *barke* (*baraka*, A.), which means they have spiritual power to help people. These answers are existential; they are as far as the average person seems to go. They provide sufficient answers for most purposes of life but are far from the deepest level of explanation obtainable by inductive reasoning from a wide range of data.

The example from Navajo culture previously noted would be placed at the existential level. Clyde Kluckhohn found a widespread pattern of not finishing a work which he labeled "fear of closure." Certainly there was more to the pattern than just a simple fear of not finishing work. At a deeper level, this pattern doubtlessly would be seen to fit into their conception of the cosmos or relate to some cause that would have been revealed at a deeper, or greater, level of generality. Kluckhohn saw a pattern which seemed to be sufficient for him. In world view study, one looks for the ontological reasons that lie behind the patterns. The reader will see how this methodology works out with the example of *muslaay*.

---

[20]Throughout the dissertation, a majority of the Senegambian terms used will be from Wolof. Hence, only non-Wolof terms will hereafter be identified, as follows: A. for Arabic, D. for Diola, E. for English, F. for French, L. for Lebou, P. for Pulaar, S. for Serer, Sf. for Saafi. Occasionally (W.) will be used to clarify that a word is Wolof. (This list is repeated in the Glossary, Appendix Two.)

Background

In the Redfield-Kearney approach to world view, the focus is on the existential level. In Kearney's (1984:37) words:

> He [Redfield] asked, What are the fundamental ways in which all people everywhere conceptually divide up and categorize the phenomena that they perceive? Once this universal structure of world view, this metamodel, is established, then the task would be to fill in the content of specific world views of different societies.

This approach focuses on the universals: self, other, time, space, causality, relationship, and classification. To these, I believe, have to be added EMPIRICAL UNIVERSE and TRANSEMPIRICAL UNIVERSE if world view study is to include the full sweep of culture, of what is being called here full thematic range. NATURE would be the natural world and man's relationship with it. The transempirical world would include questions of the supernatural and man's relationship to it. Although Kearney (1984:81–85) deals briefly with the supernatural and religion, he places them within his discussion of classification, which seems to relegate them to a very secondary importance. He also deals with "magical causality" but only in the context of many different concepts of causality. As these areas—of the spirits, of deity, of the spiritual, of concepts of and interaction between man and these elements, of the roles of man in the universe—are so important, even central, to so many cultures of Africa and the world, it seems to me necessary to consider them as universal categories. Although none of the universals are dealt with here in detail, they have all served extensively in the inductive and deductive processing of Senegambian cultural data.

Ontological Assumptions. The ontological assumptions, L.7, are the deepest level of explanation that a philosopher or thinker of the culture would ordinarily articulate. They express the nature of things, proper roles, and ultimate causes conceptualized by the more perceptive members of society. In Africa, the widespread concepts of vital force, or the belief that discontented spirits or ancestors cause certain illnesses, or that the supreme deity created the material universe—all these are examples of ontological assumptions.

Ontological assumptions also include constructs derived or inferred from higher levels of the culture. They relate to fundamental assumptions about reality that are perceived or known by the society, as articulated by the people themselves or by cross-cultural observers.

Continuing with our example of *muslaay,* one finds that the names of Allah (ninety-nine are known) are both powerful and found in the Qur'an. Each name is imbued with specific, magical powers, imparted to it by Allah himself, that can be released through proper technique. Thus, the true marabout, as Allah's appointee in such matters, knows precisely which verse of the Qur'an is necessary to provide the client with the desired power and protection, and prepares the amulet accordingly. To the marabout and his client, these interior meanings of the Qur'an and the names of Allah reflect their most basic assumptions of reality.

Ontological Absolutes. The set of the culture's universal assumptions, that is, those few assumptions that underlie all the culture, all higher-level assumptions, and all levels of themes, are labeled ontological absolutes, L. 8. They are the conceptual and foundational pillars, or assumed ultimate causes, of the whole culture. METACAUSES is a term that could also be applied to them, to parallel the term metatheme. They are limited in number, whereas higher level assumptions are doubtlessly very large in number, with, of course, existential assumptions and folk explanations being rather beyond enumeration, given the breadth, diversity, and complexity of any culture. They are termed "absolutes" in that they are absolutely assumed to be true by the culture; not that they are absolutely true, say, in a theological sense. If it could be determined that certain ontological absolutes were found in all cultures, these could be called ONTOLOGICAL UNIVERSALS. At the present stage of development, the ontological absolutes discussed here apply only to Senegambian culture.

Ontological absolutes are theoretical constructions of the widest possible generalization. While a culture makes many more-or-less general ontological assumptions, these can be reduced and reformulated to make one small, systematic set that articulates the most fundamental causal issues dealt with by the culture. This set would comprise those few principles that explain the totality of the ultimate meaning of people, matter, and transempirical beings and forces, that is, of the full range of perceived reality. Informal, yet insightful, deep-level understandings could well be formulated by a perceptive holder of a culture, but people who are part of a particular culture seldom have need to so analyze their own culture. They know, with little questioning, what their culture has inculcated in them as the content and meaning of reality.

A formal set of propositions would ordinarily be formulated only by individuals who come from outside the culture, such as anthropologists or

Background

other cross-cultural scholars. Examples are: (1) George Foster (1965 and 1972) attempted to formulate an ontologically absolute assumption of Mexican peasant culture, which he claimed had pervasive influence throughout that culture. This was called the "image of limited good." (2) Cora DuBois (1955) posited a set of four assumptions she called the "dominant value profile of American culture." These four assumptions were shown to underlie many dominant American behaviors.

For Senegambian culture, ten ontological absolutes have been identified. They have been arrived at by a process that has been inductive, deductive, and iterative. This process has been employed with the full abstractive range of world view levels, but its end point is the ontological absolutes. It is a process of formulating, testing with philosophically minded informants, reformulating and retesting, until a degree of satisfactory understanding and articulation is reached.

The ontological absolutes are:

1. God *(yàlla)*. God is transcendent, remote, and little concerned with, or at least little involved in, the daily affairs of his creation. For Sufi Muslims, although God *(Allah,* A.) is transcendent, the divine reality can be experienced through proper action.
2. Universe. The universe is composed of both visible and invisible reality (to man), but the invisible is of greater ontological significance than the visible.
3. Peace. Peace is the ideal state, and harmony is the ideal relationship of the universe.
4. Integration. At all levels of the universe, the ideal condition is integration. That is, all parts need to be brought together through interdependence.
5. Destiny. Every being and part of the universe has an assigned role that needs to be filled. For Muslims, submitting to divine law will provide assurance of approval on the Day of Judgment.
6. Hierarchy. The universe is organized on the basis of hierarchies of position and power on every level and within each domain.
7. Power. The universe is administered through the exercise of inherent and derived power.
8. Reality. All reality is dichotomized into exterior and interior.
9. Human beings. Man is the ceremonial center of the universe.

10. Transfer. All spiritual good or evil and abstract qualities are transmitted through the principle of transfer, by means of the mechanism of intent.

These ontological absolutes for the Senegambia are not, of course, limited to the culture of this particular region. Many scholars have found similar features in other African cosmologies and elsewhere in the world. Among the many that could be cited is Geoffrey Parrinder, a recognized specialist in African religions. He describes the following as present in African ideologies: "Belief in life beyond the grave, ... that men were not meant to die ... that death is not the end ... that life force is indestructible" (1976:38). All four of these assumptions would be included in number two, universe, under the concept that the invisible is of more significance than is the visible.

What is presented above is not meant to be a set of all-inclusive basic causal assumptions; rather, it is a set that has been derived from Senegambian data. These absolute CASUAL PRINCIPLES are touched upon in chapters three and four, but the main analysis of Senegambian world view is built upon the ORGANIZING PRINCIPLES of the culture, that is, on the themal propositions.

The division of deep-level culture into four levels is admittedly partly, but by no means wholly, arbitrary. What is in focus in proposing such a four-level scheme is not a precise separation into discrete levels, or the formulation of a set of questions that will elicit the proper responses at each level. Rather, the levels are designed more for heuristic purposes and as elicitation aids, not as some kind of representation of a preexisting structural system. Their main purpose is to serve as constructs of increasing generality leading to the formulation of primary world view assumptions. At each level valuable insights are disclosed about the culture, but in world view study the goal is to discover basic assumptions, with the focus on the deepest levels and the greatest generalizations.

The main point is that continued and systematic probing will reveal explanations, then explanations behind the explanations and the assumptions behind the explanations, until the questioning participant observer finds the deepest-level explanations and assumptions that explain and reveal the deepest layers of the conceptual system.

This is not just a subjective exercise, but at this juncture it is not possible to articulate anything like a precise formulation of the layers of culture and the processes that lie between behavior and ultimate assumptions about

Background

reality, or what the nature of such layers would be. What cannot be clearly defined, however, at least can be inferred with sufficient clarity to provide insights with a valuable degree of explanatory power. The process does require much inductive reasoning and familiarity with large amounts of data. It requires a willingness to pursue intuitive judgments and much testing of tentative hypotheses, until the patterns and consistencies begin to emerge. Then, with further reworking and crosschecking, the generalizations emerge and can be adequately confirmed across the culture.

Before leaving this section, the example of *muslaay,* the protective amulet, needs to be related to ontological absolutes (OA). At the beginning of the section, OA were said to be "those few assumptions that underlie all the culture." This means that all ten OA underlie *muslaay.* Yet, if OA are made to apply to everything, they may become trivialized in the process. I do not mean, for example, that all ten OA underlie the way Senegambians tie their shoelaces. But as the foundational, causal principles, they permeate the whole culture. Therefore, in all significant cultural behavior the traces of all ten OA can be found.

As *muslaay* are a major part of a significant behavior, traces of all ten OA can indeed be seen, to a greater or lesser extent, in this complex of beliefs and practices, as follows:

1. God. To the Muslim, Senegambian God is in and part of everything. Even when wearing an amulet which may invoke the help or power of a spirit being, the Muslim is very conscious of God having ordained the powers and the system in which they function. In spite of this constant awareness of the greatness and power of God, however, he is not addressed directly for the ordinary matters and concerns of life. This is believed to be the way God has ordained it, whether because he is too busy, or the matter too small to be of interest to him, or whatever.
2. Universe. *muslaay* relate directly to the reality of both the visible and the invisible. They are visible reminders of the power of the invisible, and provide a sense of identification with, or allegiance to, these greater realities.
3. Peace. An amulet is an implicit admission that there is or can be a spiritual problem, that is, a breach in the peace and harmony between the individual and the unseen world. The amulet is provided as part of the prescription obtained by revelation of the state of affairs in the

transcendent realm in order to assure the maintenance or the reestablishment of such transcendent peace.
4. Integration. *muslaay* are also reminders of man's dependence upon greater beings and forces; even as man is dependent upon these transcendent beings, so the transcendent beings are dependent upon the ritual initiative of man.
5. Destiny. This whole scheme of things, and the actions taken, are part of the established nature of visible and invisible reality, that is, of destiny.
6. Hierarchy. *muslaay* are also an implicit acknowledgment of the law of hierarchy. The citizen goes to an ordained intermediary who ascertains the explanation and the required prescription, of which the *muslaay* is a part. Hence, there is acceptance of the cosmic scheme, which includes the recognition of God as over all, the revelation to Muhammad, the revealed Qur'an and its supernatural powers, the roles of invisible spirits, and the necessary direct appeal to humans who have been given interior vision.
7. Power. All of these roles and operations involve inherent, derived, or delegated power. And at the end of the line, the amulet itself becomes a locus of delegated power.
8. Reality. It is clear that visible and invisible (to ordinary mortals) realities are integral elements of this belief system.
9. Human beings. Although in a sense man is at the bottom of the hierarchy, his place is central, as imbalance and nonpeace will continue until he initiates rituals that are required to restore balance. The *muslaay* is a very commonplace, if not hackneyed, example of such ritual action.
10. Transfer. *muslaay* do not remove, eradicate, or annihilate imbalance, or forgive evil. Rather, they transfer ritual impurity or, more precisely, they transfer ritual or cosmic imbalance. Perhaps exchange would be a valid synonym. Peace and balance are received in exchange for disharmony and ritual impurity. I have not been able to elicit satisfactory answers to the question of just where the nonpeace goes when it is transferred. The answer seems to be lost or unavailable to man. Such theoretical matters are of little importance; Senegambian religion deals with practical matters. The wearing of *muslaay* is deemed above all to have practical benefits.

Background

Themal Propositions

In deep-level analysis of causes, one probes the culture for reasons behind the reasons behind the reasons for behavior, while attempting to infer what the assumptions are that underlie that behavior. The resulting formulations represent the generalized principles that underlie (not to say determine) cultural behavior.

With the study of themes, the analytical method is similar, but the generalizations are built upon a determination of the organizing principles found in the culture that tie disparate behaviors together, forming patterns of behavior. Rather than searching for the reasons behind behaviors, the goal is to find the principles that are followed to organize and unify behaviors. The most general organizing principles that are used across the full range of cultural activity are sought. The end products of themal analysis are metathemes, plus a set of themes of lesser generality, organized hierarchically to reflect degrees of affinity and generalization. For Senegambian culture, eight metathemes have been identified.

There is a key difference between the constructs of ontological absolutes and metathemes. Each reveals closely related but quite distinct features of the culture's principles. The ontological absolutes are those few principles that underlie all the culture. They constitute its ultimate CAUSES. The metathemes express the principles that organize all cultural behaviors. They therefore express the ultimate RELATIONSHIPS, encompassing classification. Both constructs are essential components of world view. With the one, we are looking for the causes behind the causes. With the other, we are looking for the relationships behind the relationships.

The eight-level model, then, is derived from the Redfield-Kearney seven world view universals, although its organization is quite different. See figure 7 for a comparison of the Redfield-Kearney and eight-level models. Four basic differences stand out.

First, the general approaches are different. Kearney, in his case studies on California Indian and Mexican peasant world views, analyzes the cultures and their world views in terms of the seven universals, plus a few other features of the culture that he believes are of special note. The eight-level approach is, to start with, a comprehensive examination of the entire culture. Then its organizing principles and ultimate causal assumptions are ascertained.

Redfield-Kearney Model		Eight-Level Model	
			Thematic range
1. self		relationship-	⎱
2. other	are	classification	⎰ metathemes 1, 2, etc.
3. time	treated		
4. space	linearly,	self	⎫
5. classification	in	other	⎪
6. relationship	sequence	time	are dealt with
7. causality		space	within themes
			in full thematic
		empirical	range
		universe	
		transempirical	
		universe	⎭
		causality	> ontological absolutes

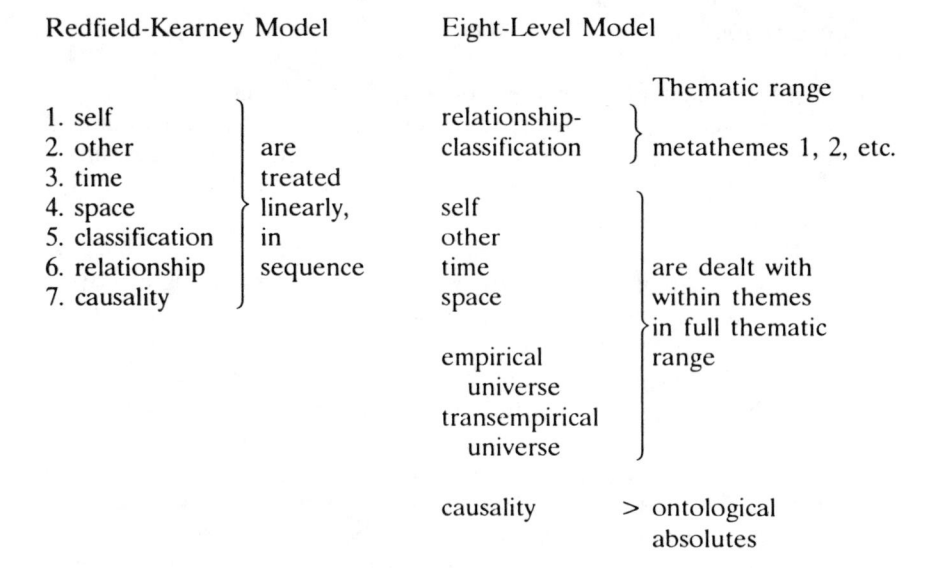

Fig. 7. Comparison of Redfield-Kearney and eight-level model of world view

Second, Redfield-Kearney treats universals linearly, basically describing world view in terms of examining how each universal is reflected in the culture. In contrast, the eight-level model handles the universals, along with culture-specific categories, in an ethnoscience approach.

Third, another basic difference lies in the treatment of relationship and causality. The eight-level approach considers them the primary articulations of world view. When one notes that three of the Redfield-Kearney universals (classification, relationship, and causality) cut across the other four, it seems apparent that they are of a different order. By cutting across, I mean that relationship and causality can hardly be separated from self, other, time, and space. Relationships and causes are integral elements of all categories. This problem of analyzing incommensurate universals is solved by treating the isolable universals in relation to those that are embedded; the principles of the eight-level model are then more clearly brought out. Instead of considering classification-relationship and causality as dependent variables cutting across the other universals, as Kearney does, in the eight-level model they are both treated as independent variables. Other aspects of the culture are thus considered in relation to them, rather than vice versa. The result is that all the culture (i.e., its basic assumptions or world view) can be examined in terms of them, as they constitute the organizing principles and foundational causes, respectively, upon which the whole culture is structured. From this, a definition emerges: world view is the composite of organizing principles and ultimate causes upon which a culture is constructed.

The fourth difference lies in the treatment of classification. In the eight-level model, classification is treated as a subcategory of relationship. Classifications are considered to be expressions of relationships. If or when elements of classification are found to be separable from relationships, they can be handled within themes, as are self, other, time, and space.

The concept of cultural themes was developed by Morris Opler (1945, 1959, 1968). He (1945:198) defined themes as:

> a limited number of dynamic affirmations, which I shall call *themes*, [that] can be identified in every culture and that the key to the character, structure, and direction of the specific culture is to be sought in the nature, expression, and interrelationship of these themes...
>
> The term "theme" is used here in a technical sense to denote a postulate or position, declared or implied, and usually controlling behavior or stimulating activity which is tacitly approved or openly promoted in a society.

Opler (1945:199) gives as an example of a theme the Apache belief that men are superior to women, morally and mentally as well as physically. This theme can be found throughout Apache culture as an organizing principle in family matters, and in social, religious, economic, and political life. Hence, this one proposition has great explanatory power for the behavior of both male and female Apaches.

In his essay "Component, Assemblage, and Theme in Cultural Integration and Diffusion," Opler (1959:964) proposes a hierarchy of concepts which can be used in the analysis of cultures, especially aspects of integration, variation, and process. Although Opler's proposal presents many additional analytical and contrastive terms, the core terms and concepts are theme, event, assemblage, and component. Figure 8 presents a schematic outline of Opler's textual description.

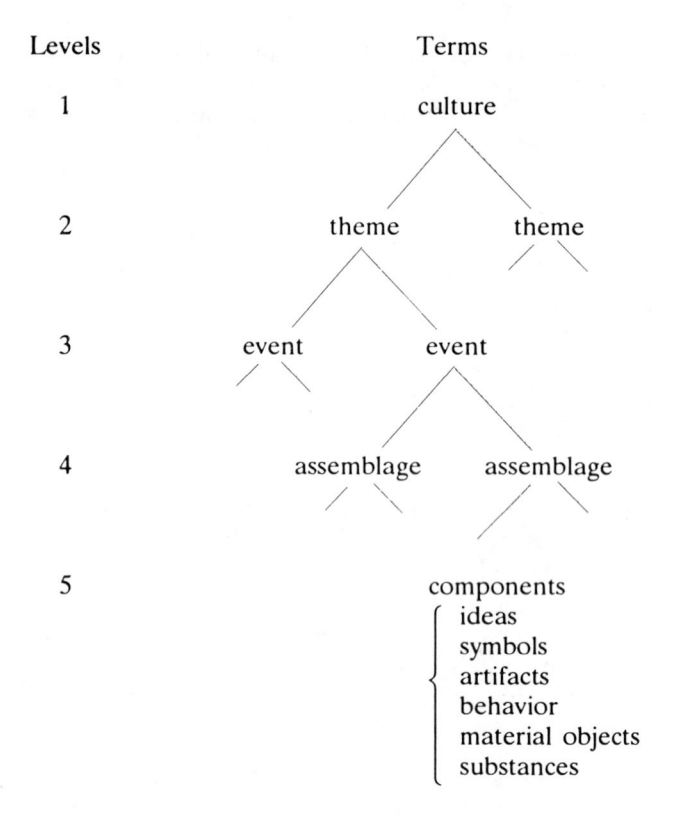

```
Levels                          Terms

   1                           culture
                                 /\
                                /  \
                               /    \
   2                        theme    theme
                             /\       /\
                            /  \     /  \
   3                     event  event
                          /\     /\
                         /  \   /  \
   4                  assemblage  assemblage
                       /\          /\

   5                           components
                              ⎧ ideas
                              ⎪ symbols
                              ⎨ artifacts
                              ⎪ behavior
                              ⎪ material objects
                              ⎩ substances
```

Fig. 8. Schematic outline of Opler's thematic model of culture

THEME has been defined. EVENTS are major cultural happenings, such as life-cycle events. An example Opler provides is the complex of behaviors that accompany a death among the Apache. An "assemblage" is "the total group of components which are activated by the event and are considered appropriate in coping with it or referring to it" (1959:962).

Opler proposes a five-level analysis of cultural institutions. This has served as the basis for analyzing world view on a number of different levels, even though there is little definitional correspondence between Opler's levels and those of the eight-level model.

The hierarchy of thematic levels that are used in the present essay are shown in figure 9.

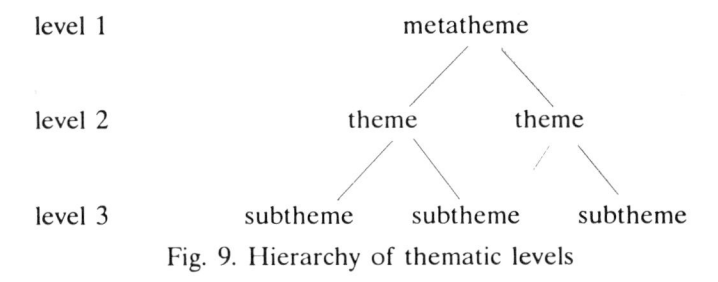

```
level 1                    metatheme
                           /      \
                          /        \
level 2              theme          theme
                    /     \        /     \
                   /       \      /       \
level 3      subtheme   subtheme       subtheme
```
Fig. 9. Hierarchy of thematic levels

The prefix meta- in its most general sense means changed, transposed, or derived (Guralnik 1984). It has been applied to social science in various ways. For example, James Buswell (1989:27) employs the term metaanthropology. His usage follows David Bidney (1953:164), who defined the term as follows:

> metaanthropology ... is not merely another name for anthropological theory, but refers to a special kind of theory, namely, the theory concerned with the problems of cultural reality and the nature of man.

The term METATHEME, used here, is derived from the usage of Everett Rogers (1983:127), who defines metaresearch as "the synthesis of empirical research results into more general conclusions at a theoretical level." This may be paraphrased as a definition of metatheme, theme, and subtheme as the synthesis of empirical, phenomenological research results into three levels of general conclusions of increasingly/decreasingly abstract theoretical levels.

Metathemes are therefore defined as the most generalized propositions that can be formulated regarding cultural behavior. They express both the principles involved in organizing behavior and the basic relationships that underlie it. Themes and subthemes have no particular conceptual or theoretical significance; they are simply propositions of greater or lesser encompassing scope that relate to a particular metatheme. Although the concepts of themes and levels were borrowed from Opler, the way they are used in the eight-level model is very different.

Opler's event, assemblage, and components are found directly in the culture, as with his example of taking as an event the complex of life cycle behaviors that accompany a death. These contrast conceptually with his category of theme, which is a construct of the anthropologist that expresses a principle found to operate widely across the culture, as in the proposition that men are superior to women. It is not a single behavior found within the culture.

In the eight-level model the metathemes, themes, and subthemes correspond to Opler's themes; they are propositions constructed on three levels of generality, derived from behavior (see figure 4).

Thematic Range

Thematic range refers to the scope that is covered by the metathemes (including their subsets of themes and subthemes). By SCOPE is meant the gamut of cultural elements for which such metathemes can be constructed. For example, a world view study might focus solely on concepts or themes of the supernatural, or of man's relation to nature, in a particular culture. These would be narrow range studies.

It is posited in the eight-level model that a full study of the world view of a culture must include cosmic themes, social themes, and naturalistic themes (see figure 4). Cosmic themes refer to the relationships between man and transempirical beings and forces. Social themes include relationships between individuals and social groups. Naturalistic themes reflect the relationships of man, individually and collectively, with the natural order. These definitions are not meant to be rigid or complete. A culture's themes can probably never be neatly subsumed under these three categories of thematic range with no overlaps or fuzzy borders. Rather, they are meant to show that world view study includes the full sweep of relationships of man and culture in their full worldly and cosmic context. A world view is not just, for example, the culture's basic concepts regarding the supernatural or its concepts about time or space. World view is the complex of basic assumptions found in a culture that relate to all its perceived reality. The range of the metathemes of a full description of world view will be inclusive of all such reality.

Doubtlessly, for some cultures, a full thematic range would require the inclusion of diachronic themes (historical, futuristic, or eschatological) as well as the synchronic themes which are almost exclusively in focus in this work. In Senegambian culture, historical themes (relating to kinship and ancestors) and eschatological themes (relating to the Islamic doctrines regarding the coming of the messiah *(mahdi)* and future judgment for all humans) are identifiable, but they are not given particular analytical attention as none were found to have the importance of a metatheme.

The thematic distribution of the metathemes defined for Senegambian culture is now given. Cosmic themes include the following:

Metatheme 1: Senegambians seek to have a personal transcendent peace, which is experienced through a moral conscience, a spirit of personal peace, and social peace.
Metatheme 2: Peace, happiness, and success are achieved by means of power granted by supernatural beings and forces of the transempirical world.
Metatheme 8: The uttered word has inherent power that can be set in action through its proper formulation.

Social themes include:

Metatheme 3: Humans should live in inter-dependent community.
Metatheme 4: Social peace is achieved through an integrated community life.
Metatheme 5: Man is defined in terms of kinship and in relation to the cosmos.
Metatheme 6: The unique nature of being Black-African man, and of being Senegambian man in particular, has profound implications on thought patterns, on comportment, and on the emotions.

Naturalistic themes are subsumed under one metatheme:

Metatheme 5: Man lives in symbiosis with nature, which is for him his source of physical life and survival.

Metathemes and Ethnoscience

The approach to culture followed in constructing metathemes has some features in common with ethnoscience. Ethnoscience is an emic approach that seeks to understand a culture's terminological systems and the "conceptual principles that generate them" (Frake 1972:192). Its methodological focus is on objects and domains, although on a theoretical level it is especially concerned with methodological rigor, replicability, and verifiability (Berreman 1972, Sturtevant 1974, Tyler 1969). It seeks to discriminate and categorize objects of the culture according to the same systems as are followed in that culture. The starting point is the terms used for objects, events, and concepts. These are sometimes referred to as the MICRO meaning systems (Spradley 1972:206). Spradley gives an example of distinguishing between different categories of university classes in the students' own terminology: snap, mickey mouse, and tough. Ethnoscience thus seeks to understand the discriminative criteria used in separating items in sets of related terms; that is, what are the distinguishing characteristics of snap, mickey mouse, and tough courses?

Ethnoscience also focuses on taxonomies. If man did not categorize as well as discriminate, he would be reduced to dealing constantly with the infinite number of particularities that exist in all human environments (Bruner, et al. 1972:169).

Gerald Berreman (1972:229) describes ethnoscience as having its focus on "particular domains rather than on general accounts of the cultures studied." Charles Frake (1972:202–203, quoting Goodenough 1957:167) has characterized it as the:

> presentation of observed and elicited events according to the principles of classification of the people he is studying. To order ethnographic observations solely according to an investigator's preconceived categories obscures the real content of culture: how people organize their experience conceptually so that it can be transmitted as knowledge from person to person and from generation to generation. As Goodenough advocates in a classic paper, culture "does not consist of things, people, behavior, or emotions," but the forms or organization of these things in the minds of people.

World view study in the eight-level model is the study of the classification system or principles of the whole culture. This statement can be more meaningfully rephrased by substituting "relational system" or "organizing principles" for classification system, as the term classification system hardly seems appropriate when applied to a whole culture. It denotes the organization of items within a particular class. It ordinarily refers to the organizational system found within a particular domain of the culture, used to discriminate units by culturally determined criteria. Hence, it seems more appropriate to think in terms of the relational system, that is, the ways in which disparate items relate to one another, or how disparate items are organized within a culture, than to think in terms of classification.

Background

In ethnoscience, the boundaries of the classification systems of the culture are analyzed emically, that is, using the principles derived from the culture. The boundaries that separate domains are those that exist in the culture being studied, not analagous boundaries existing in the culture of the foreign anthropologist.

The same principle is followed in constructing metathemes, basing descriptions and analyses upon cultural units that are found in the culture. But these units are not just selected domains. The whole culture is examined (comprehensively but not exhaustively) so that the domain boundaries themselves, not just domain contents, are those that are found in the culture.

Taking a Senegambian example, the participant observer notes that most people wear amulets. This becomes the starting point for a domain. In ethnoscience the study of the domain of amulets would lead to a collection of native terms for amulets and the features in the culture that define each type. These distinguishing features are called "dimensions of contrast" (Conklin 1969:52).

With metathemes, the domain of amulets would include the various types and their dimensions of contrast, but would be extended to include everything associated with amulets, in a way analogous to Opler's components that make up an assemblage. Thus, the amulet maker, the contents of amulets, the beliefs associated with them, their purposes and uses, other objects that function similarly or contrastively, and the overlap and ambiguity of criteria are all placed in the amulet domain. The goal is to understand the place of amulets and their relationships to as many other aspects of the culture as possible. Such mega-domains can be called DOMAIN CLUSTERS. The goal is to find as many as possible of the major domain clusters. These become the basis for the inductive process that leads to the formulation of the metatheme propositions.

In ethnoscience, and its major methodological tool, componential analysis (Goodenough 1967, Nida 1975), finding the differences between components of a domain is a central concern. The differences are believed to lead to discovery of the organizing principles behind the culture (Tyler 1969:3). The principles are assumed to be revealed largely within domains, according to the criteria used to discriminate, or separate, the various elements. The unifying features are taken as givens. In metatheme analysis, the goal is also to find the organizing principles, but they are assumed to be seen largely across domains. The uniting features, that is, relationships, are in primary focus. The separating features are largely ignored.

This can be summed up by considering both of these processes as componential analysis. Then, what has been defined as componential analysis would now be called componential separation, as that is largely what the process is all about. And the process used in inferring metathemes would be called componential clustering, as in figure 10:

```
                componential
                 analysis
                  /    \
                 /      \
      componential    componential
      separation      clustering
      (the old
      componential
      analysis)
```

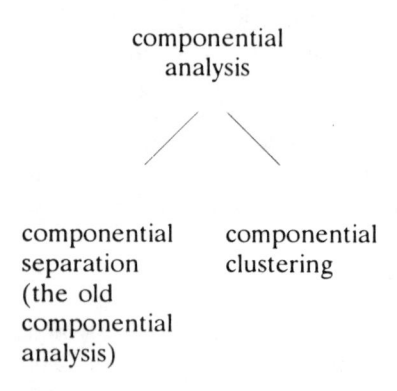

Fig. 10. Componential clustering

Verification and replicability have been primary concerns of the practitioners of ethnoscience. In metathemal analysis these concerns can be addressed. The end products, those limited number of metathemes that have been generalized from the full range of the culture, are subject to verification and replicability by other researchers. Ontological absolutes, at the other end of the spectrum of generalization, can also be compared, verified, and replicated. Although the process of constructing the metathemes is inductive and intuitive, the end results are open to comparison by other scholars working in the same culture and with metathemes constructed from other cultures. Metathemes and ontological absolutes are units that can be compared cross-culturally. Thus, major goals of traditional anthropology, of making the real social lives of others intelligible, can be met and some of the many objections raised against ethnoscience (e.g., Harris 1979:265ff.) can be corrected in the metathemal approach. The goals of anthropology and the objections to some uses of ethnoscience are expressed well by Malcolm Crick (1982:299):

> Functionalism saw meanings as lubricants in an interconnected set of social activities. In some modern anthropological traditions the opposite pole has been reached with lifeless taxonomies or elegant

symbol structures presented with no indication of how they are a part of the ongoing life of social groups. Clearly all the while the main aim of anthropology is to make social life intelligible, knowledge must be seen in social context. Culture, after all, is a continuous creative, inventive process, it is not a dead representation.

In metathemal analysis, the symbol structures are sought after in real life contexts. It is also asserted that such analysis can make "social life intelligible" and be "seen in social context." In the following chapters such a metathemal analysis is carried out in the Senegambian social and cultural milieu.

Culture versus World View

The terms CULTURE and WORLD VIEW are referred to throughout the study; hence, they need to be defined and contrasted at the outset.

The definition of culture used here will follow James Lett (1987:58), who describes cultures as

the routinized, adaptive, patterned forms of interaction among the members of a society—forms of interaction that are supported, rationalized, and transmitted by shared beliefs and perspectives. Symbolic systems [are a subset of culture and] are made up of learned, shared, patterned sets of meanings that enable people to perceive, interpret, and evaluate life—sets of meanings that are both explicit and implicit and that are embodied and expressed in both beliefs and behaviors.

We will say, therefore, that culture is composed of the behaviors and the interactions in human society and the meanings that are used to interpret them. A further reduction of the definition would simply define culture as learned behaviors and their underlying beliefs.

In contrast, world view is the assumed and/or deduced structure that accounts for the patterned sets of meaning behind behavior. World view is, for each culture, its "specific set of existential assumptions" (Lett 1987:118, interpreting Geertz). Therefore, culture is learned, patterned behavior. World view is that part of culture constituted by the structured assumptions that inform behavior.

3
Metatheme 1:
Personal, Transcendent Peace

Metatheme 1. Senegambians seek to have a personal transcendent peace, which is experienced through a moral conscience, a spirit of personal peace, and social peace.

One short Wolof proverb sums up to a remarkable extent the most basic value of the Senegambian belief system: *jàmm ci la lépp xejj* 'everything is contained in peace'. Another proverb underlines this desire for peace, *bakkan jàmm lay laaj* 'the soul aspires only to peace'. Peace is the social and individual ideal. It is a philosophy of life. It is the ultimate desire for life in this world, as well as in the next. Without peace, life is but existence.

The desire for peace is the organizing principle on which family, kin, community, and society-at-large are based. In traditional African society peace is also central to relationships with ancestors and beyond them to all transempirical beings and forces.

The highest compliments relate to peace. Among these are *bëgg na jàmm* 'he loves peace' and *nitt u jàmm la* 'he is a man of peace'.

Peace requires tolerance of others, of their behavior, faults, weaknesses, and idiosyncrasies. It seeks a position between all extremes. It respects others and in turn requires respect. It is profoundly humanistic, that is, prohuman.

Peace is based on reciprocal need and service. It is inclusive of everyone: small and great, humble and proud, stranger and slave, rich and poor, spiritualist and materialist, needy and affluent, the dead and the living.

Peace requires personal sacrifice, the giving of oneself and one's means. Senegal has long been called, and still calls itself, the home of *teraanga* 'hospitality'. Gamble (1957:74) notes:

> All travelers from earliest times mention the generosity and hospitality of the Wolof. Mollien (1920, p. 89) writes: "Hospitality is so generally practised... that it is not regarded by them as a virtue, but as a duty imposed on all mankind; they exercise it with a generosity which has no bounds and do not even make a merit of it." [ellipsis in Gamble]

Hospitality is practised, not as an end, but as a means of living in peace with others, with whoever comes into the community or to an individual's home. Senegal calls itself the country of dialog *(waxtaan)* and especially one of hospitality *(teraanga)*. Christian Saglio (1980:6) in a book about Senegal writes that Dakar's "tradition of *teranga* [sic] (hospitality) remains a reassuring reality."

Theme 1: Alliances Needed

To possess peace, human beings need to establish alliances with the forces and beings that govern the world.

Subtheme 1-A. Peace in this world must be sought in accordance with the fundamental, superior, and unchangeable laws of the transempirical world.

Subtheme 1-B. Man's role is to initiate and execute appropriate, specific actions (cults and ceremonies) that can serve to reestablish and maintain communion with the beings and forces that operate in the world of man.

Subtheme 1-C. The beings and forces of the transempirical world confer on initiated individuals a consciousness awakened to the supernatural realm that makes them masters of the laws of the seen and the unseen.

A prerequisite of peace is recognizing the existence of the cosmic order, where every being has an established role to play. Beyond the mere recognition of the existence of these beings, man must accept the suzerainty of those beings that are above him or more powerful than he.

Metatheme 1: Personal, Transcendent Peace

The beings that Senegambians recognize are described in the following sections.[21]

Supernatural Beings

Senegambians are no exception to the probably universal African belief in a Supreme Deity (Mbiti 1969b). Among the Wolof, the name for God *(Yàlla)*, although it appears to have come from the Arabic *Allah*, is believed to be the pre-Islamic word for the Supreme Deity (Gravrand 1983:224, Sylla 1978:48ff). The concept of angels *(malaaka)* doubtlessly came with Islam. This also applied to Satan *(ibliis)* and the devils *(seytaane)*. In Wolof, whatever may have been the concepts and words used regarding lesser divinities has been lost.

The focus of many beliefs and practices in African traditional religion centered around spirits and ancestors. Much of this has continued under Islam, partly altered and partly intact. The main attention given to the spirit world among Senegambian Muslims is to *jinne*, which constitutes a separate supernatural order of creation, made by Allah from fire, who can be either good or bad. These spirits are frequently referred to in the Qur'an (Ali 1983 6.128–30, 15.27, 55.15, etc.,). The English word genie is derived from the Arabic term *jinni* (pl. *jinn* or *jinns*) (Guralnik 1984). Other spirits are common to the Senegambian belief systems. Each ethnic group or language has multiple general and specific terms for spirits, e.g., *rab, pangool* (S.), *kumpo* (Diola), *gino* (Mandinka) and *u-mthaï* (Mancagne). These may be protector spirits *(rawane)*, personal spirits, doubles or spirit shadows *(qarina,* A., *takkandeer,* etc.), family spirits *(tuur)*, possessing spirits *(rab-ndëpp/njuuma)*, or family or clan totems *(mbañ)*. This by no means exhausts the types, which are appealed to by both Muslims and traditionalists, although with significant differences that are described later in the essay.

That spirits are given important attention in daily life, as well as in the belief system, is brought out by Schaffer and Cooper (1980:37) in their ethnography of the Senegambian Mandinko:

> The widespread use of charms is one indication of the great danger that Mandinko perceive in their world. Much of the danger is due to demon-spirits *(gino)*, which can bring death and suffering to humans.

---

[21]The classification followed in this instance for these supernatural beings is not necessarily Senegambian.

"Everything, every person has a demon-spirit." People are shadowed by these spirits, and one of the principal duties of the *marabout* is to protect his clients from them with various charms and blessings. This is not easy. Whole villages such as Karantaba, Soumboundou, and Dar Silamé have double villages of demon-spirits lying nearby. In Pakao[22] the especially religious places have more, not fewer, demon-spirits... Karantaba, the holiest Pakao village, has a reputation for having the most dangerous demon-spirits. Its mosque is thought to shelter many demon-spirits at night and is the only Pakao mosque off-limits after dark. The fifth, night-time prayer cannot be said there.

Souls of the Dead

Souls of the dead, ancestors *(maam)*, manes (disembodied spirits of the dead), shades (souls or shades of the dead), the living dead *(noonoh*, Sf.), reincarnation of the dead, and related concepts, have been important in the Senegambia. Some, or all of these kinds of beings, and related concepts are still important concepts of the belief systems of certain ethnic groups.

Islam is much less ambiguous about cultus to the ancestors and ancestor spirits than to *jinn* and other classes of what could be called disembodied spirits. There is much overlap between devotion to the spirits and that related to ancestors, so part of the attention traditional religion gave to ancestor veneration has been displaced to the more nebulous spirit realm. Another large part has been redefined or reinterpreted as part of Islamic beliefs and practices. This part is analyzed in succeeding pages. A third part has been suppressed and seems to have either disappeared or been sublimated in acceptable Islamic forms. An example is the *gàmmu*, a major traditional celebration of illustrious ancestors, which is now a major annual event in the Muslim calendar but reconstituted in ways acceptable to Muslim orthodoxy. This is the subject of chapter five.

Human Intermediaries

The suzerainty of transempirical beings refers to the belief that these beings are in a position of spiritual authority or power over human beings. Different supernatural beings exercise authority of various kinds on several

---

[22]Pakao was a precolonial Mandinko kingdom in present-day south-central Senegal. It retains its identity as a traditional region.

Metatheme 1: Personal, Transcendent Peace

levels and in separate or overlapping areas of jurisdiction. Suzerainty refers to all these roles and authorities. There is little distinction between what is Islamic and what originated with African traditional religion (ATR), except where a pre-Islamic concept clearly contradicts Islamic doctrine and, even in some of these cases, if the belief is central to traditional religion, such inconsistencies may be overlooked. An example would be black magic *(jibar)*, clearly prohibited by orthodox Islam, yet prevalent, albeit in the "shadows" of society. And, as with all the domains of the transempirical, the concepts are seldom clearly defined.

This suzerainty takes many forms and is recognized in many ways. An example is the role angels and deities are believed to have in assigning a particular preexisting soul to each human couple at the time of each conception. They are in charge of choosing the quality, type, and particular soul that will be placed in the person to be born, according to moral and other cosmic criteria.

Submission to marabouts is part of the recognition of the cosmic order of authority structures. This is seen, for example, in the oath of allegiance *(jébbal)* required in the Mouride order and the acceptance of the maraboutic yoke *(nangu)*. Even the celebrations of the anniversaries of the Prophet's birth and the commemorations of the anniversaries of death of Sufi saints fall at least partly under this rubric.

Suzerainty is not just a momentary relationship. It is also not just one relationship, but is multiform. One such relationship is presented in some depth below, as probably the most prominent one in the culture and one of the most common and far-reaching in life.

Recognition of the suzerainty of superior beings includes the establishment of proper long-term relationships with certain members of the spiritual, cosmic hierarchy. In Muslim Senegambia this is most commonly carried out by having a marabout.[23] It is very important for the Senegambian Muslim to have a good marabout.

But having a marabout is not a light burden. It involves accepting the *nangu*, the maraboutic yoke. This yoke is defined as acceptance of, obedience to, and submission, without complaint, to the requests of the marabout. The sought-for accolade is called *kii taalibe bu nangu la*, that is, a disciple who is very submissive.

---

[23]The word marabout is derived from *murabit* (A.), a term used in the historical Muslim West to designate "a man who went into the state of *ribat*, a sort of conventual retreat coupled with ascetic practices and, occasionally, with military exercises which formed a training for holy war" (Gibb and Kramers 1965:325).

The goal is to have the *ngërëmu sëriñ bi*, the appreciation-benediction of the marabout to whom the disciple is attached. The *ngërëmu sëriñ bi* is the assurance of entry into Paradise, but much more. It also results in a visible and palpable material blessing. The disciple gives his effort, his obedience, and physical work in the marabout's fields, and receives the benediction in exchange. Everything he receives in his life of material and social good, and of (esoteric or occult) protection, will come to him through his marabout. These are considered to be the earnings that come from the supramundane forces available through the intermediary powers of the marabout. For the disciple, this is the way of the good future *(yoonu ngëneel)*. The greater the degree of obedience and acceptance of the marabout, the greater will be the recompense and benediction.

One of the most evident facts of life in the Senegambia is the multitude of Muslim clerics found wherever Islam is present, which is all of the region except small enclaves of or within the small non-Islamized ethnic groups. These clerics are called MARABOUTS in French and English. This is the term used throughout north and west Africa to designate a Muslim holy man, or cleric. The widespread occurrence and importance of maraboutic Islam is described by Vincent Monteil (1980:153):

> 'Maraboutism' appears... as a very general phenomenon in the Muslim world. It includes religious personages of various degrees of Islamic learning, who are called by various names. They may be more or less magicians or healers, sometimes authentic mystics, often affiliated with a Sufi order. They are called *shaykh* in North Africa and Mauritania, *molla, faqir, akhund* by the Irano-Indians and the Turks, *guru* or *shekh* in Indonesia, *ahong* in China. Contrary to the spirit and the letter of the Qur'anic revelation, these have appeared everywhere as intermediaries between the creature and the Creator.

Most of Islam is organized in this part of Africa on the basis of Sufi orders, called *tariqa* (A.), and *tariixa* (W.). Marabouts constitute the leadership class of the orders, on different hierarchical levels.[24]

There are many kinds of marabouts, from the relatively orthodox to those who are practitioners of what would clearly be, to an objective observer, African traditional religion with a thin Islamic veneer. The term is also applied to men of great Islamic learning with millions of followers,

---

[24]For descriptions of Sufi Islam see M. Hodgson 1974, F. Rahman 1979, and J. Trimingham 1971.

Metatheme 1: Personal, Transcendent Peace

as well as to rural marabouts who barely know the rudiments of Islamic teaching and practice.

As marabouts are such an important and ubiquitous fact of life in the Senegambia, reference is made to them in numerous sections of the essay. The purpose is not to describe marabouts as an institution; rather, the discussion must include them where they significantly intersect various world view themes.

The Sufi orders and their marabouts crossed the Sahara with the implantation of Islam. The concept of marabout meshed easily with the terms and concepts used to designate an officiate of traditional religion in the Senegambian region, whose role also included that of intermediary between man and deity. In Wolof this is *sëriñ*, and *tierno* in Pulaar. The term *sëriñ* designates 'religious teacher, spiritual leader, husband'. The maker of traditional amulets was a *sëriñ*, as were other types of religious specialists. A traditional woman would, and still does, call her husband her *sëriñ*, as he was the spiritual head and family ritualist, charged with maintaining a proper relationship with the family deities.

The term *marabout* was brought by those who introduced Islam into the region. It was applied to men with Islamic learning, whether rudimentary or advanced. But the term *sëriñ* was also retained. A *sëriñ* could be a Muslim or a traditionalist. This duality was facilitated by the fact that Islam readily adapted itself to local belief systems, so that at many times and places dualistic or parallel systems were present.

> The process was one of accommodation associated with parallelism and this came about through African Muslims themselves. They did not so much adapt Islam, a legalistic religion, as secure the acceptance of certain Islamic customs in such a way that the customary framework of society remained intact... The result is a fusion in life but not a true synthesis, the unyielding nature of Islamic institutions precluding this. The parallel elements bear the mark of their indigenous origin. Everywhere the traditional world remains real and its emotional hold vivid. There is, therefore, an ultimate dualism in life, since this rests upon a double foundation. [Trimingham 1980:46]

Colvin characterizes the Wolof as not having been converted to Islam so much as having been initiated into it (1974:590). This is a very penetrating insight and one that corresponds precisely with Senegambian world view.

In this section I am considering personal, transcendent peace as a function of alliances with transempirical forces and beings. A large part of the function of marabouts is to serve as intermediaries between Allah (and/or between lesser beings and forces) and the average Muslim. The marabouts are designated intermediaries; peace results when a man or woman has secured an effective alliance with them.

The non-Muslim adherent to African traditional religion also has intermediaries between himself and the deities and the High God. It is difficult to find a basic distinction between the Islam practised by the majority of Senegambians and ATR, in this area of alliances and intermediaries. As this is not meant to be a comparative study, this statement is only made in passing.

The area of INTERMEDIARIES covers a wide range of roles, from orthodox functions of Islam, down through various levels of popular Islam, down to traditional religion. In using the terms such as orthodox, high Islam, popular Islam, and low traditional religion, the purpose is not to pass judgment or evaluate their appropriateness as religious systems, but simply to use terms that reflect what is considered to be the relative content of REVEALED religion as contrasted with TRADITIONAL, non-codified, beliefs and practices. One of the problems of determining what is orthodox in Islam is that there is no single authority to define orthodoxy. There are local or national *ulama* 'councils of doctors of the law', but they have taken many different positions about many points of law in various times and places.

If the role of intermediary is so important in the conceptual system of the Senegambia, one would expect to find the concepts to be well developed, with an accompanying extensive vocabulary. This is very much the case. The extensive list that follows, with brief corresponding descriptions, is by no means exhaustive. Even so it certainly shows the breadth of the concepts and the corresponding importance of intermediaries. The distinctions between the categories are not always unambiguous, as might be inferred from the listing. Islam and ATR have each so penetrated the other that clear distinctions are frequently difficult to see in practice, if not in theory.

1. Intermediaries: Orthodox Islam
    sëriñ charia: a marabout qualified to teach the Qur'an and other Islamic subjects.
    sëriñ ndaw: the low hierarchy, or lesser marabouts. This term covers the marabouts who have very limited learning, being limited to the

recitation of the Qur'an and rudimentary notions of its meaning and translation, and of law and theology.

sëriñ daara: a marabout capable of instructing children in Qur'anic school.

yelimaan or *imam*: one who directs Muslim cultus, usually group ritual prayers in a mosque; chief of a Muslim community. These are ordinarily considered to be marabouts.

serif: someone who is descended from the prophet Muhammad and is thereby in a privileged spiritual category, above that of normal mortals.

sëriñ alxuran: a marabout of the Qur'an, i.e., one who is perceived to be orthodox in his practices.

2. Intermediaries: Sufi Islam

sëriñ bu mag: the high hierarchy, or great marabouts. This term covers the marabouts learned in Islamic sciences, such as law, theology, and exegesis of the Qur'an.

xaalif: a founder of a *tariixa*, Sufi order, or branch of an order; grand patriarch or head of an order.

sééx: title for chiefs of several levels who have the authority to initiate members into the order, in the Mouride and Qadri orders. The term partially overlaps with *xaalif*.

wasila: an intermediary between God and man; the marabout to whom one has allegiance.

muqàddam: in the Tijani order, three levels of chief who have the authority to consecrate new members.

boroom barke: one who holds divine blessing, a holy and prosperous person. This term is often applied to a marabout with a charismatic personality, but can also be applied to a layman who is seen as a moral person living under God's blessing. Such a person may be approached by others, who ask that the person bless them. A holder of *barke* (*baraka*, A.) is believed to be capable of acting as an intermediary with divinity.

3. Intermediaries: Islamo-Traditional

sëriñ xaatim: a marabout who makes talismans and amulets on the basis of Qur'anic or cabalistic writings.

4. Intermediaries: African Traditional Religion

sëriñ tariax: a marabout who uses esoteric practices in connection with vows and employs the names of God in clairvoyance.

doomi soxnayi: the children of saintly or virtuous women. These are believed to have inherited special virtue, protection and prosperity from their mothers.

sëriñ jibar or *jibarkat*: a marabout who is a practitioner of black magic.

xérémkat: a practitioner of traditional cultus. *xérém* refers to objects used in connection with traditional cultus; *kat* means agent, specialist, practitioner. *kat* contrasts with *sëriñ*, in that the former focuses on the *practice* involved, while the latter focuses on the knowledge required. There is considerable overlap in the meanings of the two terms.

boroom tuur: a chief of a family traditional altar.

saltige: a chief of traditional cultus; a shaman chief.

ndëppkat: a practitioner of ceremonies of spirit possession.

5. Intermediaries: Neutral[25]

seetkat: a clairvoyant, whether Islamic or traditional.

luggkat: a practitioner who is a specialist in counteracting poison and stings.

mocckat: a specialist in counteracting pain.

boroomi reen: a practitioner of herbalistic medicine and touchings.

The two dozen varieties of intermediaries given above by no means include all the categories found in Senegambian society, but they do indicate that this concept touches all of life and applies equally to Islam and ATR. Together these intermediaries occupy a central place in Senegambian culture and world view. They are part of the dominant organizing principle of Senegambian culture—transcendent peace.

Note that the categories are not discrete. They sometimes overlap, often have fuzzy borders, and vary with the practitioner. Often, even typically, individual practitioners function at different levels or in more than one category. The categories are better thought of as roles rather than as individual specialties.

The way these intermediaries relate to peace and the alliances they conclude with their clients can be shown through several examples.

---

[25]The term "neutral" refers to a belief or practice that is not considered to have its basis in Islamic or traditional religion but rather to merely be part of the cosmically ordered system of the universe.

Metatheme 1: Personal, Transcendent Peace

The Senegambian Mouride Sufi order has features that are commonly found in Sufi orders from Senegal to Indonesia, but some have been developed to a striking extreme.[26] Since its early establishment in Islam in the eleventh century in the Middle East, Sufism has taught that the disciple must give complete obedience to his master. This is commonly expressed in the saying, "Thou shalt be in the hands of thy shaykh like a dead body in the hands of its cleanser" (F. Rahman 1979:154). The particular form this takes in the Mouride order is in the oath of allegiance that an initiate takes of his marabout *(jébbal)*. The disciple kneels before the marabout and repeats this oath: "I give my life to you. I submit to you body and soul. I will do all you request of me and I will abstain from all you forbid" (Coulon 1981:105). In other orders, the oath of allegiance is less personalized but at base requires a high degree of submission to the Sufi master.

In addition to giving allegiance, the disciple gives the legal tithe *(asaka)*, the offering made to one's marabout *(addiya)*, and the special obligations required by the order *(sas)*. He also gives his time to work the marabout's fields. This is ordinarily carried out as collective work one day a week in the Wednesday fields *(toolu àllarba)*. The spiritual purpose behind these acts of allegiance and devotion is to assure the disciple that he or she will be a recipient of the benefits of intermediacy that have been bestowed upon the Sufi master.

The disciple *(taalibe)* expects to receive multiple returns on earth and in paradise for all this allegiance, effort, and money given to the intermediary between Allah and man *(wasila)*. The writings of Amadou Bamba, the founder of the Mouride order, make clear what returns are offered. The following lines are extracted from several of his poems, the main vehicle used by Bamba to propagate his doctrines:

> Blessed is the Mouride that God calls to attach himself to me!

> Blessed is the Mouride that hastens to bring me the best of himself, without reproaching me afterwards!

> Every Mouride that takes refuge in me will be happy and kept from evil.

---

[26]This order has been frequently described in general news media, histories of West Africa, scholarly journals and in monographs. See for example P. Clarke 1982, C. Coulon 1981, D. Cruise O'Brien 1971 and 1975, Kirtley and Kirtley 1985, and C. T. Sy 1969.

Every man that affiliates with my order will be saved from calamity in this world and from problems on the Day of Judgment.

Cursed is everyone who turns back and flees, after having been a Mouride!

Anyone who neglects to be initiated by a marabout will be unfortunate.

Anyone who does not have a marabout as his spiritual director, Satan will be his master wherever he goes.

Obey your spiritual director with diligence, even if you have no taste for it.

Do not cease to offer gifts to your spiritual director as often as possible.

Receive with open arms, as a devoted slave, all those who are attached to your marabout.

One loving glance from a marabout renders the recipient worthy of esteem and elevates him to a sublime rank.

Abandon yourself to your marabout as a cadaver in the hands of the body washer, and you will be happy.

Be to your marabout as a slave. For this servitude you will attain the rank of a king.

To the extent you honor your marabout, to that extent you will obtain what you desire. It is through him that you can attain good fortune. [A. Samb 1972:466–467]

The concept of alliances with transempirical beings and forces did not come just with Islam. In traditional religion there were and still are alliances established between man and divinities. This is clearly seen in the *ndëpp*, the healing-spirit possession ceremonies still practiced by some Wolof, Lebou, and Serer.[27]

The *ndëpp* usually originates with someone in the community becoming sick with one of the particular illnesses known to be caused by *rab* 'spirit, ancestral spirit'. The illness is brought on by a *rab* in order to get the attention of the person or of the community. It is imposed when either:

---

[27]Other less-Islamized ethnic groups in the Senegambia also maintain such rites.

Metatheme 1: Personal, Transcendent Peace

(1) a particular *tuur* (the traditional altar to the *rab,* or the family spirit itself) has been neglected, and the *rab* attached to it feels slighted; or (2) a wandering *rab* selects an individual to establish a *tuur* where he will be honored. In the terms of the proposition we are discussing here, the *rab* desires a renewed or a new alliance (M. C. and E. Ortigues 1984:119–130).

The alliance is consummated in the *ndëpp* ceremony, where the *rab* identifies himself by name, where blood sacrifices of a goat or a beef are made to him, and with which the spirit is thereby induced to inhabit the altar rather than the person. The person is then free from the illness, but must continue to honor the *rab* who thus remains domesticated and appeased.

> The principal, if not exclusive, motive for causing the illness is to bring about the renewal of the alliance with the *rab* or *tuur,* the ancestral spirits of the uterine or agnatic lineages. The illness is experienced as an ambivalent appeal made through the invasion of the human body space. The *rab* love those they punish for having forgotten them. They 'inhabit' and 'torment' whomever they elect to honor them. [Zempléni 1985:664]

Even when an intermediary or practitioner is sought for a transitory problem, an alliance is involved. The alliance relationship has two facets. Take, as an example, the common practice of a university student facing an examination. He goes to his marabout to enlist his help in passing the exam. One side of the alliance is that the student has already established this marabout as his spiritual advisor, so there is a long-term relationship, analagous to having a family doctor. The doctor looks out for the health of the family, makes suggestions, gives advice, takes time with family problems, and warns of dangers. In the same way, the student's marabout is not just involved in today's exam but in the long-term health, wealth, and success of the student.

The second facet of the relationship is that the marabout will find out what is going on in the unseen realm, so that he will know if there is a problem with transempirical beings and forces. He will follow the indicated procedures (normally some kind of sacrifice is involved) that will ensure peace between the student and these powers, so that success will be assured. Thus a kind of alliance is established or maintained in the relationships:

transempirical beings and forces
|
intermediary
|
man

One may ask what is Muslim and what is ATR in these concepts and practices. It is beyond the scope of this essay to answer this in detail, but a brief comment seems in order. Basically, Senegambians do not think in terms of orthodox Islam and traditional religion. They see life as a whole, with various practices, specialists, powers, and human needs. It is similar to health care in the United States. There are medical and osteopathic doctors, chiropractors, dentists, druggists, and nurses, to name a few. One uses the services of each as needed for various problems and in different situations. The layman is not concerned with where they did their training or with which professional association they are affiliated.

There are blatant pagan practices that Islam has forbidden, such as certain traditional dances and blood sacrifices, but many of these practices are still carried on and, when needed, one can find the required specialized practitioner. It is not that people have ceased to believe in the efficacy of these practices, but that Islam frowns on them, and most spiritual needs can be met in other ways unless there is a crisis. An elderly Muslim Senegalese man once confided to me, "We have never had good rains in this country since we gave up our *tuur*."

There are what seem to be both Islamic and non-Islamic elements in the alliances. Many Senegambian people, especially those who have had Western-type education, are conscious of certain practices being considered unorthodox to Islam, yet permitted. Others are forbidden as blatantly pagan. Still, the wide range of extant practices are not ordinarily thought of in terms of their degree of orthodoxy but just as part of life, taken for granted as multiple threads of its complex fabric.

Even when we look at historical Islam from the Muslim heartland, it is difficult to find a clearcut boundary between what is considered orthodoxy and traditional, pre-Islamic religion. Certainly, the concept of a human intermediary has always adhered at least to Muhammad, in practice if not in strict doctrine.

H. A. R. Gibb (1969:42) contrasts the teaching of orthodox Islam with the accommodation of the near-universal practice of approaching Allah through intercessors:

Metatheme 1: Personal, Transcendent Peace

[the] presentation of the awful reckoning [of the terrors of hell] is heightened by repeated assurances of the Divine Mercy and by hints of the power of intercession which God will grant to those whom He pleases... In no passage of the Koran, however, is the power of intercession specifically attributed to Muhammad.

Gibb characterizes the doctors of the law (*ulama*, A.) in modern Islam as generally taking an intermediate position on the question of intercessors, rejecting both Wahhabi fundamentalism and ecstatic Sufi saintship. These doctors thus assert that "reverence for the saints and prayers for their intercession are lawful" (1969:116).

Saints

Another class of intermediaries with whom disciples can establish allegiances are Sufi saints. They overlap with the category of marabout but are so important to Senegambian culture and world view they warrant a separate discussion.

Strict orthodox Islam includes no concept of a hierarchy of believers. Such a concept would seem to be in contradiction to its basic doctrine that all created men must submit to the Creator. Yet, since the 12th century, Islam has accommodated the Sufi doctrine of sainthood (Gibb and Kramers 1974:629–630).

All Muslims are equal before Allah. Confession and prayers are made directly to Him, with no one placed between them. No man has the power to withhold Allah's forgiveness. There is no one to administer baptism into the faith, and no one to order excommunication. Each believer is responsible for his or her own actions at the Judgment. This is orthodox teaching (Lippman 1982:2–3).

Yet, since very early in Islamic history, the revered position of some men besides Muhammad (and occasionally of women) who exhibited special spiritual knowledge or piety made them objects of extreme veneration and even of worship. This has been the case throughout the Muslim world. In fact, the worship of saints is not expressly prohibited in the Qur'an. This has allowed it to be accepted by Muslim theologians under the rationalization that it is permissible as long as the saints are held to be inferior in rank to Muhammad and the prophets.

An early definition of a saint (*wali*, A.) was one "who possesses knowledge" and "he who knows God" (Gibb and Kramers 1965:629). A saint is a Muslim who possesses three basic virtues: freedom from slavery to his passions, influence with God to bind and loose the affairs of men, and miracle-performing power.

The most common miraculous gifts (*karamat*, A.) ascribed to saints are: self-transformation, self-levitation, self-transport, ability to speak in diverse tongues, reviving the dead, thought-reading, telepathy, prophesying the future, and ability to make a dry stick grow leaves. In contrast to some other belief systems, these powers are considered to be gifts from God rather than resulting from the saint's merits or ascetic practices. Such Islamic beliefs were easily adapted to the Senegambian world view.

Subtheme 1-A: Peace, in Accordance with Laws

> *Peace in this world must be sought in accordance with the fundamental, superior, and unchangeable laws of the transempirical world.*

There are many principles underlying this central area of Senegambian culture. The following are some of the most important, at least to the cross-cultural observer.

1. There is a hierarchy of transempirical beings, with specific, complementary roles assigned to each within the cosmic order.
2. Man has need of intermediaries who can bridge the gap between the empirical and transempirical worlds through their understandings of both interior and exterior realities. (See subtheme 2-A: interior radiance of peace.)
3. There is a hierarchy of human intermediaries (i.e., human intermediaries of a lower level have lesser intermediary power, others on higher levels have greater powers), although the levels are not at all clearly defined.
4. There is a gamut of human intermediaries (i.e., within a given level intermediaries have roles, powers and specializations). (See subtheme 1-C: masters of the seen and the unseen.)
5. Every human being has a defined place and role in the cosmology. A Wolof proverb states *nitt ku nek juddom a ko mag* 'for every human being there is a superior birth'. This proverb means that every person is born with something higher than himself or herself, that is, with a destiny in life. It is described in African conceptual terms by Alassane Ndaw (1983:159–160, citing Bâ 1972), a Wolof university professor of philosophy:

Metatheme 1: Personal, Transcendent Peace

> The person is not an entity in itself, like a sealed box. Rather the person possesses several dimensions and is oriented in several directions, that are at the same time "exterior" and "interior." The several beings and states to which these correspond relate to the worlds of man and Creator... In the African conception of man and the universe, these are tightly integrated and at the same time dependent and part of the supreme power, and in fundamental relationships of equilibrium, exchange and interdependence.

6. Peace is founded on human comportment and virtue. (See theme 3: harmony with established laws.)
7. God will accept the intercession of a saint *(wàlliyu)* or other authorized intercessor on behalf of a disciple, as he would be ashamed *(ruus)* not to. Allah is too loyal not to heed the request of a saint that has worked on earth for Him.
8. Peace is inextricably linked to material well-being. (See theme 4: spiritual and material blessing.)
9. In the Islamic system, a genealogy of high ancestry is a prerequisite to the position of intermediary. The ancestry can be by blood from a recognized saint through descent from Muhammad, from a spiritual pedigree *(silsila,* A.), or in the second type of spiritual genealogy, by being "born" from close association with a particular saint, with that saint's baraka being transmitted to and then through the associate and his descendants.
10. In the traditional religious systems, an intermediary can be selected and ordained (tacitly) through several mechanisms, including heredity, apprenticeship, initiation, and special appointment by a spirit itself (Ray 1976:102ff).
11. Man has been placed at the cosmological center. This is explained by H. Gravrand (1983:219), describing the cosmology of the Serer:

> At the center of the universe stands living man, *O kiin,* surrounded by relays[28] of transcendence: the sun, the moon, mother earth, *Kumba Njay* (the rain), running water, fire, the winds, the rocks of *Roog*[29], the planted poles or stel of *Roog*, the sacred trees. [These] symbolize the visible world.

---
[28] Or re-transmitters of universal energy.
[29] God, or the Energy of the Universe.

> The contours of the energies of the universe [of the invisible world] pass through the equator [of the cosmos] and are concentrated in the world of the dead... Thus the energies of the universe reach the dead through the mediation of the living. The dead are therefore maintained by the living... The ancestors... in their turn re-emit the vital energies back to their lineages, to ensure their longevity, permanence and prosperity. The cult of the ancestors is founded on this vital exchange.

12. Being wellborn *(juudu bu réy)* or badly born *(juudu bu tuuti)* has much to do with peace and prosperity. No one will admit to being badly born, and various strategies are used to deny it if there is any hint that this might be the case, as defined by the social rules. Also, to call someone badly born is one of the deepest insults that can be inflicted on another. One of the most important aspects of being wellborn is to have a mother of recognized ancestry, piety, and submission. A banal example is the motto *bonne mère* (F.), painted on countless buses, taxis, and trucks. It literally means 'good mother', but implies much more—that both driver and passengers are protected because of good, exemplary ancestry, that the inherited upright character of the driver or owner are attested to by Allah, as His material blessing has been on them.

Subtheme 1-B: Man's Role to Initiate Action

> *Man's role is to initiate and execute appropriate, specific actions that can serve to reestablish communion with the beings and forces that operate in the world of man.*

The appropriate actions are contained in the cultus and ceremonies that are carried out as acts of allegiance and veneration to transempirical beings and forces. These include rituals, verbal expressions, dances, chants, sacrifices, and any other practices of phenomenological religion. The term CULTUS will be used to cover all these religious phenomena.

The cultus is analyzed under the three major religious expressions in the Senegambia: Islam, Sufi Islam, and ATR. The three systems are contrasted schematically in figure 11.

Metatheme 1: Personal, Transcendent Peace

Category	Islam	Sufi Islam	ATR
1. Object(s) of veneration	Allah	Muhammad and the saints	drivinities and spirits
2. Manner of access	the declaration of faith	creed *(wird)*	cosmic nodes
3. Requests and thanksgiving	prayer	prayers	prayers and private rituals
4. Offering of means	alms and offerings	alms and offerings	sacrifices and offerings
5. Ascetic requirements	fasting	fasting	ritual purification
6. Public allegiance	pilgrimage	pilgrimage	public ceremonies and rituals
7. Religious purpose	paradise	blessing and prosperity	harmony with ancestors and spirits

Fig. 11. Comparison of Islam, Sufi Islam and ATR as systems

Islam. Islam is the way of correct praxis and reason; exterior religion. Under Islam the cultus falls easily under the supreme God and the five pillars of Islam.[30]

1. Allah, the Creator. The name used is *yàlla*, as well as the Arabic word, Allah. The name *yàlla* is said by several scholars to pre-date the arrival of Islam (cf. A. Sylla 1978:46ff).
2. The declaration of faith (*téewe ci sa làmmiñ* and *shahadah*, A.). This is the obligatory declaration: "There is no God but Allah, and Muhammad is the apostle of Allah."

---

[30]See F. Rahman (1979) for one of the best of the countless treatments of the "five pillars."

3. Prayers. There are five prescribed daily ritual prayers (*julli* and *salat*, A.). Extemporaneous prayer is called *ñaan* and *du'a* (A.). There are also other words in Wolof to cover various other kinds and concepts of Islamic prayer.
4. Alms and offerings, both legal and voluntary. The legal alms, or welfare tax, are called *asaka*. The voluntary alms are *sarax*.
5. Fasting. Ramadan is the month of fasting during daylight hours. It is called *woor*, and *sawm* (A.).
6. Pilgrimage. Every Muslim has an obligation to make a pilgrimage to Mecca during his or her lifetime if he or she can afford it and is physically capable. In Wolof this is *aj*, and in Arabic *hajj*.
7. Paradise: To achieve Paradise (*àllaaxira* 'the abode of the dead' or *àjjana* 'paradise') and pass the Day of Judgment.

Popular or Sufi Islam. This practice of Islam is the way of correct relationships and emotions; interior religion. Under Sufi Islam (also referred to as popular Islam), the five pillars are practiced, as is of course the worship of Allah. C. Adams (1976) distinguishes between three types of Islam: orthodox, popular, and Sufi. In this essay I am following a slightly different three-fold classification: orthodox Islam, Sufi Islam, and ATR. Some of the beliefs and practices that Adams describes as characterizing popular Islam would here fall within Sufi Islam and part within ATR, or even in both. As my interest is to analyze Senegambian world view, I use the classification that best fits this region, whether or not it fully corresponds to Islam elsewhere.

From a world view classificatory viewpoint, Islam and Sufi Islam are parallel systems. Following the same seven points that were followed under Islam, Sufi Islam is revealed as having a parallel system which even Senegambian Muslim theologians recognize. Serigne B. Mbacké (1981) outlines the two systems as follows:

Islam	The Sufi Path
ihsan virtue	*hakika* the law of divine essence
|	|
iman faith	*tarika* the mystical path
|	|
islam submission	*shari'a* the formal law

Metatheme 1: Personal, Transcendent Peace

Seyyed Nasr (1975:133-134) considers the three steps Mbacké places in Islam as the major steps of the mystical progression of Sufism, in a nearly identical sequence: *islam* is the starting point; *ihsan* is the ultimate awareness, the possession of virtue and attachment to Allah, which is attained by only a few.

ihsan	living in the Divine presence; extinction in the Divine	(greater)
iman	faith in Divine unity	participation in religion, attachment to Allah
islam	submission to the Divine will	(lesser)

1. Muhammad and the saints. The objects of veneration are Muhammad and the Sufi saints, who are the appointed intercessors. The veneration is carried out through a variety of special prayers, poems, chants, oratory, hagiographies, and other forms. Whatever veneration is given to these humans is not considered idolatry *(biddaa)*, as there is always recognition of but one, supreme Allah.
2. Creed. Each Sufi order has a unique litany, or prayer, called a *wird* (W. and A.). This litany is the distinguishing practice of the order and de facto statement of faith and practice that will lead to enlightenment and to communion with Allah. True membership in an order is based on being initiated into (i.e., being authorized to use, and being instructed in the use of) the *wird* of the order.
3. Prayers. There are a number of special prayer litanies, called *sikar, jàng, wasifa,* etc. They amount to special Sufi prayers of one or more orders. There is also the prayer for supernatural guidance or knowing the will of Allah, *listikar,* which has many forms and can range from the orthodox to the esoteric.
4. Alms and offerings. The Sufi orders have nonobligatory (in principle but certainly not in practice) alms of submission that are due to be paid to the chief(s) of the order. In Wolof this is *addiya*. It is defined as the "gift one offers to a holy person in expectation of receiving some of that person's baraka" (A.-B. Diop 1981:300). The *barke (baraka,* A.) is the spiritual or material benediction received through a Sufi saint.
5. Fasting. Mystical (Sufi) Islam has a special rite called *xalwa,* through which the marabout, or even the disciple who has been initiated into its

mysteries, can enter into contact with *jinn* and, then through the mystical names of Allah, employ these *jinn* to resolve specific problems (see subtheme 2-B). The *xalwa* rite involves fasting and other ascetic practices.
6. Pilgrimage. A very frequent event in the Senegambia is pilgrimage to many different Sufi holy sites. During pilgrimage, the disciples expect to receive *barke*. These pilgrimages come under various names, depending on the Sufi order and the specific event that is being commemorated. The most common Wolof terms are *siyaare*, general term; *màggal*, the great annual Mouride pilgrimage to the mosque and headquarters at Touba; and *gàmmu*, the annual pilgrimage of the Tijani order to commemorate Muhammad's birth.
7. Blessing and prosperity. To be *texe* (blessed, prosperous, saved), and obtain *barke* are two ways of indicating religious purpose.

African Traditional Religion. ATR expresses itself through the realm of intermediaries. A similar classificatory scheme as found in Islam and Sufism can be followed, although the contents are quite different. All terms are Wolof unless otherwise noted.

1. Divinities and spirits.
   yàlla: God or the Supreme Spirit.
   rab: spirit; protecting divinity.
   rawane: personal, protecting spirit.
   jinne: genie; spirit; a supernatural being either good or bad.
   baatin: the hidden world; the practices of esoteric science, reserved for the initiated, that renders this world accessible to humans.
2. Cosmic nodes (points of concentration between the visible and the supramundane, through which cosmic power may be transmitted).
   gisaane: divination, clairvoyance.
   mbañ: totem; an ancestral spirit attached to a particular family.
   mbind: writing; a magic text.
   muslaay: a talisman (generic term); any object employed in protection against esoteric forces.
   saafara: magic potion; medication; remedy prepared by an initiate.
   tuur: traditional altar; the spirits attached to the altar.
   xàmb: a place or object serving as spirit locus.
   xérém: objects used in traditional cultus; idol.

Metatheme 1: Personal, Transcendent Peace 83

    xonjom: objects that have been embued with esoteric power (generic term).
3. Prayers and private rituals.
    jibar: black magic.
    jat: esoteric formulas for charming animals.
    kaar: formula used to counteract the evil tongue.
    léemu: bless; recite protective prayers.
    liggéey: to cast a spell on someone.
    lugg: to heal through pronouncing antipoison formulas.
    mocc: to ward off evil by use of counter-pain formulas.
    móolu: formulas or special words used in esoteric protection (generic term).
    ñaanu làmmiñ: oral prayers (generic term).
    topp: the principle of transfer of evil or of evil consequences. The complex of beliefs concerning evil tongue, mouth, eye, and touch, and the related principle by which these evils are effected, constitute one of the most pervasive belief clusters in the region. One Saafi healer who specializes in treating these ills revealed to me treatments for *topp*, from either the "side" (as he put it) of ATR or of Islam. The treatments are presented in parallel columns, as follows:

Traditional offerings for *topp*:	Islamic offerings for *topp*:
milk	white or red cola nut
white or red cloth	candle
white or red chicken	white or red cloth
white or red goat	milk
millet-sour milk porridge	sugar
chicken egg	cookies

    The following are explanations as provided by the healer: No explanation was given for the use of milk. The white or red cloth depends on the preference of the spirit, who dresses himself in the cloth. The chicken and goat, or a beef, may be required as part of the therapy. The malefic spirit drinks the shed blood of the animal, which restores it to a normal, peaceful state. The spirit accepts the animal's blood and frees that of the human. The millet-milk porridge is only needed in cases of the death of an infant. It serves to nourish the malefic spirit who thus allows the infant's spirit to be liberated (to return to the abode of souls). This offering must be renewed each year. The egg is to be broken at a crossroads. When two spirits are in contradiction with each other or, when fortune is not smiling, it unites both spirits in support of the offerer.

topp is cured in much the same manner whether by specialists in ATR or by marabouts using Islamic rites, except that with the latter there are no blood sacrifices. The marabout uses either *xalwa* or *listikar* rites, through which the spirits will communicate the offerings required in each particular case.

wojj: to bring back (e.g., a wife) or to conjure by esoteric means.
xarbaax: personal magic.
xuli bët: formula used to ward off the evil eye.

4. Sacrifices and offerings.
sarax rab: an animal sacrifice.
sarax guinaar, xar, nag, béy: sacrifice of a chicken, sheep, beef, goat.
tuur deret: a blood sacrifice.
weexal: honorarium or offering paid for esoteric operations.
xam-xamu baatin: ceremonial magic.
xor: honorarium or offering paid to a healer.

The reader may question why sacrifices are shown only as being characteristic of ATR and not of Islam or Sufi Islam (see figures 11 and 12). After all, both of the latter religious systems include tabaski (*id al-kabir*, A.), the major annual sheep feast at which time each family "sacrifices" a sheep. I queried many Senegambians about this rite and conclude that it is seen merely as a commemoration of what Abraham was prepared to do in sacrificing his son, and of Allah's provision of a ram.

Three basic differences, at least, separate the concept of commemoration from that of sacrifice. Commemoration: (1) is carried out on a calendrical basis, that is, on the same day every year and worldwide; (2) is a public religious rite that was given millenia ago by Allah to the whole *umma*, the universal community of Islam, and without reference to the spiritual state of the community; and (3) is carried out primarily to remember and identify with Abraham, Muhammad, and the *umma*. These features contrast point by point with sacrifice which: (1) is carried out at critical junctures when called for by ritual specialists; (2) is usually a private matter; and (3) is made to eradicate a particular case of *umute,* disturbed equilibrium, that has arisen between man and some part of the transempirical world, with the expectation that appeasement will thereby be achieved. The differences between the traditional concepts of sacrifice and the Muslim rite of commemoration are great enough to account for the people not considering the latter as being a sacrifice. Etically the Muslim rite is sacrifice; emically it is not (Pike 1967). These distinctions may not hold true for all of the Muslim world; rather, they may be another example of a universal Muslim form having a particular local meaning.

5. Ritual purification.

   baaw-naan: ceremonies and rituals to ensure there will be plentiful rains during the coming season.

   ndëpp: rites of spirit possession; thaumaturgical ceremonies, including purification of the spirit.

   sangat: ritual bath used to eliminate esoteric impurity, as a means for achieving desired ends.

6. Public ceremonies and rituals.

   gàmmu: a traditional holiday of games of strength (related to concepts of fertility), dancing, chanting, drumming, alcoholic drink, and libations that have largely disappeared or changed in character under pressure from Islam.

   njong: the rite of circumcision.

   ngénte: naming ceremony carried out eight days after birth.

   lël: initiation into manhood, now largely abandoned under the influence of Islam, cultural change, and urbanization.

   tyamaba (P.): cultus of the river deity-serpent-ethnic totem, means of communication with the supramundane (Kesteloot, Barbey and Ndongo 1985).

   xooy (S.): gathering of several neighboring villages before the rainy season, where shaman chiefs (*saltigi,* S.) reveal the state of the community's spiritual condition and the prospects of good rains, and during which the community reaffirms its belief in and adherence to the esoteric powers (Sène 1978).

7. Harmony with ancestors and spirits: *mucc* salvation (in the sense of living in peace and prosperity); *jot ci maam ya* 'touch the ancestors', that is, to go in peace to the abode of the ancestors.

Note that although the elements in this section are classified under ATR, many in fact are also practiced under Islam with certain changes that make them acceptable within Islam. For example, a *saafara* under ATR will be made on the basis of natural materials, like tree leaves or roots, while a *saafara* made under popular Islam is made on the basis of water poured over Qur'anic writing.

A number of questions are raised implicitly in the preceding presentation of Islam, popular Islam, and ATR.

Recognized scholars of African traditional religions, such as E. B. Idowu (1973) and E. G. Parrinder (1954), have proposed classificatory schemes that are widely quoted. The structure of ATR that Idowu proposes is as follows: (1) God (Idowu insists that ATR is monotheistic, even if a modified form); (2) divinities who are derivatives from God, and who have governing roles in the universe, with different local names and forming various local pantheons; (3) spirits, the apparitional entities "who may use material objects as temporary residences and manifest their presence and actions through natural objects and phenomena" (Idowu 1973:173); (4) ancestors, who are the deceased spirits of family members, closely related to this world but part of the supersensible world, who "abide with their folk on earth invisibly, to aid or hinder them, to promote prosperity or cause adversity" (1973:184), and who receive veneration verging on, or becoming, worship; and (5) the practice of magic and medicine. This is the tapping and harnessing of the power of elemental forces to serve desired ends, using appropriate techniques, "seeking to secure the proper means to the end [of] control over these elemental forces" (1973:189), rather than through the communion and communication that is used with divinities.

Idowu's structural analysis, or that of Parrinder, could be applied to ATR in the Senegambia. They have not been followed here because my goal has been to analyze world view assumptions, rather than to describe the religious system(s). My purpose is to deduce the basic assumptions behind the ceremonial and religious phenomena. These assumptions do not necessarily correspond with the religious structure. Take a computer as an analogy. The hardware designer is interested in the mechanical structure. The programmer is interested in the operating system. Each involves a different approach to the same subject. Here, the assumptions are analogous to the operating system. As an example of this difference in approach to ATR, all the supernatural beings can be considered together as one world view assumption applies to them as a group: that man has access to them only through intermediary human beings. It is unnecessary

Metatheme 1: Personal, Transcendent Peace

to consider them separately, as in Idowu's scheme. The purpose here is to consider the data as much as possible in the way the Senegambian people do, and as reflected in the deduced presuppositions.

Next, clarification needs to be made of where Islam, popular Islam, and ATR fit into the religious practices of the Wolof and other Islamized peoples of the area. If the peoples under consideration are about ninety-seven percent Muslim, just where the practice of ATR fits in needs to be made explicit. Figure 12 compares the practices of Islam and African traditional religion, indicating the degree of correspondence between their respective phenomenological expressions. It shows that there is a very high degree of correspondence, reflecting a near-identity of world view assumptions supporting the two religious systems.

As this study is primarily one of world view rather than of religious systems, no particular attempt has been made to determine what belief or practice belongs to one system or another. Neither has any particular attempt been made to determine which people or what percentage of the people are following one practice or another. What has been in view has been to ascertain as many of the significant phenomena (and under the proposition being discussed in this section, ascertain the significant RELIGIOUS phenomena) as possible, and then make deductions from them about world view.

What has been identified as pertaining to ATR are practices for which there are currently used local terms, and for which there are current practitioners to be found. That they can be called practices of ATR is clear upon perusing the abundant literature, some of which has been cited. My primary purpose is not to put one religious label or another on them, but to analyze the underlying, deep-level belief system.

Still, one wonders how, among these overwhelmingly Muslim peoples, so much of ATR still seems to be present. An observation made by Malise Ruthven is pertinent. He (1984:265) notes that ritual will be Islamized before beliefs will be, as a general rule:

> In Islam, syncretism in ritual is much more difficult to justify than syncretism in theology. Whereas every kind of religious belief can be accommodated within the framework of Islamic concepts merely by the adoption of Islamic terminology or symbols, the outward recognition of these symbols in formal religious observance is a matter on which orthodoxy is severe and uncompromising.

This certainly applies to the Senegambia, where religious practices seem clearly to be more Islamic than are the underlying beliefs.

Islam	Correspondence*	Traditional Religion
Confession of faith:	0	
teewe ci sa làmmiñ/shahadah (A.)	0	
Prayer to Allah:	≠	Prayer to spirits and divinities:
salat ritual prayer	0	
ñaan/du'a (A.) free-form prayer	≈	*ñaan* free-form prayer
ñaan-yàlla prayer to Allah	≠	*ñaan ci rab yi* prayer to spirits
tuub ask pardon for self	≠	*jógal ci sa bopp* undertake occult measures
	0	*léemu* invoke spirits
Fasting:	0	
sawm (A.)	0	
koor	0	
Tithes, offerings:	0	
asaka, zakat (A.)	0	
Pilgrimages:	≈	Annual public assemblies:
Mecca	0	
siyaare, màggal, gàmmu	≈	*gàmmu* feast days
	0	*xooy* (S.) rains prognostication
Miracles:	=	Occult wonders:
kéeman miracle of Allah	=	*kéeman* a mystery
kawtef miracle of Allah	=	*kawtef* a supernatural act
Spirits:	=	Spirits:
jinn genies	0	
rawane protector spirits	≈	*rab* spirits
Cultus of spirits:	=	Cultus of spirits:
xalwa retreat	≈	*tuur* altar
	0	*xàmb* place of cultus
	0	*xérém* object of spirit residence
Divination:	≈	Divination:
listikar divination by dreams	=	*tëddale* divination by dreams
Interior knowledge:	=	Interior knowlege:
xam-xamu baatin magic	≈	*xam-xam buñul* black magic
Amulets and talismans:	≈	Amulets and talismans:
xaatim talisman	≈	*xonjom* talisman
Occult remedies:	=	Occult remedies:
*[biddaa]*** superstitions	≈	*cosaan* traditions
[araam] forbidden things	≈	*rab yi daañu ko bañ* taboos
saafara magic potions	≠	*tul* magic potions
gàllaaj occult protection	=	*gàllaaj* occult protection
Destiny:	≠	Destiny:
àtte-yàlla the edicts of Allah	≠	man's ceremonial role in cosmos

(continued)

Metatheme 1: Personal, Transcendent Peace

Islam	Correspondence*	Traditional Religion
Malediction, benediction:	≠	Malediction/benediction:
barke blessing of Allah	0	
toskare the product of a curse	=	*toskare* the product of a curse
tuyaaba divine recompense	0	
Circumcision *njong****	≠	Circumcision *njong****
Sacrifices:	≠	Sacrifices:
	0	*tuur deret* blood sacrifice
	0	Black magic:
	0	*jibar* black magic
	0	*liggéey* occult actions
Transfer of malevolent intent:	=	Transfer of malevolent intent:
cat evil tongue	=	*cat* evil tongue
bët evil eye	=	*bët* evil eye
laal evil touch	=	*laal* evil touch
topp principle of transfer	=	*topp* principle of transfer
	0	Initiation rites *kasag, lël:*
	0	*njong* circumcision
	0	*siru* secret lore
	0	*kanam gu ñu yaat* masks
	0	*maas* age-grades

Notes:
  * This column indicates the degree of correspondence between the Islamic and Traditional elements:
      = equivalent   ≠ distantly related
      ≈ roughly equivalent   0 no equivalency
  ** [ ] indicates a forbidden item.
  *** Circumcision occurs in both Islam and traditional religion but on different ideological bases; only the physical operation is common to both.

Fig. 12. Comparison of practices: Islam and ATR

A common Wolof saying aptly serves to close this discussion: *Liggéeyal àddina ba mu mel ni doto dee, liggéeyal àllaaxira ba mu mel ni suba ngaay dee* 'work for the world as if you were not going to die; work for the future life as if you were to die tomorrow'. This expression, even said to be a *hadith*, is used to justify many actions. The world it refers to includes any earthly desires and any earthly means, including those that are esoteric. Working for the future life as taught by Islam means practicing the five pillars of Islam *lislaam*. This is concise evidence that many Senegambians accept Islam as the means to gain paradise, while traditional practices are believed to provide the means to gain the essential spiritual power needed for life in the here and now. One can thus conclude that the pre-Islamic belief system is still fundamentally intact, at least at the deep, ontological levels. ATR had little concept of a hereafter. That came with Islam and was added on to ATR. It remains the primary domain of Islam. ATR was a religion of and for the living, and it remains so today.

It is of note here that of the sixty-three themes identified (on the three levels of metatheme, theme and subtheme) in the course of Senegambian world view analysis, none can be said to denote a particularly Muslim deep-level assumption. Islam, per se, appears only at more specific, that is, less abstract, levels of the culture. See figures 13 and 14, where specific Islamic elements are presented. It can be asserted, therefore, that Islam has not changed the basic historical world view of the Senegambian peoples. This assertion is made, not on the basis of a historical-comparative study, but on the basis of none of the deep-level assumptions being perceptibly Islamic, or different from those of ATR.

The question of where Islam fits into Senegambian world view can be analyzed in the framework of the eight-level model that was presented in chapter two. In the analysis here, two representative cultural Muslim elements are considered, the pilgrimage to Touba which pertains to popular Islam, and the Qur'an which belongs to orthodox Islam. Both fall under the same propositions at the levels of metatheme, theme and subtheme.

The examples in figures 13 and 14 show from levels one to seven the basic beliefs of Islam and ATR which underlie the conceptual system. At level eight, however, the deepest level of assumptions—ontological absolutes—Islamic assumptions are not different from those of ATR. What this indicates is not yet clear. A number of comparative studies of ontological absolutes would seem to be necessary before many assertions would be justified. What does seem to emerge is that Islamic world view was compatible with that of ATR, or perhaps it accommodated itself to the world view of ATR, and so did not change at the deepest level. This could be examined by means of comparative studies. What this compatibility of world views may have meant to the acceptance of Islam by Senegambians will also have to await further study before an answer emerges. One would assume it had much to do with the implantation of Islam, but this assumption is only mentioned as an intuitive judgment.

The second example of where Islam fits into the Senegambian world view is given in figure 14. It needs to be emphasized that the assumptions presented on the different levels in figures 13 and 14 are only samples of the many that can be adduced for all levels, except on the level of ontological absolutes.

Metatheme 1: Personal, Transcendent Peace

World view propositions:	Themes and assumptions relating to one particular surface-level behavior
1. Metatheme 1	Senegambians seek to have personal transcendent peace.
2. Theme 1	Human beings need to establish alliances.
3. Subtheme 1-B	Man's role is to initiate and execute appropriate, specific actions that can serve to reestablish communion with the beings and forces that operate in the world of man.
4. Surface level element	Pilgrimage to Touba at the Magal (described in detail in chapter five).

Deep level assumptions:

5. Folk explanations	Obtain *barke*. Give offering of loyalty *(addiya)*. Keep in favor with Allah, Amadou Bamba, and my marabout. See friends, maintain social network, enjoy. Attend the *màggal*—a duty for a good Mouride.
6. Existential assumptions	Bamba was a great man, statesman, savior-prophet, saint, founder of the order. A disciple needs to practice his faith before Allah and fellowman. Bamba and my marabout guarantee well-being now and Paradise later. I would be criticized and ashamed if I didn't go. Praying and otherwise participating is uplifting to body and spirit.
7. Ontological assumptions	God has ordained intermediaries that are the guarantors of Paradise. Peace and prosperity are essential to a good life. Peace and prosperity are attainable through the Mouride way, and through its saints. Blessing *(barke)* needs to be renewed and built up at Bamba's tomb.
8. Ontological absolutes	(The ten universal assumptions identified for Senegambian world view are given in the left column of figure 15, as well as in appendix five.)

Fig. 13. Abstractive levels:
Example one, pilgrimage to Touba at the Magal

World view propositions:	Themes and assumptions relating to one particular surface-level behavior
1. Metatheme 1	Senegambians seek to have personal transcendent peace.
2. Theme 1	Human beings need to establish alliances.
3. Subtheme B	Man's role is to initiate and execute appropriate, specific actions that can serve to reestablish communion with the beings and forces that operate in the world of man.
4. Surface level behavior	The use of the Qur'an in religious life.

Deep-level assumptions:

5. Folk explanations	It is the eternal word of Allah, in Arabic, revealed to Muhammad. Memorization and recitation win merit against the Day of Judgment. It is the basis of earth fertility. A very common belief is that the earth is fertile because Allah "sprinkled" it at creation with the Qur'an (S. Diop 1987). It contains the 99 powerful names of Allah.
6. Existential assumptions	It contains all the knowledge of the world, but only initiated saints understand the powerful, hidden meanings. Marabouts know which Qur'anic verses to use to prepare amulets and potions for illness and health, prosperity, and success. If the Qur'an (plus Sunna and Shari'a) were perfectly practiced by Muslims, Islamdom would be united, living in prosperity, and leading the world (Hodgson 1974). The eternal purpose of the Qur'an was to reveal the five pillars needed to be righteous before Allah.
7. Ontological assumptions	The Qur'an is a book of powerful, hidden meanings that only initiates can uncover and unleash. The average Muslim cannot, and does not need to, understand the meaning of the Qur'an. The Qur'an reveals Allah as very merciful towards Muslims, who therefore do not have to be unduly concerned about the Day of Judgment. As Arabic is a language of heaven (as shown by the fact that the Qur'an was given to Muhammad verbatim, from the Eternal Qur'an extant in heaven), so Arabic and Arabic writing have mystical and authoritative value.
8. Ontological absolutes	(The ten universal assumptions identified for Senegambian world view are given in the left column of figure 15, as well as in appendix five.)

Fig. 14. Abstractive levels:
Example two, the use of the Qur'an in religious life

Metatheme 1: Personal, Transcendent Peace

We see, therefore, that Islam is very visible at the surface level. This goes without saying, as by definition our world view analysis starts with surface level, cultural phenomena. At the levels of folk explanations and even of existential assumptions, Islam is still clearly and importantly visible. But at the ontological level Islam begins to fade out. And at the level of ontological absolutes (which are the structural equivalents of the operational propositions, or themes), Islam is distinguishable only in assumptions about Allah and destiny. The conclusions that can be drawn from this are: (1) in regard to ultimate relationships, expressed in metathemes, Islam and ATR are basically identical; (2) in regard to ultimate causes, Islam required no changes from ATR in ontological assumptions, but it did require adoption of additional concepts regarding Allah and paradise; and (3) the forms of Islamic rituals are very important, while the deeper meanings are more susceptible to accommodation with local belief systems.

This means that the deepest-level assumptions are more general than Islam. Said another way, Islam seems to be the expression of assumptions that are broader than just that one religious expression. Perhaps it could be said that a number of religions could be practiced on the basis of the deepest-level assumptions found in the Senegambia. And in fact, as seen above, at least two religions are being practiced on the basis of one set of world view assumptions. If popular Islam is considered to be a separate religion from orthodox Islam, there would be three religions built on one set of assumptions.

Although this is not a comparative study, a parenthetical comment seems in order. It should be enlightening to consider whether or not Christianity could be practiced on the basis of the world view assumptions found in the Senegambia. There are, of course, many quite distinct belief systems calling themselves Christian. What is considered in this parenthesis is Evangelical Christianity which, as one of the more conservative expressions of Christianity, could be expected to have assumptions that contrast with those identified for the Senegambia.

In figure 15, the ten Senegambian world view ontological assumptions are presented in one column and their assumed compatibilities with Christianity are briefly commented on in the second column. The reference work for Christian doctrine is Donald Guthrie (1981). This summary analysis does not address the question of whether or not any of the ten Senegambian assumptions is indeed part of the Evangelical Christian world view or not, but only whether or not each one would or would not be compatible with this expression of Christianity.

Ontological Absolutes	Compatibility with Christianity
1. *God.* God is transcendent and remote.	Incompatible.
2. *Universe.* The universe is composed of both visible and invisible reality (to man), but the invisible is of greater ontological significance than the visible.	Incompatible.
3. *Peace.* Peace is the ideal state and harmony is the ideal relationship of the universe.	Substantially compatible; reconciliation with God is of utmost importance; peace is an ideal but not such a supreme value; love and truth would probably rank above it.
4. *Integration.* At all levels of the universe, the ideal condition is integration. That is, all parts need to be brought together through interdependence.	Partly compatible, in that unity is an ideal, but only if centered on Jesus Christ.
5. *Destiny.* Every being and part of the universe has an assigned role that needs to be filled.	Partly compatible, in that all parts and beings of God's creation were created for a purpose, but much of the concept of destiny is incompatible.
6. *Hierarchy.* The universe is organized on the basis of hierarchies of position and power on every level and within each domain.	Basically incompatible, in that the equality of men and women before God is stressed, as is their direct access to Him, yet hierarchies of spirit beings is taught.
7. *Power.* The universe is administrated through the exercise of inherent and derived power.	Basically incompatible, in that God is far more immanent and effectively active, and therefore secondary powers are unneeded.
8. *Reality.* All reality is dichotomized into exterior and interior.	Basically incompatible although the reality of an invisible world of spirit beings, and even of forces, is taught.
9. *Human beings.* Man is the ceremonial center of the universe.	Incompatible, except in the sense that man is a primary actor in the cosmic battle between good and evil (God and Satan). The ceremonial center is the death and resurrection of Jesus.
10. *Transfer.* All spiritual good or evil and abstract qualities are transmitted through the principle of transfer... through the mechanism of intent.	Incompatible, although Christianity recognizes the constructive/destructive effects humans exercise over one another; love toward others is an eternal principle.

Fig. 15. Senegambian world view: Compatibility with Christianity

Metatheme 1: Personal, Transcendent Peace

The ontological absolutes of Evangelical Christianity are, therefore, seen to contrast with those found in the Senegambia. Thus, the world view assumptions identified for the Senegambia cannot be considered to be universal. The main point of this parenthetical study has been to examine this question, however briefly, to remove any doubt about the world view described in this essay as being universal.

Subtheme 1-C: Masters of the Seen and Unseen

> *The beings and forces of the transempirical world confer on initiated individuals a consciousness awakened to the supernatural realm that makes them masters of the laws of the seen and the unseen.*

The key word is MASTER. Three conditions must be met before one can be considered to be a master *nittu xam-xam* 'a person with understanding' of the laws of the seen and the unseen. These are, first of all, to have *gis* or *xam-xamu biir* 'double vision' (interior and exterior). In order to be a great leader, an individual must understand reality. Reality is divided into hidden, spiritual reality *(baatina)* and exterior, visible reality *(saxiira)*. Hidden reality is more important ontologically than that which is visible. A common proverb states *lu yëngu la ko yëngal a ko ëpp doole*, 'every existing thing and life is the product of a higher reality'. This means there is something higher behind all visible reality. Consequently, it is crucial to have knowledge of the hidden realm for the really important events of life, but it is only accessible to chosen, initiated, elite individuals. With their understanding of the hidden world, these enlightened individuals also have a greater understanding of the visible world as well. Hence, a major spiritual leader, as well as a diviner, must have double vision or "double view," the term used by Niane (1978:1). The Wolof say of their renowned leaders *xalifatou saxiira wa baatina* 'that he had the spiritual grade of having the interior and exterior vision of the world'.

Second, he must have a personal revelation and endowment of power from deity. Double vision comes from revelation. Revelation, in the form of inner illumination, is the main attraction and *raison d'être* of Sufi, or mystical, Islam. The teaching of the well-known marabout Bokar Taal is clear about the primacy of revelation and illumination (interior vision):

> Mysticism originates from two sources: Firstly, a Revelation sent by God to an elected prophet of his choice, that will teach and propagate the revelation; secondly, a direct intuition of the divine

Light given to the predestined believer, as the fruit of long meditation and religious practice. [Bâ 1980:131 and Brenner 1984:174]

Amadou Bamba was the founder of the Mouride order and dominant personality of the Senegambian region for the entire postconquest period, 1886 to the present. Amadou Bamba is a master figure on many counts. His origins could hardly have been better. His family was part of the Tukulor *torodbe* (P.) class or caste, which dominated the Senegal River valley kingdoms for centuries. Torodbe warrior-saints were the principal leaders of successful military jihads all across west Africa from the 17th to the 19th centuries (Clarke 1982:80ff). Bamba was from an illustrious Torodbe line. Heredity is a very important concept in Senegambian world view, as it is believed that spiritual and material blessing can be transmitted hereditarily through the father or especially through the mother. Bamba's mother, Diarra Bousso, was considered to be a virtuous woman and was also descended from Muhammad (Cruise O'Brien 1971:39). Clearly, Bamba fulfilled the requirement of being *juudu bu réy* 'wellborn'.

Bamba claimed to have had one spiritual revelation, or perhaps many spiritual revelations, directly from the prophet Muhammad. This is made very clear in his writings, even if the dates and times of the revelations are never specified. The following lines, extracted from several poems, need to be understood in the Wolof context. Wolof serious communication is like the proverbial iceberg, i.e., nine-tenths is hidden below the surface. Bamba's disciples do not just accept the words, but look behind them for the greater, spiritual significance.

> The apparition of the Prophet [Muhammad] and his Companions protected me from my enemies.
>
> The Prophet accompanied his servant [Bamba] all the time of his exile, far from his people.
>
> The Prophet granted me favors for which I addressed to him extraordinary and just praises of admiration.
>
> Before this a voice seemed to say to me, "Be the Servant of Him that will protect you from all harm, by the grace of God the protector."
>
> The Prophet gave this order: "Teach the Mourides and all your contemporaries that will accept your words..." [Samb 1972:464-65]

Third, a master must demonstrate signs that testify to the revelation. Not everyone who claims to have had a revelation is believed. Visible signs are necessary to prove that Allah has indeed chosen the individual and endowed him with power. Many miracles are attributed to a *wàlliyu* 'saint', or *sang-bi* 'master, lord, king': healing, communicating with *jinn*, defeating foes, etc. Amar Samb (1969:745) recounts what he heard of an orator telling of the miracles of Bamba during the pilgrimage to Touba:

> Is there an equal among the human race, of him whose exile lasted 7 years, 7 months, 7 weeks, 7 days, 7 hours, 7 minutes? Of course there is not! The first miracle of the *Sérigne* took place just at noon, when he was served a plate of roast dog [by the French, while in detention]. As soon as the plate was put in front of Amadou Bamba, each piece of meat began to bark and to growl like a ferocious dog... They locked Amadou Bamba in a cage with an enormous lion. The next day when they opened the cage the beast attacked the guards, but *Khadim-er-Rasul* [the servant of the Prophet] was untouched. Out of pity he left the cage, grabbed the lion by the mane and made it lie down at his feet like a docile sheep. At that point, the *toubabs* [Europeans], trembling with fear, bowed before him and praised him for his courage and holiness.

Of course, many accounts are more serious than that of this orator carried away by his oratory, but the many oral and printed hagiographies abound with every kind of miracle imaginable, which are clearly believed by many disciples.

Bamba is the model, if not the archetype, of a charismatic, master figure of the modern era. There have been others in Senegambian history. There are also living masters, especially certain of the caliph-generals of the orders, who are judged to exude the blessing and prosperity of Allah, mediated through Muhammad.

The second key word to be noted is INITIATED. This is a key word throughout the Senegambia. Knowledge is understood in terms of general knowledge, *saxiir* 'the visible world' and hidden knowledge, *baatin* 'the hidden world'. The hidden world is the truly significant one. This was discussed above.

The Iranian scholar Seyyed Nasr (1975:58–59) describes the exterior-interior dichotomy as central to Islamic thought, both Sunni and Shi'ite:

> To penetrate into the inner mysteries of the Quran *is* precisely to reach back to its Origin because its Origin is the most inward, and

the revelation or manifestation of the sacred text is at once a descent and an exteriorization of it. Everything actually comes from within to the outside, from the interior to the exterior and we who live 'in the exterior' must return to the interior if we are to reach the Origin. Everything has an interior *(batin)* and an exterior *(zahir)*, and *ta'wil* is to go from the *zahir* to the *batin*, from the external form to the inner meaning... The idea of penetrating into the inner meaning of things is to be seen everywhere in Islam, in religion, philosophy, science and art.

Although the Wolof terms for interior and exterior knowledge are derived from Arabic, it seems unlikely the concepts originated with the advent of Islam. The dichotomy is deeply rooted in the Senegambian conceptual system and is also fundamental to the concepts of ATR as seen in the region. Therefore they would seem to be both Islamic and traditional.

Every substantial event of life has significant hidden meaning, probably surpassing the surface meaning. Humans need to understand the hidden meanings, to live and plan their lives to their best advantage, and to avoid reverses. They also need to understand any hidden meanings that might be directed against them by others. These hidden realities, the more significant realities behind apparent realities, apply to illnesses, prosperity, setbacks, success, physical attractiveness, intelligence—everything of life.

A seemingly related phenomena is the cultural pattern of using hidden meanings in everyday speech. Probably all Senegambians use this communication ploy, as, for example, they consider Africans from west and central Africa to be naïvely direct and simple in their speech and manners, and make jokes about them. But Wolof from the Kajoor region (north of Dakar, along and inland from the coast) are famous, even in the Senegambia, for hiding their true meanings in surface speech forms that seem to express apparently straightforward meanings. The Wolof say *waxinwa déggin la laaj* 'for allusive speech you need an allusive ear.' Proverbs and folk stories are also filled with hidden meanings.

It follows then that if the hidden world and hidden meanings are so important, enlightened members will have a prominent place in society, and an accompanying power, prestige, and prosperity. This is certainly the case.

Theme 2: Peace is a Consequence of Harmony

Peace in the human spirit is the consequence of a condition of harmony between human beings and transempirical beings and forces.

Subtheme 2-A. When a person has the interior radiance of peace, it is manifested through coherence of thought and interior harmony, which together enable the person to counterbalance the ascendancy of transcendent forces over him or her.

Subtheme 2-B. When there is a breach in the relationship with transempirical beings and/or forces, man suffers disastrous consequences (such as insanity, chronic bad luck, and failure in life).

The peace referred to in this theme is not just an English dictionary definition of peace, "Freedom from disagreement or quarrels; harmony; concord; an undisturbed state of mind; absence of mental conflict; serenity; calm; quiet; tranquility" (Friend and Guralnik 1956). It is all of this and more. It involves material well-being, one's position in life, success— "everything" as we have seen in the Wolof saying *jàmm ci la lépp xejj*, 'everything is contained in peace'. Another proverb that speaks of peace is *bakkaan jàmm lay laaj* (W.) 'the human soul only aspires to have peace'.

It may be helpful to consider this concept of peace in terms of the basic laws of a nation. There are laws regarding individual rights, property rights, taxes, the functioning of the different levels of government, the judiciary, legislative and executive systems, regulations regarding the environment, and ad infinitum. The archaic term used for this was laws of the commonweal, or of the well-being of society. There is a sense in which the goal of the common weal is really social peace under which all citizens can live in individual peace so that they can pursue their right to "life, liberty and the pursuit of happiness," as stated in the U.S. Declaration of Independence. This is analogous to the Senegambian concept that peace is the fundamental law and goal of not just a nation but of the whole universe, and that all well-being is related to this peace, and that all humans have a part in establishing and maintaining it. The focus of this peace is cosmic not worldly, as peace on earth is not possible without peace in heaven.

So a definition of transcendent peace in the Senegambia is: The state of equilibrium and harmony between the exterior (visible) and superior (transempirical) worlds, that flows from putting into practice the set of prescriptions ordained by transempirical beings for the well-functioning of the cosmic world order.

Senegambian peace is hierarchical, as is all of the cosmology. The highest level can be called mystical peace. This is related to theme 1, above, where the alliances between humans and the supramundane were described. These alliances serve to establish and maintain peace between human intermediaries and the supramundane. This concept is basic to Islam as well as to ATR. From this alliance relationship springs the harmonious relationship servant-master, that is, the individual religious believers and the human intermediaries through whom they relate to divinity.

Hierarchical peace also means that it is related to many levels. It is not attained by just establishing a proper relationship with the Supreme Deity, or with one spirit or *jinn*. Transcendent peace involves establishing peace relationships with all levels. These include the Supreme Deity and intermediate beings, including *jinns*, angels, saints, demiurges, ancestors, and masters of the elements. This does not mean that every individual has to develop relations in all these dimensions. It means that in the Senegambia there are individuals and/or cultus relating to all these entities, and individuals fit into the system in different ways, depending on whether they are Muslims, followers of ATR, people who are more traditional, or people being urbanized.

Peace also means peace in society with family, friends, and acquaintances, including all those with whom one shares peace *(àndi-jàmm)*. This is a beautiful definition of friends.

Peace means peace with enemies or potential enemies through peace alliances, intermarriages, negotiation, and accepting responsibilities. For Senegambians the wars of conquest in their history, the Islamic jihads, and the slave raiding and pillaging were caused by disturbances brought by Arab and European forces, not by the peace-loving peoples of this part of West Africa who, when left alone, know how to live peaceably with their neighbors.

Peace is peace with, and respect for, elders from the family unit on up the social scale. They are the guardians of peace. This is their main role.

Peace is seen as continuous, from this world to the next. That is, peace flows from social peace to peace with ancestors, to cosmic peace, and back. Hierarchy does not imply compartmentalization.

Many common greetings reflect the importance of peace, such as the following (all examples are from Wolof):

mba jàmm genn yendu 'did you pass the day in peace?'
jàmm nga fanaan 'did you pass the night in peace?'

Metatheme 1: Personal, Transcendent Peace

jàmm ngeen am 'do you have peace?'
jàmm rekk 'I have only peace!'
seen yaram jàmm 'do your bodies have peace?'

The importance of peace is also seen in common descriptions of respected men.

bëgg na jàmm 'he loves peace.'
nitt u jàmm la 'he is a man of peace.'

One expected quality of a person of stature in society, a *kilifa*, is that he be known as a man of peace.

Peace is not a state of a balance of terror, as between superpowers, but the integration of society around a common consensus. Social harmony is the key concept. Sulayman Nyang (1984:87) expresses Senegambian man's desire for peace and harmony in these terms:

> Indeed, if there is ever going to be a structure of world peace, its creators must know the secret language which traditional African man has evolved over several millennia to deal with fellow men as well as nature. This language is that of tolerance and social harmony, a medium of communication which was best symbolized in the old Africa by the drum. Such a human instrument does not stimulate and excite the mind; rather it coaxes and subdues it to join the *body* of man in the rhythmical dance of nature.

So peace is not primarily a concept or a state in the Senegambia, but is really an all-pervasive way of life. Indeed, much of life's time, activities, and means are spent establishing and maintaining peace, at all levels.

Subtheme 2-A: Interior Radiance of Peace

> *When a person has the interior radiance of peace, it is manifested through coherence of thought and interior vision which together enable the person to counterbalance the ascendancy of transcendent forces over him or her.*

When discussing peace, knowledge, emotions, thoughts, values, and other abstract concepts, Senegambians frequently use the qualifying terms interior and exterior (cf. Senghor 1964:90, Ndaw 1983:35, 90, 108, 159, Ba 1972). The terms express a dichotomy that is important to Senegambian world view, yet difficult for a Westerner to comprehend. Cheikh Sy (1969:129), a scion of the Tijani order who published a lengthy monograph on the main rival Sufi order of Mourides, makes a clear statement of the importance of the interior-exterior concept:

> All orders have interior and exterior aspects. The first resides in its doctrines; it is metaphysical. The second resides in its practice, the *wird*, more easily perceptible than the doctrine itself.

The Wolof speak of: (1) interior peace *(xel mu dal)*; (2) the interior world *(baatin)*; (3) the interior vision that enables clairvoyants to interpret dreams *(gis)*; (4) the solid interior of a man of good character *(bopp bu rëy)*; and (5) the interior attitude of a pregnant woman that will determine the future character of the child and adult *du ëmbu neen* (lit. 'not pregnant for nothing'). The concept is further expressed in the Wolof proverb, *liggéey u ndey, añup doom* 'the child inherits directly (in the womb) the blessing or curse from the mother'.

The qualifier exterior is used in describing: (1) exterior knowledge *(mbaax u bitim réew)*, such as that taught in French language schools, which contrasts with the interior *(mbaax u réewmi)* or traditional values of the people; (2) the exterior elements in traditional healing ceremonies *(déebaa-déeb)*, such as dancing, drumming and chanting; (3) the exterior atmosphere or ambiance *(xumbal)*, designed to recreate an emotional state of communication; and (4) exterior peace *(jàmm biti)*, as contrasted with interior peace *(jàmm biir)*.

A third concept, superior, is also used, although not as frequently as interior and exterior, and employs a variety of terms, such as *kàttan* 'force or power' or *xam-xamu bu ya* 'grand knowledge'. It overlaps with exterior in some contexts. Examples of its usage are: (1) traditional altars to family or village spirits that are tied to *tuur* or *boëkin* (Diola), which are superior forces; (2) Senegambians seeking mystical peace who follow the directives of the interpreters (marabouts and other intermediaries) of the superior force *(kàttan)* (a common prayer is *Yàlla na Yàlla def jàmm ci kàttan u boroom* 'may God give peace by his superior power'); and (3) Senegambians following their religious convictions because of their being convinced of the existence of principles of the hidden, superior force *(doole baatin)*.

These three terms reflect a simple difference in semantics and culture as well as a difference in deep-level conceptions of reality. An example of a semantic difference would be the Senegambian expression *xel mu dal* 'interior peace' where we might just say 'peace of heart' or being 'at peace

Metatheme 1: Personal, Transcendent Peace

with yourself'. Or we might say that someone 'without internal peace' is agitated.

Beyond simple semantic differences, there are differences in basic concepts. The questions of the origins, explanations, and reasons behind diseases is a good example. Western man looks for scientific explanations and when he finds one, he considers it the complete explanation; Senegambian man looks for explanations that are spiritual or mystical. Even educated Senegambians, who understand that, say, measles is caused by a virus that is transmitted from one human to another, will also understand that the who, when, how, and even the where of getting measles may be related to spiritual, mystical forces. And they believe that those who have adequate mystical defenses will not get the disease.

Measles is a relatively trivial example but it illustrates the concept that every reality—even those with scientific explanation in the Western sense—has an interior reality behind or inside it, and that the hidden reality is generally of greater significance to man than the visible one.

The classificatory triad interior-exterior-superior can be understood in terms of: (1) man, (2) knowledge-reality, and (3) the supramundane.

Man is made of two halves. One is interior, his subjective half that is made up of thoughts, emotions, values, and dreams (including the subconscious, which was not a Senegambian concept). The other is the objective, exterior half, that which is visible and otherwise discernible by the senses, including speech. This is diagrammed on the left side in figure 16.

Senegambians are also very conscious that outside of man there is knowledge-reality. They consider it to be divided into two parts. One is visible and otherwise knowable through the senses—the exterior reality and the knowledge open to all humans. The other is behind this exterior reality—an interior one, known only to those initiated into it. Even those initiated into the interior reality understand only as much as their initiation has revealed to them. The more knowledge of the interior reality an initiate has, the greater is his (or her) degree of mastery of this reality. See figure 16.

This is explained by Ndaw in terms of a "double body," rather than exterior-interior. What he calls the double in the following quotation, I call the interior, because that seems to be the more common Senegambian usage.

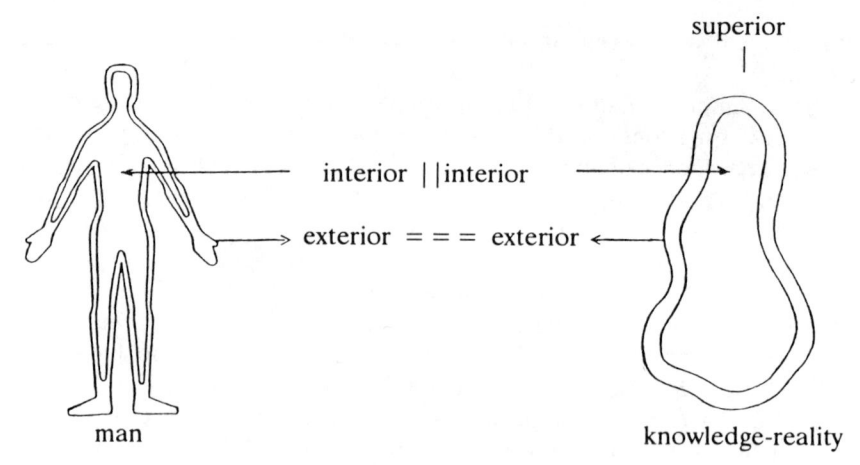

```
                                                superior
                                                   |
                              interior | | interior
     [man figure]  ←—————→                    ←—————→  [shape]
                              exterior === exterior

         man                                  knowledge-reality
```

Figure 16. Interior, exterior, and superior realities

The practice of divination is based on a conception of the human person that emphasizes one part of the soul: the double body. The transfer of the double defines various states of the person. The most extreme, that is, its permanent transfer, corresponds to death.

The double is a center where the energy and vital forces of the individual are concentrated. The mastery of the double confers on the diviner an exceptional lucidity, enabling him to pass beyond obstacles that prevent profane or less sensitive individuals from understanding the fluid, the life current that circulates between living beings.

As the double is mobile, the diviner himself becomes part of the circulation. From then on, he can penetrate man, society and the world in a kind of pan-communication. [Ndaw 1983:102]

Lastly, there is the superior reality. It is shown in figure 16 above knowledge-reality, but it is less directional than are interior or exterior. In conceptual terms, it usually refers to transempirical beings and forces, either directly or indirectly. But the interior of reality may also refer to these same beings and forces.

In terms of subtheme 2-A, transcendent peace is a major goal and reality in the Senegambian conceptual system. This peace is made accessible to individuals and to society through their penetrating into the interior of reality, in order to gain rapport with the superior reality in it or above it.

Metatheme 1: Personal, Transcendent Peace

But the average person cannot penetrate into the interior of reality. He or she must go to those who can penetrate it through their initiation into and mastery of parts of this reality. And that is much of what life—even daily life—is all about in the Senegambia.

The initiate has access to interior reality *(baatin)* through esoteric, mystical knowledge. Through dream-inducing rites *(tëddale)*, mystical Islamic procedures or prayers *(listikar)*, possession rites *(ndëpp)*, and special mystical retreats *(xalwa)*, he penetrates his own interior and thereby gains access to the interior of reality-knowledge, where he is in communication with superior beings or forces.

This is diagrammed in figure 16 by the blockage between the interior of man and the interior of reality, shown with a ||. This is simply to indicate that the interior of man cannot contact the interior of reality through the external world. Access is gained only from the interior of initiated men to the interior of reality through mystical or esoteric knowledge and experience.

Subtheme 2-A states that an interior radiance of peace is manifested through coherence of thought and clear interior vision, enabling the person to counterbalance the threat of being overpowered by negative transcendent forces. This is analogous to photographic film in a camera, where adequate and sharply focused light produce a clear image. If the interior light and focus are inadequate or absent, there will be a fuzzy image or none at all (cf. Faye 1983:58–59).

This description, and the state it describes, verges on the enigmatic, not to say the incoherent, at least from a Western point of view. The subject is obviously within the nonrational, although not the irrational. In any case, this discussion should not be taken as a precise description of mystical elements. Such a description would seem to be a contradiction of terms. Besides, it is all too easy to overly formalize a nonformal system. David Ames' (1959a:264) caution needs to be kept in mind:

> In general, it should be noted that anthropologists are often guilty of trying to make a consistent and coherent system out of the supernatural beliefs of non-literate people, where it does not exist from the view of ethnographic reality. Of course, the religious beliefs of Western peoples also are often varied and contradictory, but full-time religious specialists, with the aid of writing, have been able to standardize beliefs and practices to a greater extent.

So the wording of the subtheme is meant to be ideational and by no means precise.

The direct operation of this subtheme is limited to the initiated, the intermediary individuals described under subtheme 1-C. The concept is understood by all Senegambians, however, and so they participate in the operation through the intermediaries with whom they have alliances and to whom they credit as having this interior vision that is exercised on their behalf.

Subtheme 2-B: Consequences of a Breach

> *When there is a breach in the relationship to transempirical beings and/or forces, man may suffer disastrous consequences.*

"Man" in this subtheme should be read as both the singular and plural, as well as male and female. A breach, at least at this point in Senegambian history, is primarily thought of in terms of the individual and his or her relationship to transempirical beings and forces. This is probably due in large part to the influence of Islam, where the emphasis is on the individual's performance of his religious duty. Traditionally, breaches were defined largely in community terms. This is brought out by J. Spencer Trimingham (1980:55):

> African religion is eminently practical. Religion, whether the cult of spirits of ancestors or of nature or those of the mystery cults, sustains a moral order of society, and all ritual is designed to foster the well-being of the community. Those who conform prosper, those who rebel pay the penalty, and all this not in some future life but in the here-and-now.

So African religion is collective, individualistic, and practical. This definition applies to Islam in the Senegambia as well.

Some of the most dramatic examples of how a breach in the relationship with supramundane forces can bring disastrous consequences are seen in the many accounts of the *xalwa wird* 'gone wrong', that is, when this very powerful, yet risky and even dangerous, mystico-esoteric secret rite is not properly carried out.

A *wird* (W. and A.) is a formula of prayer recited outside of the five prescribed prayers. It also refers to the formula of prayer itself. Very early

Metatheme 1: Personal, Transcendent Peace

in Islamic history, many different litanies were built into the *wirds*[31] that included the names or attributes of Allah in Arabic, and invented or cabalistic names. These were added to the orthodox prayers because they were found by Muslims to be "efficacious" (Gibb and Kramers 1965:634).

The *xalwa* is a mystical, Muslim, esoteric retreat, that has as its center a special *wird*. There are many *xalwa wirds*, each of which has a specific, esoteric purpose.

The *xalwa* that is described here is called *ryada*.[32] Its description was provided by a practitioner who declined to give me his name, and who said it really was taboo to provide such confidential information.

The *xalwa* is carried out in secret. Preparatory ablutions are required. Each spirit to be called requires a different incense to be burned. Then names of four superior spirits are used, which represent the east, north, west, and south and thus form a magic circle. The number 1,111 is written and collected as a magic potion *(saafara)*, with which the performer washes his or her body. Next, four sheets of paper are prepared, on which are written the names of the superior spirits. These sheets are placed in front of, behind, to the right, and to the left of the performer to form a spiritual shield against external attacks.

During the rite, the performer must never go more than ten meters beyond the circle of protection. He must also keep a vow of silence and keep his eyes from looking at anything evil.

If his invocation is accepted, he must stay in *xalwa* for three, seven, or thirty-three days. He must also make an offering of millet porridge *(laax)* or sacrifice a sheep.

The spirits manifest themselves in awakened dream. The first effect the performer experiences is a glacially cold wind or an extraordinary perfume that penetrates the nose. The spirit may brusquely appear, or come in the form of an animal, or appear in frightening form.

When the spirit comes, an alliance is made, and *xalwa* after that is simpler. The performer then has the authority to call the spirit, who is at the service of the performer. When the spirit leaves, it is often in a great wind or even a whirlwind.

The gifts these spirits offer include clairvoyance, the gift of healing, a great destructive capacity (such as burning houses or separating a person from another), and even the power of life and death.

---

[31] The plural of *wird* in Arabic is *awrad*.

[32] Where this name originated or what language it represents is unknown to me.

Each *xalwa* rite must be performed in a precise manner. If not, the spirit (*jinn*) will be angry and wreak his vengeance on the perpetrator of the incorrectly performed rite. Accounts abound of people who were severely punished for breaches in *xalwa* rites. Glenn Gero (1990), a linguist doing language survey work in southern Senegal, met a Diola man and wife who had been about ninety-five percent paralyzed from the neck down for over ten years, ever since the man attempted to perform *xalwa*. At the time of attempting the rite, his wife was in the room with him, lying on the bed. The violation of the rule to perform *xalwa* alone, plus perhaps the violation of other taboos, resulted in retribution by the *ejiney* (*jinn* in Diola). In the morning following the failed *xalwa*, members of the family found them both curled up in a fetal position, paralyzed and shaking. After some days they were able to stretch out their limbs but remained almost totally paralyzed, with both of them having to be fed and otherwise taken care of by their family.

Another account I heard was of a marabout who had built a new, two-story house. Before occupying it, he made some sort of vow and chose an upstairs room for a *xalwa* retreat. The next morning his family found him dead, hanging outside the window of the room where he had undertaken the *xalwa*. He had evidently made a mistake and the *jinn* had retaliated by defenestrating him.

Many cases of insanity, chronic bad luck, failures in life and love, and deaths are attributed to failed *xalwa*. On the other hand, people believe *xalwa* is very powerful and, if done correctly, the *jinn* are obliged to perform the request made of them. This is because the names of Allah, used in *xalwa*, are more powerful than the *jinn*, and because Allah (indirectly through lesser beings like Muhammad or one of the many Sufi saints) has given this power to privileged, initiated individuals who use it on their own behalf or on the behalf of others.

Failed *xalwa* is by no means the only cause of insanity, bad luck, or failure. There are many causes, most of them related to the mystic or esoteric realm; *toskare*, *ñaan-yàlla*, and *um* are Wolof words indicating a state of curse or chronic bad luck.

Other common sources of misfortune or illness are sorcery (*ndëmm*), evil eye (*bët bu bañ*), evil tongue (*cat*), breaking taboos (*tere*), black magic (*jibar*), and spells of impotence (*xala*). There are many causes and explanations for the negative aspects of life.

These descriptions of *xalwa* may be imagined as somewhat unique to Senegambian Islam. This is not the case. J-L Triaud (1988:54) states that it is a "frequent occurrence in various Muslim regions." In his study of Muslim mystic practices across West Africa, and of *xalwa* in particular (which he calls *khalwa*, using the Arabic form), he (1988:55) concludes that:

> Mystic practices were a necessary part of the intellectual baggage of a religious aspirant, rather as a thesis and other academic exercises enhance a university career. Promotion to the highest ranks is rightly conditioned by tests taken, efforts made, and risks undergone, and also by the social recognition needed for acceptance by one's peers. In our view, *khalwa* is one such test: at the same time a rite of passage and a means to acceptance and promotion.

This citation refers to Sufi training for leadership, not in focus in this essay, but it does indicate how widespread and important the *xalwa* rite was. Certain major Muslim leaders in West Africa in this past century are known to have practiced various forms of *xalwa*. Some current leaders in the region are said to do so at the present time.

Theme 3: Harmony with Established Laws

Peace in the human soul is the result of living in harmony with the laws established by the transempirical beings and forces.

Subtheme 3-A. The state of personal peace is measured by the fullness of the soul (dënn bu yaa).

Subtheme 3-B. The condition of personal peace is experienced in terms of a spiritual revelation based on:

> Soul memory (xol du fàtte), *which is the reservoir and the sum of all the experiences of life.*

> Soul restoration (dund ag yeegu xol), *which is the recreating in an individual of a state of readiness to receive the miracle of communication with the transempirical world.*

> Soul awakening (fit wu yee wu), *which originates with initiation into the verities hidden behind the visible and sensible reality perceived by the uninitiated.*

> *The attachment of the soul* (nooy ci mbir) *to the objects and symbols of transempirical forces, which is the result of soul awakening.*

Most of the elements that are found under this theme are also found under other themes or are even found as other themes. This overlapping is because of the integrated nature of world view. Treated under this theme, the elements relate to a greater generality, that of the laws of the cosmos. But most in turn are so fundamental that they comprise a theme by themselves.

The laws that have been established for mankind to follow are basically traditional and unwritten, except for the revealed laws brought by Islam. Although they are informal and noncodified, they are considered to be much more than mere social norms, as they are believed to relate to the whole universe and to man's place in it. This innate sense of the moral law is well expressed by the African scholar, Maurice Glélé (1981:25):

> The African believes in the transcendence, and at the same time, the immanence, of God and in the divine presence in every living being and in every thing. The consequence is that man needs to show himself just and moral in his life, in his social relations. He does this out of respect for God, who is present everywhere and in everything, in the form of the soul or the vital force.

The well-being and peace that man desires are dependent upon his obeying these transcendent laws. They are analogous to a manufacturer's instructions that accompany a product; in order to get the maximum benefit from the product, they should be followed.

Writing specifically of African mysticism, which is the search for ultimate meaning, Ndaw (1983:103) states that

> The rituals, the mystical acts in general, are but the materialization of the desire that motivates man to uncover the underlying laws that govern the universe... All symbolic ritual is a refining process whose purpose is to allow man to progressively pass from a perception of the sphere of relationships between man and the world, to a comprehension of the cosmos.

These laws fall into two categories, exterior and interior.

The Laws That Govern the Exterior Life

The exterior life is that which is practiced, what is done external to the self and the body. Although a separation is made between exterior and interior, Senegambians believe there is a close connection between the two. That which is done externally will have an interior effect. There seems to be a definite concept that what is exterior fact becomes automatically interior fact. Take Islamic prayer, for instance. I have had Muslims attempt to get me to repeat the Shahadah, whether or not I believed it or wanted to convert to Islam. They believed that the exterior expression would have positive interior results. This sort of external to internal relationship is common.

The Prohibitions. The prohibitions are *lu diiné bëggul* 'that which religion does not like'. They all have their origins in Islam, except for the taboos. Black magic is of course also pre-Islamic, tolerated but largely considered to be a social evil. Following are the "thou shalt not . . ." restrictions of the moral law:

idolatry *(sirku)*. Here Islam has largely won out. Overt idolatry is definitely considered to be un-Islamic. Yet many covert forms remain, such as the near-worship of some saints of the Sufi orders.
apostasy *(tubbi)*. It is considered a serious matter to turn back from Islam, having converted or been born into a Muslim family.
alcoholic drink *(sàngara)*. The nonconsumption of alcoholic drinks is central to Islamic practice in the Senegambia. The distinction is frequently made between Christians and pagans on the one hand, and Muslims on the other hand, on the basis of nonconsumption of alcohol. It is also frequently remarked that it is easier for a pagan to convert to Christianity than to Islam, as in the latter case he will have to give up alcohol. I have heard of nominal Christians who have converted to Islam in order to deal with their alcohol problem.
eating pork *(yàpp mbaam)*. Food and drink prohibitions are called *araam* 'to be prohibited by religion'. Pork is in the same category as alcohol: it is a diagnostic taboo, that is, the consumption or nonconsumption of pork is used as a major criterion for determining who is a Muslim and who is not.
taboos (also called superstitions) *(tere)*. There are countless taboos that cover every conceivable aspect of life. Some are strongly believed in,

others are less so. Some are being questioned on the basis of scientific ideas being taught in the modern school system. Some are followed more in rural than in urban areas. But it is safe to say that many are followed and are taken very seriously. See appendix 6 for a collection of taboos selected from many in current belief in Dakar. Other scholars have collected taboos from the area (cf. Appia 1940, Bodiel 1949, Thiam 1987).

black magic *(liggéey)*. Black magic is still believed in and feared, in the city as well as on the farm. It is not too much talked about, but steps are taken against it and it is not to be taken lightly.

The Moral Life. Live the moral life, that is, live in compliance with the norms established by society. It is not limited to sexual morality or immorality as is so often the concept of morals in current American usage.

Community Life. Humans need to live in community, where each individual is given and carries out his or her duties in mutual dependence upon, and in harmony with, all members.

Practice the sunna. Muslims are required to practice the five pillars of Islam *(topp sunna)*. For many Senegambian Muslims, this practice is Islam by definition, even when the majority seem to the outside observer rarely to perform even the ritual daily prayers. They seem to internalize only their belief in Allah, Muhammad, angels, and *jinn*. From that point on, the orthodox practices complete the rest of what the Muslim faith is.

Kinship. Live loyally and in harmony with blood relatives.

Nature. Live in respect and appreciation of nature, recognizing that man cannot live without its bounty.

The Laws That Govern the Interior Life

The interior life is what we might call spirituality. It relates to the ultimate values and aspirations of life, beyond that which is visible and practicable. The interior life is not separated from that which is exterior. All internal values have external manifestations.

The Blessing. Seek the blessing (baraka, A.) of Allah. Cheikh Sy (1969:129) defines the essential nature of baraka as the "spiritual influence" transmitted from the Sufi masters to the disciples. By means of this baraka, the master is able to put the disciple in communion with God.

Vincent Monteil also characterizes baraka as central to Islam in black Africa. It is the "motor of the action of the Cheikh to his disciples" (1980:155). It expresses charismatic power, or magnetic flux, and is transmitted especially by saliva and the laying on of hands. It is accompanied by miracle working. Monteil characterizes it as that which Max Weber (1980:155–156) called "the quality that distinguishes the person that possesses it from ordinary humans and the fact of seeing them as superhuman beings, or at least exceptional ones."

Harmony. Live in harmony with the transempirical beings and forces. This topic was discussed under theme 2 above.

Esoteric Protection. Obtain a spiritual, esoteric protection *(ñagu)*. This will be dealt with in metatheme 2.

Destiny. Live in accord with your destiny. This was described under subtheme 1-A, explaining that every human being has a defined place and role in the cosmology.

Prescribed Place. Live within your prescribed place in the social hierarchy. Senegambian society is not at all egalitarian. Every person has an assigned place or level in society. Upward mobility, to the extent it exists, is a mechanism that has only come in from the outside since Western influences began to be felt in the society. In traditional society, endogamous castes and social hierarchies were the rule. The arrival of Islam, from the tenth century onwards, did bring some limited exogamy and social mobility, but mostly Muslim society and traditional society lived apart, so the effect was never great (Trimingham 1959a).

Subtheme 3-A: Fullness of the Soul

The state of personal peace is measured by the fullness of the soul.

Fullness of the soul *(dënn bu yaa)* refers to the quality of the soul and not to its dimensions, which are never a consideration. State of the soul is another way of expressing the concept. The state of the soul can basically be in balance or out of balance. Its ideal state is to be in perfect equilibrium. This is the ideal of the whole cosmic order, which includes transempirical beings and forces, society, community, family, and even the interior of the self-balance within and between all these elements. Public figures who are in the midst of difficulties are typically described in the media as being serene, the ideal state.

The key word in this subtheme is the STATE of the soul. It is this state that is in focus here, while in the next subtheme it is the CONDITION that is in focus. The state of the soul is shown through a person's will, whether strong, weak, or of other quality. The will, *pastéef,* manifests this state of the soul. A man of strong will is a *boroom pastéef* 'the owner of willpower'; while one who is weak-willed is *nit ku ëppal,* a person who violates social norms, not controlling his language and actions. This is similar to the contrast between 'forceful personality' and 'milquetoast' as an inherent trait, rather than a question of being disciplined or undisciplined in character.

The soul is referred to by the terms *noo, bakkan, xel,* and *ruu*.[33] *noo* means 'breath, soul'; *bakkan* means 'nose, life, breath of life, soul'; *xel* is the word for 'intelligence, thought, spirit, reason, soul'; and *ruu* is used for 'vital breath, soul, life'.

The task of describing the Senegambian concepts is doubly difficult. On the one hand, meanings of the individual terms and the differences between them have been very difficult to elicit. On the other hand, the English language has no parallel vocabulary. A third difficulty is the lack of precision of definition of the terms, even though they are referred to and alluded to in everyday speech. The Senegambian focus seems to be on the quality of the soul, rather than on its precise nature.

The concept of the soul in the Senegambia stands in considerable contrast to that in the West where the concept is quite undeveloped. The soul is defined as "an entity which is regarded as being the immortal or spiritual part of the person and, though having no physical or material reality, is credited with the functions of thinking and willing, and hence determining all behavior" (Friend and Guralnik 1956).

Beyond these very general concepts, the soul is totally taken for granted, at least in present-day modern society. In the realm of religion, the soul is important as it is considered to be immortal. Yet in spite of the soul's importance to historical Judeo-Christian thought, which has been foundational for the West, it is not much developed beyond being stated as part

---

[33] This word is derived from the Arabic *ruh,* meaning "the human spirit or life" (Gibb and Kramers 1974:433).

of man's tripartite being, along with body and spirit. Even in the Bible, the frequently occurring term soul is left quite undeveloped. See Matthew 22:37, Mark 8:36, I Thessalonians 5:23, Hebrews 4:12, and Revelation 20:4 (I.B.S. 1978). Biblical Old Testament usage of the Hebrew *ruwach* parallels the Wolof *ruu*, derived from the Arabic *ruh* (Strong 1984:107).

To put this in perspective, compare the development of the concept of the human body with that of the human soul. For the body, there are anatomical divisions (head, toe), terms expressing health (headache, broken foot), age (old, young), size (tall, fat), ad infinitum. Yet for the soul, which probably most people believe in, we have few descriptive or qualifying terms. It may be immortal, lost, or saved, but the soul itself is probably formless, unalterable, nebulous, and very little thought of per se.

Senegambians are much more conscious of the soul. Although they do not have anatomical descriptions that would correspond to terms for various parts of the body, they have numerous descriptive words to describe states and conditions of the soul.

Henri Gravrand (1961:36), a researcher and scholar for more than thirty years in Senegal, describes the importance of the concept of the soul:

> The Négro-African is entirely soul, as his 'self' resides inside the vital principle, which is the soul. At the same time he is entirely body, because the soul wants to be embodied, in that when it is separated from the body [as at death], it exists in a violent state and tends toward reincarnation. In all his preoccupations, he is oriented toward the invisible world, where his destiny is in play. He is at the same time implanted on earth, which is for him his true paradise.

Part of the difficulty in conceptualizing the soul resides in purely semantic differences of expression. That is, at base some of the problems of comprehension stem from differences of terminology and not of basic concepts. So, if an American says "he loves life," while the Senegambian says *"dafa topp bakkanam"* 'his soul has pleasure from his body', meaning 'he loves the world, he is a sensualist', they basically may be saying the same thing. There are many cases of Senegambians locating emotions or conditions in the soul that Americans would not precisely locate anywhere anatomically, but would conceptualize in general terms only. But beyond such semantic differences there are conceptual differences.

The body of a person is born; the soul is not, it is eternal. The soul is preexistent to the birth of the person. That is, souls exist in the supramundane world. These souls are not all alike, but come predisposed to goodness, badness, difficultness, and other qualities. At the time of human conception, a particular soul is assigned to the fetus in the mother's womb. The selection of qualities of the soul to be sent to the particular couple and, therefore, to the future adult who will have this soul all his or her life, can involve: (1) various concepts of reincarnation, (2) the role of particular deities in the assignment process, and (3) the moral status of the human parents influencing or even determining the quality of the soul being assigned.

Different ethnic groups hold to a variety of concepts within the general framework. L. Faye (1983:71), in his monograph *Mort et Naissance: Le Monde Sereer (Death and Birth: The Serer World),* describes one facet of Serer beliefs concerning the soul and reincarnation:

> The *ciid*[34] (reincarnated souls or the dead who are seeking reincarnation) are divided into two groups: the good and the bad. The latter ... are very often the cause of abnormal, rickety infants that typically do not live long. The *ciid* are manifested to women in dreams, but very discreetly. Through a dream the dead that wants to be reincarnated presents itself in human or animal form. At that point the woman will wear an amulet and will usually offer prayers to neutralize adverse action taking place during pregnancy. If the woman pays no attention, she will receive the *ciid* in her fetus.

The soul and the body are closely tied together during the life of the person. For example, if a person is happy, that is, the condition of the soul is good, this is transmitted to the body, which will be in good health and portliness.[35] Therefore, a person who is in robust form is judged to live in interior harmony and contentment of soul.

Just as the condition of the soul is transmitted to the body, any negative effects on the body are transmitted to the soul. The soul can suffer damage and changes. Although it is always a complete entity, the soul can develop in quality. The human body starts out small and grows; the soul is always complete and inclusive of all its faculties although it needs perfecting. As the soul is complete, it has to adapt itself to the limitations of the body in which it is conveyed.

---

[34] The sound represented by the "d" in *ciid* is an "implosive *d*," in linguistic terms. As this is not a linguistic study, this and other non-English sounds are represented by the standard English orthography.

[35] Thin people in the Senegambia are thought to lack God's blessing. A certain portliness is almost a requisite to being highly respected and being considered successful and prosperous.

A large part of traditional education in Africa was related to the body-soul relationship. The goal of education and initiation, and mature adulthood, was to achieve the ascendancy of the soul over the body. It was believed the body needed to be made subject to the soul. The soul was a complete, eternal principle; the body needed mastery. Ndaw (1983:113) explains this ideal of self-mastery:

> The African ethic is based on one fundamental notion: self-knowledge and its corollary, self-control.
>
> Master of himself, conscious of his value, the African acquires the feeling of power through having exercised power over himself. His sole desire, but also his duty, is to extend this power beyond himself to the world.
>
> Education is totally oriented towards this goal, toward this ethical conduct.
>
> Cowardice is a source of humiliation, of dishonor, of serious consequences for the individual and his family. Even while small, the infant learns to stoically support pain, and his self-esteem grows little-by-little, until he is proud. The trials that mark the passage from infancy to adolescence, the circumcision and excision, plus the physical ordeals of initiation, are all designed to teach mastery over the body through suffering, and disdain for pain. The counterpart is unpitying scorn for those who weaken... The indifference to pain provides the means for the domination of all feelings, and a training for overcoming suffering. Knowing how to maintain a desired expression and to control one's speech are virtues and criteria of appreciation and esteem that society has established.

One of the major problems of education introduced from the West is its exclusive attention to the practical side of life, neglecting the development of the soul. This has resulted in a lack of mastery of the exterior self (made possible by a lack of properly developed interior soul) and, consequently, has had repercussions that have led to confusion in the area of self identity.

The body-soul relationship is said to compare with that of the *kora*, the great Senegambian stringed musical instrument (which is similar in sound to a harp), and the *korist* musician. The strings of the *kora* (the body) must be controlled through tension and tuning so that the sounds correspond to the desires of the *korist* (the soul). Without this domination of the *kora*, the sound is chaotic. An uncontrolled body will lead to a failed life.

The soul can be fortified, improved, and perfected through experiences it receives by means of the body. The state of the soul is revealed in personal, interior character *(jikko)*. Good character *(jikko bu baax)* is contrasted with bad character *(jikko bu bon)*. The internal state of the soul is revealed through external comportment.

A person of good character is described as *daffa yaatu* 'he is wide'. An essential quality of a strong person, i.e., one who is wide, is that he or she makes allowances for, and is indulgent toward, others in their faults, weaknesses, and idiosyncrasies. A person with a wide soul or character is one who has control over himself or herself and who can take the trials of life in stride. The wide person is also more integrated into society, fully participating in family and community life.

A person of weak character is called *daffa xat* 'he is narrow'. The narrow person is impatient, self-centered, inconsiderate of others, does not tolerate well the negative factors of life and society, and is not well integrated. To be *dëgër fit* 'a solid soul' means to be courageous, while *amul fit* 'without a soul' means to have a fragile soul that is cowardly.

A soul that is rebellious in this life, that refuses to follow its assigned role, that is, its destiny, will be reborn as a *dëmm* 'witch, soul-destroyer'. A person who is a *dëmm* has what could be called a negative soul. The soul of such a person can leave its human body at will, and travel long distances to attack and feed on the healthy souls of other humans. Many illnesses and undesirable emotional states of Senegambians are attributed to *dëmm*. Today, this belief is held by Muslims and traditionalists alike. The news media often report cases of accusations of witchcraft, and courts of law in Senegal are frequently called upon to judge them.

At the time of writing this essay, Senegal's national daily newspaper devoted many columns to the reporting of a major witchcraft retrial, an appelate court having overturned a previous court decision (Diack 1990). Another example of media coverage is a series of articles, authored by Africans, in the magazine *Famille et Developpement* (Traoré 1984), which covered the subject from traditional to modern-scientific viewpoints in a section entitled "Witchcraft Today" (Diagne, Diédhiou, Niang and Okoumba-Nkoghe, all of 1984). Witchcraft is a very live issue, even among urbanized Senegambians. Islam seems to have done little to attenuate this belief and the fears that accompany it.

Metatheme 1: Personal, Transcendent Peace

The state of the soul is not just a matter of social compatibility or of character development. It has two other profound implications. (1) It is determinative of internal peace, which is of utmost value. An over-burdened, agitated soul means there has been a lack of development in the soul's state. A lack of peace is very undesired existentially. (2) At death the soul will not be liberated to go to the higher celestial fields and will, therefore, be required to be reincarnated, to go through another cycle of human life. The traditional and Islamic prayers for the dead, especially on the third, eighth, and fortieth days after death, are especially important in this sense, to assist the dead soul to make the transition into the higher spheres of the beyond.

Subtheme 3-B: Experience of Personal Peace

> *The condition of personal peace is experienced in terms of a spiritual revelation based on:*
>
> *Soul memory* (xol du fàtte), *which is the reservoir and the sum of all the experiences of life.*
>
> *Soul restoration* (dund ag yeegu xol), *which is the re-creating in an individual a state of readiness to receive the miracle of communication with the transempirical world.*
>
> *Soul awakening* (fit wu yee wu), *which originates with initiation into the verities hidden behind the visible and sensible reality perceived by the uninitiated.*
>
> *The attachment of the soul* (nooy ci mbir), *to the objects and symbols of transempirical forces, which is the result of soul awakening.*

This subtheme addresses the CONDITION of the soul. Soul condition focuses on emotional states, just as the state of the soul focuses on developmental states. A relationship between personal peace and personal emotions is shown here.

A complete absence of peace will be evidenced by hopelessness, despair, and disharmony. If the soul is not in equilibrium *(dal)*, it is said to be tangled, confused *(yëf yi dañu jaxasoo ci xelam)*.

The soul can be in a needy or a sated condition, but it cannot deal directly with either its own needs or satiety. Both conditions are expressed through human emotions and sentiments.[36] These needs or exuberances can only be expressed through the body. For the soul to have peace it must have the freedom to express these needs or satiety. If these conditions are inhibited or repressed, there will be negative effects in the person. A major part of the importance given to family and society lies in their being instruments through and to which the individual can express his emotions. Internal peace is believed to be possible only if the emotions can be discharged from the soul.

The needy soul requires relief through sharing its need with a person of empathy and trust. In that way the emotion is relieved and, consequently, so is the need. Needs are not just the unhappy states of life. The positive and happy states also need to be expressed. Love and joy need expression as much as do anger and misery in order for the soul to be relieved of its burden.

Negative emotions act as regulators between soul and body. They alert the body to a need or a state of which it might otherwise be unaware. This function of conscience makes the body aware of emotional states. When the body is ill, the soul becomes ill from negative emotions. And a sick soul can cause a sick body, as, for example, a deep sadness or a violent emotion is known to have the capability of adversely affecting the body.

Some bodies more easily adapt to their soul than do others. Traditional initiation rites had in view the need of helping the body adapt to the soul by increasing the mastery of the soul over the body. Where the body is less controlled, the satisfaction of bodily appetites will have the ascendancy over the soul, thus providing for less satisfaction of spiritual aspirations, to the long-term detriment of both soul and body.

The soul pertains to the realm of the infinite in man. The body is limited by time and space; the soul is not. The soul can project itself to any place in the world instantly. It can be in Dakar and go to New York and back without limit and without needing an airline ticket, as one Senegalese told me. It can think any thought, of the present or of the past. The soul, through thoughts, has no limits.

Each of the four soul qualities are analyzed separately below.

Soul Memory. Soul memory is the reservoir and the sum of all the experiences of life. The experiences of life are remembered in soul memory. They are remembered as facts plus emotions. Their emotional

---

[36]Emotions are transitory states and reactions, while sentiments are longer-term states which also involve the individual's ideals.

Metatheme 1: Personal, Transcendent Peace

content is what relates to personal peace. Thus, a major part of the memory includes the emotions related to, or remembered of, past events, both positive and negative, pleasant and unpleasant. All the experiences of life are permanently held or recorded in the soul.

The Senegambian distinguishes between sentiments *(yëg)* and emotions *(fóon)*. Emotions are short-term states of interaction between the body and the soul, often communicated through the heart, which is the point of contact between the two. Sentiments are longer-term states, attitudes, or commitments. Sentiments are more controllable than emotions; they may also involve the will.

Sentiments are thought of in terms of polarization. As a magnet can attract or repel another, so humans have inherent reactions toward others. For example, sentiments of hate or love between people are repulsions or attractions that seem to be natural states. Senegambians frequently seek out clairvoyants to ascertain the sources of an undesired polarization and the means that are required to change it.

Emotions act as regulators. For example, the emotion of shame keeps a person from satisfying other emotions and desires in ways that are contrary to the moral code. The body or the soul, or both acting together, may want satisfaction of some desire, but the conscience intervenes to bring about harmony.

Emotions are thought to have a fixed CHARGE. Each emotion, positive or negative, that is, desirable or undesirable from the individual's viewpoint, consists of a certain emotive quality, quantity, and force. If any person has hatred, for example, he or she has a fixed amount of it. It only comes in one size or quantity or degree. If, therefore, this person appears to hate one person a little and another person a great deal, it is assumed that the only difference in the amount of hatred is the amount APPARENT to others; the difference is not accounted for in terms of hating one person a little and another a lot. The same applies between people. Whatever emotions they have, they all have an equal quantity or intensity. This applies to all emotions; they are units of fixed amounts of intensity or charge.

This concept of emotions has far-reaching implications in interpersonal and cross-cultural relations. For example, little anger, disdain, or disrespect shown by a foreigner in the Senegambia may be judged quite differently from what a foreigner would expect. Conversely, a little respect, goodwill, or expressed pleasure may receive a more positive reaction than one might expect.

The concepts interior, exterior, development of the soul, and especially soul memory have close connections with religious concepts. The attention given to the interior of reality, the soul of man, etc., has as its goal communication with and experience of the transcendent.

A major factor in the growth of mystical, Sufi Islam in the Senegambia is that it allows for expression of the soul rather than following the legalistic Islam of orthodoxy. Similarly, a number of Senegambians have told me that Roman Catholic Christianity is much more appealing than is Protestant Christianity, because the former has mystery, symbols, and other elements satisfying to the senses and the spirit, while the latter is largely cerebral (besides being largely foreign to sub-Saharan African culture and sentiment).

Some Senegambian Protestants have even told me that although they believe the Bible and Christian doctrines, accepting them as God's eternal and revealed truth, they still feel this kind of Christianity is defective—having developed an exterior salvation to the neglect of interior truth. They see both as being taught in the Bible. By exterior, they mean Jesus's sacrifice of himself on the cross, His resurrection, and ascension to heaven. By interior, they mean doctrines related to Jesus's descent into hell, much religious symbolism seen in the Old Testament rituals, incense, architecture, festivals, the multiplicity of symbolic objects, and gestures and chants; also they mean the place of sacramental objects, such as icons used in the Coptic and other Eastern churches, a theology of ancestors, and the use of sung or chanted liturgy. These examples are just a few of the possibilities seen in the Bible or in other churches but rejected by many of the branches of Protestantism that came to the Senegambia.

The point is that the Senegambian believes that religious experience should involve all of the body and the soul, including the emotions, and not be limited largely to the mind. The Senegambian man wants to totally experience himself, others, and the transcendent. He believes that religion, by definition, is meant to provide the means to achieve this. He wants not just to experience an emotional high, but to be lifted and inspired to be more than he is, through communion with the infinite.

As sentiments and past emotions are stored in the soul memory, they have a lasting effect on the body, on the equilibrium between soul and body, *dal*, and consequently on personal peace. That is why emotions need to be dealt with, not just ignored or denied, and why Senegambians accept religion as normal and valid. It is meant to deal with man's emotions so that he can have peace. When the body and soul are not in equilibrium, the person is said to have things mixed up in the head *(yëf yi dañoo jaxasoo ci xelam)*.

Soul Restoration. Soul restoration is the re-creating in an individual of a state of readiness to receive the miracle of communication with the transempirical world.

The soul is the interface between man and the transcendent. It is through the soul that man communicates or communes with the supernatural. It is not located in any one body organ, but is diffuse like blood is, throughout the body, and thus blood is symbolic of the soul as well as of life. The heart, *xol,* is also tied to sentiments, similar to the concepts of the West. One can say, *sama xol neex naaci* 'my heart is content.'

Soul restoration is experienced through the creation of an exterior atmosphere that is conducive to such communication, as by drumming, chanting, and dancing.

The emotions of past events are held in the soul memory. If the individual or social unit wants to relive those emotions, they can do so through soul restoration. It enables individuals and social units to relive past experiences or to re-create or reenter into past events. Exterior means (the body) are used to achieve interior (soul) effects, through dancing, drumming, singing, chanting, rhythms, orations, touch, visible images and symbols, incense, and other sensual means that activate some or all of the senses and thereby re-create in the soul the remembered experience.

In the West we understand soul restoration, although from a very different explanatory framework. The singing of one's national anthem is meant to re-create in the citizen an emotion of patriotism, as are the pledge to the flag and the parades of soldiers on national holidays. Our societies have many events, means, and symbols, including civic, secular, and religious that are designed to produce desired emotional states; but the emotional goals are much more implicit, perhaps even denied, than is the case in the Senegambia where they are explicit, focused, and even planned.

Soul restoration is made use of for the most part in religious contexts. Religious cultus and festivals are events whose goal is soul restoration. All of the elements listed above—singing, dancing, drumming—are used to create and re-create an atmosphere that will maintain and strengthen the religious values that are believed in, and that will assist the devotee in his or her communion with the supernatural. Geographic space, times of special significance, and many forms of symbolic objects are employed.

The members of the caste of praise singers and oral historians *(géwél)* play an important part in soul restoration. They are the professional keepers and masters of the word. They provide music, dancing, rhythm, motion, and color. They recount past epic events and glories and exalt present society and its leaders. All these uplifting elements create a joyous, exuberant atmosphere which serves to release emotions, restore the soul, and promote personal peace.

The *géwél* have even been incorporated into Islam. They are used as chanters and orators, and in some Sufi orders, as musicians, in all-night religious chants, and at other religious gatherings.

Soul Awakening. Soul awakening originates with initiation into the verities hidden behind the visible and sensible reality perceived by the uninitiated.

Soul awakening is limited in a definitional sense to those chosen or initiated individuals who serve as intermediaries between the visible and invisible worlds. Definitional sense means that, strictly speaking, soul awakening involves only the elite few who are these intermediaries but, practically speaking, everyone in society is involved because the fruits of soul awakening pass on to everyone in society through the intermediaries. Hence, it is a subject of common understanding to everyone who is part of the Senegambian belief system.

The spirit of man *(xel)* reads or interprets the needs of the soul *(bakkan)*. This is done through the thoughts and the interior vision. The needs that are not being met are transformed into imaginations, dreams and visions. The Wolof say *lu loxo mënul jot dooni gént* 'the reality that the hand cannot touch becomes a dream'.

This subject was generally covered under subtheme 1-C above, even though the term soul awakening was not used in that discussion.

Soul Attachment. Soul attachment is defined as the attachment of the soul to the objects and symbols of transempirical forces, which is the result of soul awakening.

Although the soul is resident in, or attached to, the body during a person's life, it is considered to need additional attachment to objects in this world because the soul is fundamentally a spiritual entity. It needs to be encouraged to appreciate and value visible realities. And in the Senegambian conception, it is thought that the soul actually has a propensity to attach itself to worldly objects. So it is up to society and individuals themselves to provide the soul with objects to which it is proper for it to be attached. Otherwise, the soul will attach itself to objects that are unworthy of or detrimental to itself and the person as a whole.

The objects the soul attaches to are the symbols of life. In religion they were traditionally the altars to the spirits and the rituals that accompanied them. The altars and idols did not just serve as objects of veneration representing deity, but also served as symbols to which the soul would be attached.

All the elements that function to restore the soul become elements to which the soul is attached. They thus serve a dual function. It is, therefore, clear how an imported religion that seems to lack symbolism and that even seeks to minimize it in its cultus, as was described for Protestant Christianity under Soul Memory above, is judged to be unsatisfying and deficient to Senegambians.

Where symbols are abundant and meaningful, the soul is not tempted to wander or develop in undesired directions. It will be content in familiar and meaningful surroundings. It will be at peace.

Theme 4: Spiritual and Material Blessing

Transcendent peace results in spiritual and material blessing (barke), *social supremacy* (daraja), *and a high place in the social hierarchy* (martaba).

In the development of this section, a number of related topics are presented, after which a synthesis is provided. Last of all the concepts of blessing and social supremacy are analyzed in relation to the overall social context.

Socioeconomic Dynamics

Success, which frequently is defined in visible, materialistic terms, is thought to have a spiritual origin. This contrasts greatly with the Western notion, often called the Protestant work ethic, as described by Max Weber (1958).

Several mechanisms in Senegambian society operate against an ethic of hard work as a means of economic and social advancement. The fear of envy, particularly through the mechanism of the evil tongue *(cat)*, the related fear of witchcraft *(ndëmm)*, the requirement of sharing material goods, a strongly hierarchical social organization, and the fear of social quarantine *(tong)*, are some of these mechanisms. They are all discussed under their relevant themes. Together, they add up to a formidable impediment to an ethic of achieving an accumulation of wealth or a means of production through hard work and getting ahead economically. Senegambians have a great desire to get ahead, to be successful, to live comfortably, and to have material plenty, but the means the culture legitimizes for their realization are spiritual rather than physical, that is, through personal effort.

Although the term 'getting ahead' was just used, it was meant as a term meaningful to an American reader. Senegambians have no concept of getting ahead in the Horatio Alger tradition. What material blessing means in this part of Africa is a far different way of material advancement. Some description of this material context is needed before material blessing can be understood. William Foltz (1969:149) describes a core element:

> Money is important only as something to display or give away, not as anything to be sought for itself. This attitude toward money has nothing to do with conservative gentility or with the 'Protestant Ethic.' It is the spending or giving away of money that is highly valued, not just possessing or acquiring it. Only through spending it ostentatiously for public display or to increase the size of one's entourage of personal clients can it serve to enhance one's status.

People certainly want to live better, dress better, and be prosperous in every way, but society puts severe limitations on them. Even those who manage to have well-paying jobs or income from any source are under constant pressure to share their food and finances with extended family and friends who are less fortunate, or who are facing a major expense like a wedding, or who have any kind of pressing financial need or even claim to have such a need. No one is immune from the system unless he deliberately cuts himself off from society to live in isolation. Anyone who wants to be a respected member of society must give. The degree and the spirit of the giving will determine the respect which the person is accorded by his or her society.

David Ames (1959b:232) writes of the Wolof in The Gambia, "Most Wolof would rather be poor but proud of their conspicuous display or consumption of wealth than rich but shamefaced." Not only is prestige gained by conspicuous consumption but, more basically, the shame that comes from not sharing the means one has available or can borrow for even normal needs is so severe that holding back can hardly be contemplated.

Metatheme 1: Personal, Transcendent Peace

The financial situations of most families of the region are graphically described by Chi-Bonnardel (1978:475):

> During the course of a year, in every family, there are three to four family or religious feasts that are extremely expensive. In a world where for the great majority daily existence involves deprivation and destitution, festivities accompanied by a surfeit of food provide a compensatory mechanism, a relief, while at the same time it is a typical African festivity, a total feast where the individual in the midst of his social group experiences the individual and collective joy of life.
>
> Besides the feasts, simple civil relations and the required hospitality are occasions necessitating expenses of prestige without thinking of avoiding them with loss of one's honor. These seemingly exceptional expenditures are in fact very common and occupy a major place in the family budget. Often their unexpected nature means there are not resources at hand to cover them, so the money must be borrowed. So whether in the city or in the country, all Senegalese, by the imperative of custom, live above their means ...
>
> The obligation of providing hospitality creates a situation that frequently results in family parasitism. A man that well knows how to take care of guests gains a flattering reputation. He is called *téguine* if he is a jovial and courteous host. He is called *bakhe* if he is indulgent, and *yévène* if he is totally generous. In Baol, when a guest enters the house, he should be offered a pitcher of water, two red and two white cola nuts, then a platter of food, of which the wife will incite him to eat as much as he can. The guest is lodged and fed as long as he wishes to stay, provided he does not make it his home.

The outcome for most families of this unbridled pressure to provide for others and to spend is further described by Chi-Bonnardel (1978:480):

> The 'social' expenses related to family celebrations and feast days are the principal source of Senegalese indebtedness. Whatever the social level, whatever the financial revenues, the normal budget cannot meet the demands; they can be covered only through recourse to credit and borrowing. In this regard, the highly placed government officer and the farmer in the peanut basin alike live in a permanent state of debt, obligated as they are to constantly cover extraordinary expenditures and spend today against future revenues.

People who have any job or any means, therefore, are under constant financial pressures from all sides. I have had many Senegambian friends, acquaintances, and even strangers, ask to borrow money from me for one need or another. They are conscious of their plight, but consider themselves helpless to act differently from what is expected of them. To go against the expected pattern would mean rejection, condemnation, scorn, and social isolation from their society.

National Economics

Part of the pressure comes from the precarious nature of the economy and the lack of employment possibilities in the region. As difficult as the system is on the individual who has any means, it does serve of inestimable value to those who are without means. It also serves those who have lost their employment, or who face a sudden financial crisis. They can turn for help to those they helped when they had the means to do so. If you refuse someone in need today, he will refuse you when you are in need. It is an exemplary social security system spun out of anyone's control, subject to manipulation by those without strong principles.

For the average Senegalese, the economics of life are objectively difficult. The average per capita annual income is only approximately four hundred dollars U.S. (Adams 1984). The uneven distribution of income further aggravates the situation: 62.5 percent of national income goes to the top twenty percent of the population and only 3.2 percent goes to the bottom twenty percent. And the lowest, 22.3 percent of the population, receives less than fifty dollars income per year (Bugnicourt et al., 1987:43).

Employment figures confirm the gloomy economic picture: The urban employment picture for the country of Senegal in 1980 is shown in figure 17.

	Employees	Percentage
Privately owned business	107,200	18.80
Government and government-owned enterprises	88,400	15.50
Informal sector	275,700	48.35
Unemployed	98,900	17.35
Total, employed and unemployed	570,200	100.00

Fig. 17. Employment in Senegal

Metatheme 1: Personal, Transcendent Peace

The informal sector is considered to be largely underemployed; actually little more than disguised unemployment for many. It includes shoeshine boys, street vendors, and anyone else regularly engaged in any effort to earn some money so as to keep body and soul together. It also presumably includes some self-employed people of adequate income. If half of the informal sector is considered to be adequately employed, probably far above the facts, then unemployment plus underemployment would total about forty-two percent of urban adults. This is certainly a conservative figure, yet one that puts the Senegambian social security system in its true African context.

How this complex social situation relates to transcendent peace and material blessing is a very complex issue. A world view study can only partly delineate underlying causes. Here, I only sketch some of the factors I have adduced on the subject.

Minimizing Risk

Peace is of such value that society cautions the individual against doing anything that will provoke inner turmoil. This emphasis mitigates against risking present peace in the hope of a future of greater prosperity, with the concomitant of living with present tensions and hardships, for oneself and for one's family, in the long-term hope of getting ahead. And rare indeed is the individual who has opportunity to get ahead, given the constant imperative of spending on others.

Apropos of this is the Wolof proverb, *mag lu dal xelam-a koy may yaram* 'only that which inspires inner confidence will permit a person to develop personally'. A. Sylla (1978:105) explains that this proverb "is frequently evoked to remind someone to take sufficient precautions, or to not make commitments beyond his possibilities, in order to live without too much worry, but rather with a tranquil and calm spirit."

Yet another proverb teaches caution rather than risk: *def la nga man, wax la nga xam, boo tëdée nelaw* 'do only what you can, speak only what you know, and in bed you will sleep tranquilly'. Sylla (1978:105) interprets this as strongly recommending that a person should live within his means and talk only of those things he is sure about, if he wants to live in peace and happiness.

In spite of this caution prescribed by society, it is clear that the ideal of life is to achieve material blessing and social supremacy which are believed to be attainable through spiritual means. Consequently, the efforts undertaken to achieve them are focused on spiritual means rather than on human physical effort. These spiritual means constitute the major subject of chapter four.

Living for Appearances

This concept is called *ngistal* in Wolof. CLAD (1977) defines it as "ostentation." These are examples of *ngistal:* (1) a marabout, walking down the street dressed in a fine robe *(boubou)*, walking with dignity and pride, followed by a retinue of disciples; (2) a richly dressed woman, gold jewelry in evidence, attending a wedding party, distributing gifts all around, to the flattering verses of the caste of praise singers; and (3) the government bureaucrat, who has gone deeply in debt in order to buy more expensive clothes, a better car, and a dream house.

Consequences

One of the consequences of the spirit of competition, the will to impose oneself, and the need to put on appearances, is that friendship is hard to measure. It is difficult to determine to what extent the words and actions of friends and even of relatives are sincere and to what extent they are pretenses, or even a ploy for their self-advantage. Senegalese conversations are replete with disparaging words about those not present. One Senegalese expressed the difficulty of ascertaining the true nature of friendship in these terms:

> It is sufficient to listen to a group of individuals talking together to be convinced. If you only heard in what manner they slander those not present. It is extraordinary. Intrigues, plots, lies, and treachery of all sorts are common in this society. [Anonymous]

In this context, anyone can be sure that he or she is receiving the same treatment when absent from such a group.

Metatheme 1: Personal, Transcendent Peace

Concept of Prosperity

The Wolof concept of prosperity can be explained on the basis of the meanings of three key words: *barke* 'blessing', *daraja* 'social prominence', and *martaba* 'spiritual prominence'.

Living in a state of benediction inherently includes a material dimension, or one can even say, material proof. Material blessing is the visible, exterior proof of an interior reality. Prosperous and socially prominent people are automatically, almost by definition, judged to be possessors of *barke*.

Blessing *(barke)* can originate from three sources. One is from either the father or the mother of a person, but especially from the mother. A Wolof proverb states *liggéeyu ndey añu doom* 'the acts of the mother are the dinner of the child'. It means that the child directly inherits either benediction or malediction from the mother. It is not inheritance in the physical sense, but the inheritance of spiritual qualities. Much importance is attached to what is called *liggéeyu ndey* 'mother's work', or *jëfu ndey* 'the mother's acts and deeds'. Having a moral, obedient, submissive (to her husband), and pious mother is extremely important. Another well-known proverb states *nit ku ne juddom ako mag* 'to everyone's birth there is something precedent'. This proverb means that there is more to a birth or to a person than the physical facts. That is, that crucially important, inherited, spiritual factors greatly affect and even determine all that an infant will become in life.

It follows then that probably the greatest insult in Wolof society is to make disparaging remarks about someone's mother. To call someone *juddu bu tuuti* 'badly born' is extremely insulting. Everyone wants to be considered *juddu bu réy* 'well-born' of a *yaay ju baax* 'woman of high esteem'.

Secondly, *barke* can be inherited. This source is different from a mother's or a father's good deeds or acts. Inheritance of *barke* is largely a Muslim concept. Bloodlines that can be traced back to Muhammad are deemed to transmit *barke* but, in the Senegambia, *barke* is mainly adduced to the descendants of the founders of the Senegalese Sufi brotherhoods. Such saints pass on their *barke* patrilineally.

Thirdly, *barke* can be transmitted from a holder directly to another, usually to a disciple of a Sufi saint. This aspect is examined in some detail in the phenomenon of the pilgrimage to the saintly city, Touba, in chapter five.

Material prosperity is, therefore, above all a spiritual concept. The spiritual man possesses everything, both the spiritual and the material, at the same time and inseparably. Material prosperity is the visible sign of the interior reality—*barke*. Spiritual well-being or blessing in the midst of poverty is unthinkable in the Christian sense, as taught by Jesus in the Sermon on the Mount. That is, the poor are blessed because they hold correct spiritual values and therefore please God, with material prosperity being a separate issue. In the Senegambian world view, God is the ultimate source of *barke* 'spiritual blessing', but if He grants it, it is complete—material as well as spiritual.

Even when an apparent rogue is materially successful, spiritual explanations are invariably adduced to explain the success. Somewhere at some time the prosperity had a spiritual origin. Many stories circulate that serve to describe the hidden, spiritual basis behind the seeming paradoxes of rich or prominent people who, to everyday appearances, lack positive spiritual qualities.

Possessors of *barke* fall into two classes. First, there are those who have what could be called a surplus. The Sufi saints, the leaders in brotherhoods, and especially the founders and present general caliphs, who have inherited *barke,* usually both patrilineally and matrilineally, are not just possessors of *barke* but are also transmitters of it to those who do not have it but desire it, that is, their disciples. These receivers constitute the second class. They receive and possess it, but seemingly only temporarily or in insufficient quantity. As a consequence, they must renew their supply by periodically making pilgrimages to living saints personally or to the tombs of deceased saints where *barke* resides permanently and may be received by the disciples. These two classes can be designated respectively, transmitters and receivers of *barke.*

Since the transmission of *barke* is so important to individual and community well-being as a major factor in the realization of individual and collective prosperity and peace, there are, as one would expect, constant evaluations being made by members of society to determine who are important holders and transmitters of *barke*. People want to identify them and be associated with them.

This identification and evaluation process is all the more important and necessary because the inheritance and possession of *barke,* even within the families of leading Sufi saints, is not automatic. Not all sons of even the leading saints possess *barke,* at least in quantities that make them valid transmitters. Being a 'child of a venerable mother' *(doomi soxna bi),* or

Metatheme 1: Personal, Transcendent Peace

being born into an illustrious line of *barke* holders only provides the potential of becoming a transmitter of *barke*. Hence, people are always examining and evaluating leaders and potential leaders for the spiritual qualities they may manifest.

The opposite of *barke* is *toskare*, which is the state of being accursed, like a blind beggar who became blind as the physical consequence of evil or immoral acts. There is much fear of *toskare*, and in part *barke* is sought to avoid falling into an accursed state.

There are a number of qualities and concepts that relate to the potential and the manifestation of the innate spiritual powers of individuals. The two most important ones are *daraja* and *martaba*.

The concept of *daraja* is basically the positive qualities of personality that are inherited through the mother, received at birth. It is a charisma that leads its holder to an especially respectable and honorable life. People around this personality will throughout his life defer to him. As the proverb says, *boroom daraja des koy teral* 'one must honor the man of *daraja*'. The possession of *daraja* will enable a person to occupy a high social position. A person's ultimate high esteem in society and his social prominence are signs of the innate presence of *daraja*.

The presence of *daraja* is determined by what seems to an outsider to be circular reasoning: the possessor of *daraja* obtains a prominent social position; a high social position is the result of the existence of *daraja*. To the Senegambian insider, this view is not circular because of the assumption that every exterior fact has a greater interior cause, so that anyone who is prominent in society has become so because of transempirical reasons, not just by such factors as genetic makeup, force of personality, training, and education.

The second concept is that of *martaba*. If *daraja* means high social status, *martaba* means high spiritual status. Only the exceptional person is a holder of *daraja* in the full sense, although there is a sense in which all honorable men are *boroomi daraja* 'men of honor'. Few individuals have (by destiny) the quality of *martaba*. A man who is *martaba* is considered to be a friend of Allah. His quality is demonstrated by his *barke* and his *daraja*, which are both prerequisites to the state of *martaba*. He exhibits high qualities of blessing and of goodness and personality. He is a great leader of men and women, attracting a mass following, becoming a pole of attraction in his generation, like a magnet attracting iron particles. The greatest possessor of *martaba* becomes *wàlliyu* 'a saint, a friend of Allah'. Amadou Bamba is believed to have been both a holder of *martaba* and a wàlliyu. Men who are *martaba* are the ideal, model men of Senegambian society. Even though few individuals have a full measure of *martaba*, they are especially important for two reasons. First, they are role models of ideal Senegambian manhood. Second, they function as poles of attraction, as described to me by Senegambians, that is, as leaders of large numbers of people. As iron particles participate in a magnetic field surrounding a magnet, so followers of men of *martaba* participate in the spiritual field of these leaders. The followers, by somehow being aligned with the leader, participate in his spiritual and material blessing.

In summary, theme four points to the inseparability of spiritual and material well-being. Even prominence in society is inseparable from spiritual factors. Spiritual values and concepts cannot be divorced from those that are secular. All values that would appear to be merely secular are absolutely believed to rest on spiritual factors, even if their precise nature is hidden from the majority of the members of society. Men and women with high spiritual qualities and material blessings do not live just to themselves. They are not just holders of spiritual and material means; they are expected to exercise these gifts on behalf of others, responsibly, in a stratified, yet ideally an integrated and interdependent society, with leaders dispensing spiritual and material benefits to their followers.

Theme 5: Laws of Cosmic Balance

Transcendent peace is a consequence of meeting the demands of the laws of cosmic balance. These laws emanate from the normal functioning of transempirical forces. Their purpose is to effect corrective action, when needed, that will lead to superior justice in relations between humans.

The realization of the much sought-after transcendent peace is recognized as being dependent upon giving proper attention to all the assigned roles that man is destined to fill in the cosmic order. Deity is not just interested in "religious" activities. Life is not dichotomized into the sacred and the secular. To a significant degree it can be said that all of life is conceived of in religious terms. African man is essentially a spiritual being, seeing all of life in spiritual terms (Zahan 1970:18). So cosmically ordained responsibilities and roles constitute the essence of social life and even of physical life. Hence, they are part of the whole of Senegambian world view, as well as being particularly in focus in this theme.

Metatheme 1: Personal, Transcendent Peace

The cosmic laws are phrased in the following lines in the form of commandments to emphasize their constituting the sine qua non of the establishment of peace, of balance, and of justice in human society. They are diffused throughout the world view and at the same time they constitute the core of beliefs underlying the culture's principal value, transcendent peace.

Individual peace is attained through human beings living and working together in mutual dependency and consideration. It cannot be achieved through personal effort alone. Personal peace in isolation or independent of others is unthinkable. Real transcendent peace can only be achieved when all beings and forces are in balance. Such ultimate cosmic balance is attained through the members of society living according to the cosmic rules. They can be called the Decalogue of Cosmic Balance:

1. You shall recognize the suzerainty of transempirical beings and forces. Man is not an autonomous being. His well-being is dependent upon his living in recognition of his place in the cosmic order.

2. You shall accept the status of intermediaries between the transempirical and human levels of the universe. Although man must accept the suzerainty of superior beings and forces, he must recognize that he relates to them indirectly, through the individuals designated for their mediatorial roles.

3. You shall submit to knowledge gained or transmitted through initiation. When instructions, revelations, predictions, prescriptions, or explanations are provided by superior beings through designated intermediaries, it is incumbent on humans to comply with the superior will.

4. You shall live in proper comportment in community. Part of man's cosmic duty is to live in harmony, understanding, and helpfulness to his or her community, including close and distant family.

5. You shall manifest correct verb, that is, correct manifestation of veneration of worthy beings and objects. Recognition of the suzerainty of both supernatural and natural hierarchies includes not just mental assent, but also proper outward demonstration of compliance with the superior will. Such compliance may include verbal, gesticulatory, symbolic, aural, or other phenomena, as determined by superior beings and forces.

6. You shall offer of your means. Honoring and praising deity and deity's agents are not enough. The faithful must also give of their means. This is in recognition of deity's suzerainty and their power over the distribution of good in the material world.

7. You shall render proper devotion to forces of growth and natural elements. As the earth and the natural elements are the source of life for mankind, man must live in recognition of this fact.

8. You shall accept your destiny, especially as revealed through clairvoyance and other direct means of communication with transempirical beings. Each human being, each soul sent to earth in a human body, has a purpose behind its existence. Besides, the major events of life have destined purposes. These purposes can be revealed to humans through designated individuals and established procedures. When so revealed to an individual, he or she must conform, or be willing to suffer adverse consequences.

9. You shall recognize transmitted symbols and signs. Superior wisdom is not just transmitted ad hoc for specific cases or in times of crisis. Such wisdom is also revealed through traditions, myths, proverbs, historical events, and many direct and indirect signs and symbols (Sylla 1978:104ff). These signs and symbols may be generally or only esoterically understandable. It is up to individuals or to the society as a whole to recognize what is being transmitted and to take any action that may be required by the superior will.

10. You shall find self- and social-identity through transmitted wisdom. The term "transmitted wisdom" includes origin myths, folktales, proverbs, oral history, genealogies, epic poems, and praise songs that make up the corpus of orally transmitted knowledge. Together they constitute traditional African literature.

The Senegalese linguist and folklorist, Oumar Dia (1982:60), in his essay "The Educative Function of the Folktale among the Wolof," describes the traditional role such transmitted knowledge played in society:

> The folktale, called *léeb* in Wolof, occupies an important place in education. The storyteller was a respected man, esteemed for his sense of humor, the power of his speech, and his teaching abilities.

Metatheme 1: Personal, Transcendent Peace

> Story-telling events passed from village to village... They were announced several days in advance, generally taking place during the *leer gu ndaw* (light of the moon). Everyone in the village attended...
>
> Celebrated storytellers, like Kor Koumbe and Madaawour Faal, presided over these cultural evenings that served to sharpen the collective conscience. They contributed powerfully to the education of children in putting the finger on the different forms of taboos and warning of the consequences to those who were recalcitrant. Long after the spectacle, of which certain elements were veritable mini-dramas, children would warn their comrades that they were acting against the teaching of the *léebkat*, the storyteller.

Although both rural and urban society are changing and the place of transmitted wisdom has been greatly weakened, governments, cultural associations, universities, and educators are making concerted efforts to preserve traditional values and increasingly to integrate them into the modern educational curriculum (Kane 1981:7ff, Kesteloot and Mbodj 1983, Sylla 1978:110ff).

The whole decalogue is meant to bring the unification of men with men, men with deity, and men with nature. The identity of self and society are tied to this cosmic meaning of the universe. Origin myths and other media of transmitted wisdom are major means of assisting in the building of this identity.

In sum, transcendent peace is experienced as the result of communion with transcendent spirits, as a prerequisite of peaceful human existence. The greater the degree of communion, the greater the peace. Communion itself is established through the execution of the prescribed exterior gestures (actions) which stimulate the proper interior attitudes in which the communion can take place.

These laws serve superior justice in their being constituted as a complex system that serves to create or reestablish both horizontal (human to human) and vertical (human to the transcendent) balance. This balance is accomplished through carrying out these laws that mandate such horizontal and vertical interdependencies and interactions, that is, that bring about the integration and harmony of the whole cosmic order, which is the superior goal of the whole system.

4
Metatheme 2:
Peace Achieved by Means of Power

Metatheme 2. Peace, happiness, and success are achieved by means of power granted by supernatural forces of the transempirical world.

Theme 1. It is possible to obtain knowledge about one's personal destiny, to understand the origins and causes of the events of life, and to obtain prescriptions for improving or altering future events in one's favor. The same principles and processes apply to community destinies and events.

Theme 2. It is possible and desirable to exercise control over one's destiny, over the events of life, and over the events of the community.

Theme 3. Humans should have protection through esoteric power at personal, family, and community levels, in order to: (a) be defended against destructive cosmic forces; (b) resist esoteric attacks set in motion by enemies; and (c) avoid or challenge chronic misfortune.

Introduction to Peace, Happiness, and Success

Under metatheme 1, it was stated that Senegambians seek to experience transcendent peace through carrying out ritual actions that maintain or reestablish harmony between human and transempirical beings. The consequence of this action is not only peace but spiritual and material prosperity as well. Metatheme 2 can be considered as part of this peace process of seeking cosmic harmony. Senegambians closely associate the themes of I with those analyzed here under II. But because these themes constitute a rather integrated complex of beliefs, practices, and assumptions relating to power, it seems best to consider them in a separate chapter.

The ideal of seeking peace is so strong in the Senegambia that, it seems to this observer, its people frequently fail to see what seems quite clear to an outsider: the themes under II lead to actions that go beyond merely seeking peace. Senegambian world view could be caricaturized in terms of "Peace is the greatest value and good, so the more you can get the better off you are." When does one have enough peace? When has one achieved enough harmony? When does one have enough mystical protection? There do not seem to be easy answers to these questions, especially as they include the desires for success and happiness. So the search for peace frequently becomes, in real life, a quest that turns into a continual pursuit of transempirical power, and the search for more power. Fears of imbalance between one's self-interests and of retribution from the unseen world give rise to a search for a better and better balance, or even a tilt against one's competitors, just to be sure of not falling short of achieving and maintaining what is needed or wanted.

Consequently, many Senegambians become involved in what could be called a preoccupation with transempirical, or esoteric, power. It is analogous to the ideals of capitalism being betrayed by greed, as we have seen in recent years in the United States. In the Senegambia, it seems that the ideals of peace sometimes are betrayed and become quests for spiritual power. Perhaps this is a misjudgment, or the expression of a position unwarranted in an anthropological essay, but when a society appears to accept as normal and condones the commonplace use of a broad range of operations whose purpose is to harm or destroy others, a value judgment seems justified.

Peace through Assertion versus Peace through Submission

Under metatheme 1, the direct goal was transcendent peace. Under metatheme 2, the direct goal is transcendent power which will then lead to transcendent peace. The distinction seems reasonably clear to the outside observer, but such a distinction is not apparently made by Senegambians themselves. They rather understand peace and power as being two facets of the same transempirical reality. To them, peace and power are inextricably linked. Even if they admit to a separation, they consider power as the means to peace, not an end in itself. Hence it would be possible to treat metatheme 2 as a theme of metatheme 1. Ideologically this would be satisfactory; on the level of praxis, they need to be separated.

A qualitative difference can be seen between the seeking of peace and the seeking of power even if there is no sharp demarcation between them. Under the previously considered metatheme, SUBMISSION was a major underlying principle: submission to transcendent beings and forces and their designated human agents, and submission to the established social and moral orders. Under this metatheme, ASSERTION is the corresponding major underlying principle. Submission is still required, but the purpose behind it is the achieving of specific social, or more typically personal, goals.

Power is believed to be useful, even essential, in enabling its possessor to gain what is needed and desired in life and to avoid what is undesired. Given the nature of human relations, this can sometimes pass over the line of what is implicitly in the possessor's interest to what is explicitly against the interest of another. In the first case, one person getting ahead may simply leave another person behind. For example, only one person can be promoted to the directorship of a government department at a given time. In the second case, one person seeks the decrement, misfortune, or even the destruction of the other, to leave no room for doubt about who will get ahead. The means used in the first case includes what is called *xam-xamu baatin* 'interior knowledge' magic; that of the second includes *xam-xam bu ñuul* 'black knowledge', black magic.

Peace, happiness, and success in the Senegambia are highly valued qualities, but they are very different from the equally valued American concepts of well-being and success, even though they appear to be equivalent categories in the two cultures. Material well-being is inextricably linked to success and happiness in the United States. Arensberg and Niehoff (1971:212), in their study of American cultural values, list "material well-being" as the most typical value. They (1971:212) attribute the development of this value to the underlying natural wealth of the nation.

> The rich resources of America, along with the extraordinary growth of its industrial economy, have brought a widespread wealth of material goods such as the world has not seen before . . . Americans seem to feel that they have a "right" to such amenities.

Cora DuBois (1955:1233) found that material well-being was a major component of the first of four basic premises upon which American culture rests. Stewart (1972:64) and many others report similar findings.

As was previously described, the Senegambian economy and history have been those of relative poverty and long-term disruption. We would expect that a much different ideology, culture, and set of world view assumptions would be developed under such conditions, greatly contrasting with those of the United States. Although Arensberg and Niehoff make the assumption that the American concept of a right to material well-being has as its foundation the rich resources of the country, I hesitate to make an analogous, reverse, assumption for the Senegambia. If the long-term presence of abundant resources of one country engender a world view assumption that human beings have a right to material prosperity, what do the even longer-term scarcities of resources engender in another?

The longitudinal research carried out by Milton Rokeach at the time of the war in Vietnam strongly suggested that the value WORLD PEACE increased in importance during the war. Likewise, Rokeach and other researchers have found that many values are held to be of greater importance when the corresponding needs are greater. So, for example, the values of comfortable life and cleanliness are of greater value to people of lower socioeconomic status than for those of higher status (Rokeach 1979:144–145). This would suggest that the extreme desire for peace that is characteristic of the culture indicates that the typical Senegambian has a profound sense of lack of personal peace.

It is beyond the scope of this essay to attribute Senegambian world view assumptions to any causal factors, but I further suggest that the profound desire for peace that dominates their world view must somehow be related to the scarcity of resources and, in addition, to the long-term precariousness of existence, the centuries of wars and slavetrading, the heritage of colonialism, the widespread oppression of black people, and to other extremely disquieting factors that people perceive to this day as threatening.

The overwhelming dependence on esoteric means to solve intractable problems may reflect a perceived and experienced long-term impotence to deal with the manifold problems of the environment, society, and life. If problems are understood to defy human solutions, the only alternative is to search for supernatural solutions, if they are available. It is left to other scholars to elucidate these causal factors and their relationship to particular world view assumptions.

Metatheme 2: Peace Achieved by Means of Power

Peace, as a personal value, is probably not particularly focused on in American culture. I would even consider it probable that a majority of Americans expect that a certain amount of tension, hence non-peace, is the price one has to pay for success and material well-being. Getting ahead in business, a profession, or a graduate study program all require sacrificing at some time various comforts in the hope of gaining such ends as success, wealth, happiness, and a good retirement. There may even be a widespread implicit assumption that the more an American sacrifices now of ease and luxury, the more likelihood of greater well-being in the future.

Peace, happiness, and success in the Senegambia stand in marked contrast to the American concepts. There is a basic concept that success is a result of esoteric power.

The term ESOTERIC used throughout this essay can be considered to be a synonym of occult, but the latter term is thought to unavoidably imply a value judgment and its use has therefore been avoided. The intended meaning is provided under the dictionary definition of occult (Friend and Guralnik 1956):

> 1. hidden; concealed. 2. secret; esoteric. 3. beyond human understanding; mysterious. 4. designating or of certain mystic arts or studies, such as magic, alchemy, astrology, etc.

Consequently, when the term esoteric is used it should not be understood as a negative adjective. It is meant to be a descriptive term, more or less synonymous with mystical. Occult forces may be benevolent as well as malevolent. Occult means are used in seeking either blessings or cursings as it is through them that human beings have access to the invisible world of absolute power. Occult, or as used throughout this essay esoteric, is a methodology, not a value, in Senegambian terms.

Description of Peace, Happiness, and Success

Success is the result of spiritual, esoteric power rather than the result of hard work—getting ahead by one's own efforts, planning ahead, and saving and investing one's money. Sylla (1978:58) sums up the concept:

> Of two adversaries that are in competition (politics, sports, gaining influence, etc.) or two enemies that fight, the one that concentrates on himself the greatest mystical force will of necessity gain the victory. He is described as *mop ëp bopp*, "he has more of a head than the other."

Success is the natural result of living in a state of peace and harmony with transempirical beings and forces. Peace, happiness, and success are inseparable. Success without internal and external personal peace is a contradiction in terms. Happiness cannot be conceived of in the absence of peace and success. So, in the following discussion, success will be understood to cover the trilogy peace-happiness-success.

Success in life is considered to be a supernatural gift, realized on the basis of the charismatic potential of a person rather than on his or her personal qualities. Success is the result of the direct intervention of the transcendent in the affairs of an individual. It is analogous to magnetic waves and magnets. A successful person is one who has the qualities of a magnet. Therefore the transcendent power of magnetic waves that generate success will naturally cause the charismatic alignment necessary for the achievement of success. In such a state, the person does not just have success, and especially peace, but is in peace, or is possessed by peace. Peace brings alignment and alignment brings peace. So there is a constant quest by individuals to live in a state of alignment with the transcendent. This requires constant attention to all relationships:

> man ↔ transempirical beings and forces
> man ↔ man
> man ↔ nature

In reviewing the world view propositions of this study with Senegambians, the most persistent comment received was "you need to give greater emphasis to the primacy of the relationships man—transempirical beings and forces—nature." They see success as the result of comprehensive, even cosmic, harmony, and not at all as something to be isolated and pursued in reduced terms, such as mere wealth and fame. Hence, it is understandable that Senegambians consider the propositions of metatheme 2, the quest for transempirical power, as part of metatheme 1, the desire for transcendent peace. Yet, as has been stated, the quest for power so often goes beyond just seeking good for oneself that the power propositions have been separated from those of peace for analytical purposes.

Explanation, Prescription, and Control of Destiny

The article by Robin Horton, "African Conversion" (1971), stimulated a series of articles on African religion and conversion of Africans to Islam or Christianity (cf. Fisher 1973, Horton 1975a and 1975b, Linares 1986). Horton uses the phrase "explanation, prediction, and control of space-time events," borrowed from Peel (1968), to describe the essential characteristics of Yoruba religion. From this, Horton (1971:95–96) applies the phrase to ATR in general. Although Horton does not define the terms, he does give a few examples of what they refer to. His purpose is to determine the dynamics of the conversion of Africans to Islam or Christianity, but his core concepts are eminently applicable to the purposes of the present study. It is not my purpose to examine the process of Senegambians converting to Islam, but to find the essential characteristics and assumptions of the Islamic and traditional belief systems. Horton's scheme provides an excellent core framework.

Figure 18 presents the examples given by Horton (1971:86–91) from Aladura and similar Zionist churches in Nigeria, as they relate to explanation, prediction, and control. Note that Horton gives only one example of PREDICTION so it seems this is a relatively infrequently used feature of the Zionist religious system.

Although Horton does not use the term, he provides several examples of PRESCRIPTION in church life in his data. Horton's proposition includes the phrase space-time events, but in Senegambian religion, events outside the space-time world are also of fundamental importance, so it is omitted from the formulation. This, then, gives as the essential characteristics of the Senegambian belief system—the search for explanation, prediction/prescription, and control of events that affect individuals and society.

This can be stated as a proposition in these terms: *Senegambian traditional religion at its most fundamental level seeks explanation, prescription, and control of forces and events that affect the well-being of man in the space-time world.* This is essentially identical in meaning to theme 1 below.

Explanation

Diagnose causes of misfortune.
Moral lapses bring God's punishment.
Misfortune is a sign of God's wrath.
The forces at work in a situation are identified through dreams, visions, and utterances by the Holy Spirit.

Prediction

Imminent disasters are foretold.
Actions are needed to avert or remedy misfortune.*
Prayer to God brings definite and predictable results: cures disease, brings financial success, secures promotion.*
Success of prayer depends on observing taboos.*

Control

Power of averting disasters.
Healings through prayer.
Power to remedy the ills of individuals and of society by the power of God.
Protection against sickness and misfortune.

* These items are listed under prediction but they are more prescriptive than predictive.

Fig. 18. Explanation, prediction and control in Zionist churches

Theme 1: Understanding and Controling Events of Life

It is possible to obtain knowledge about one's personal destiny, to understand the origins and causes of the events of life, and to obtain prescriptions for improving or altering future events in one's favor. The same principles and processes apply to community destinies and events.

Explanation and Prescription

Theme 1 speaks especially to the functions of EXPLANATION and PRESCRIPTION. Explanation first involves looking into the hidden world of transempirical beings and forces through the gift of interior vision. It is almost exclusively the realm of the designated intermediaries between the visible and invisible worlds to carry out these operations. This was described in a previous section.

Metatheme 2: Peace Achieved by Means of Power

It usually involves one of many forms and varieties of divination that are widely available in the society. The process of explanation through interior vision is, by definition, divination.

The only major exception to the use of divination for obtaining an understanding of the present spiritual state is augury, or omens. Many of these are also called superstitions. Their interpretations are open to ordinary people, even if most people lack a developed sense or gift of reading these signs accurately. Many experiences, events, and actions are taken as omens or potential omens of what will happen, as, for example, "The youngest son of a family should never just wear one shoe, as that is liable to cause the death of one parent" (Maranz 1989).

Once the intermediary has determined the current state of affairs in the spirit world, he or she also ascertains what action is required to effect the desired result, that is, ascertains the prescription that will lead to the desired goal: the control of destiny.

Two examples will illustrate the sequence of practices involved. The first is followed in cases of chronic, serious illness; the second in cases of mundane problems.

When a man or woman suffers chronically from a serious malady, that is, is ill for a period of some months, the typical conclusion is that the illness may indicate the existence of a major spiritual problem. Prior consultations with diviners or healing practitioners will not have led to a permanent cure. The diviner or healer will recommend that an *ndëppkat* be consulted. The *ndëppkat* is a healer, man or woman, but usually the latter, who specializes in healing rites that involve illnesses that are the consequence of spirit possession.

The services of such a healer are engaged. Entering into a trance, the healer is informed by a spirit whether a possessing spirit is the cause of the illness and, if so, what sacrifices and other actions the spirit requires, immediately and/or periodically in the future, that will allow the person to regain and then maintain his or her health. Thus, we see how in this example of serious illness, the elements of explanation, prescription, and control are the fundamental operations carried out. Senegambian *ndëpp* rites have been frequently described in scholarly literature, for example, Mercier and Balandier (1952), Ortigues and Ortigues (1984), Sarr (1980), Zempléni (1966 and 1985), and Dione (1990). My own research has also encountered descriptions of such rites.

A mundane case would be that of a person who wanted to ensure that a trip would be successful and consulted a diviner *(tanikat)* to ascertain what had to be done to ensure such success. The diviner reads the pattern of cowrie shells cast onto a woven mat. The pattern reveals to the initiated the information needed for a successful trip, including any prescribed actions that are required of the consultee. Again, even in a simple case, the elements of explanation, prescription, and control are involved.

Explanation and prescription are never separated. Probably the only Senegambians who are interested in understanding explanation for its own sake are the very few who have studied philosophy at a modern university, like Sylla (1978) and Ndaw (1983). Explanation has always been sought for practical reasons: the revelation of the mystical causes of disharmony and the steps that are required of humans by the supernatural powers to restore harmony. The prescription leads to the desired goal, the control of destiny. To a Westerner, control of one's destiny may seem like a contradiction. For us a destiny is unchangeable, implacable. Senegalese explain their concept quite differently. Every normal human being has a good destiny, but imbalance in the transempirical realm can block its realization. Hence, there may be need at times to take specific steps to assert control over one's destiny.

Figure 19 provides a comprehensive listing of the religious practices found in the Senegambia, including those of Islam, Islamo-traditional, and traditional religion. It demonstrates the applicability of the formula explanation, prescription, and control to all Senegambian religious phenomena. I have found no practices that do not fit the scheme. This demonstrates a consistency between the three belief systems that points to the existence of a common set of underlying assumptions about reality.

Explanation	Prescription	Prevenient Action	Control	
			Self-Increase	Other-Decrease

ISLAMIC ELEMENTS

divination:				
listikar	> >	—	> >	> >
mystical retreat:				
xalwa	> >	—	> >	> >
		regret:		
—	—	*tuub*	> >	—
		fasting:		
—	—	*koor*	> >	—

(continued)

Metatheme 2: Peace Achieved by Means of Power 149

Explanation	Prescription	Prevenient Action	Control Self-Increase	Control Other-Decrease
		formulas:		
——	——	aar	> >	——
——	——	astafurlaa	> >	——
——	——	jébbalu	> >	——
——	——	subbóoxun	> >	——
——	——	Qur'anic words (etc.)	> >	——
		intercession:		
——	——	rammu	——	——
		holy work:		
——	——	tarbiyu	> >	——
			divine protection:	
——	——	——	tawféex	——
			religion:	
——	——	——	lislaam	——
			miracles:	
——	——	——	karama	——
			benediction:	
——	——	——	barke	——
——	——	——	tuyaaba	——
			protector spirit:	
——	——	——	rawane	——
			prayer:	
——	——	——	duá	> >
——	——	——	ñaan-yàlla	> >
				magic text:
——	——	——	< <	mbind
				malediction:
——	——	——	——	toskare
——	——	——	——	repp

ISLAMO-TRADITIONAL ELEMENTS

augury:				
gaaf	> >	——	> >	> >
kuus	> >	——	> >	> >
jig	> >	——	> >	> >
ubiquity:				
yëg	——	——	> >	> >
		taboos:		
——	——	tere	> >	——

(continued)

Explanation	Prescription	Prevenient Action	Control Self-Increase	Control Other-Decrease
		vows:		
—	—	*yéene*	>>	>>
		formulas:		
—	—	*kaar*	>>	—
—	—	*kuf*	>>	—
—	—	*maandu ci*	>>	—
		(etc.)		
		newborn rite:		
—	—	*toqental*	>>	—
		prayer:		
—	—	—	*ñaan*	>>
		talismans:		
—	—	—	*xaatim*	>>
			(etc.)	
			miracles:	
—	—	—	*kawteef*	>>
—	—	—	*kéeman*	>>
			protection:	
—	—	—	*gàllaaj*	>>
—	—	—	*saafara*	>>
—	—	—	*yiir*	>>
			protector spirit:	
—	—	—	*rawane*	>>
			personal advantage:	
—	—	—	*kiss*	—
				execration:
—	—	<<	—	*cat*
—	—	<<	—	*bët*
—	—	<<	—	*laal*
			transfer:	
—	—	—	*topp*	—
				domination:
—	—	—	<<	*xiirtal*
—	—	—	<<	*jiitu*

TRADITIONAL RELIGIOUS ELEMENTS

divination:				
gisaane	>>	—	>>	>>
tani	>>	—	>>	>>

(continued)

Metatheme 2: Peace Achieved by Means of Power

Explanation	Prescription	Prevenient Action	Control Self-Increase	Control Other-Decrease
tëddale (etc.)	> >	——	> >	> >
possession-rite:				
ndëpp	> >	——	> >	——
ritual bath:				
sangat	> >	——	> >	——
traditional cultus:				
tuur	> >	——	> >	——
xooy (S.)	> >	——	> >	> >
miis (Safen)	> >	——	> >	——
personal magic:				
xarbaax	> >	——	> >	> >
black arts:				
jibar	> >	——	——	> >
xérém	> >	——	> >	> >
——	——	——	< <	*kort*
——	——	——	< <	*liggéey*
——	——	——	< <	*noob*
——	——	——	< <	*xala*
		formulas:		
——	——	*jat*	> >	——
——	——	*lugg*	> >	——
——	——	*mocc*	> >	——
——	——	*móolu*	> >	> >
		totems:		
——	< <	*mbañ*	> >	——
		talismans:		
——	——	——	*xonjom*	> >
——	——	——	*téeré*	> >
		victory potion:		
——	——	——	*déeba-déeb*	> >
		conjuring:		
——	——	——	*wooj*	> >
		rainmaking:		
——	——	——	*baaw-naan*	——
		protection:		
——	——	——	*ñag*	——
——	——	——	*róonu*	——
——	——	——	*tul*	> >

(continued)

Explanation	Prescription	Prevenient Action	Control	
			Self-Increase	Other-Decrease
——	——	——	——	separation of affection: *dëddale*
——	——	——	< <	domination: *noot nit ki*
——	——	——	——	drive insane: *xër-lo*

Key:
    > >   = the element is also used in this category.
    < <   = the element is secondarily applicable to this category.
    —— = the element is not used directly in this category.
    (etc.) = there are other items not listed that also fit this category.

Fig. 19. Religious elements used for explanation, prescription, and control

Knowing the Future

A presupposition lies behind the search for explanation, prescription, and control of one's destiny. Senegambians assume that if future events can be known and if power is available to control them, it goes without question that to do so will be good for one's personal well-being. It is a universal feature of human nature to act in self-interest, yet there is a need for balance. What is best for me, and best for each individual of the society, may not be best for the collectivity. Personal interests must be balanced with group and society interest. Obviously, this is also a universal need. In the Senegambia, although there is much search for greater esoteric power, most people are unwilling to pay too high a price to obtain the maximum amount.

Mercier and Balandier (1952) recount the rumored story concerning the origins of the Layenne Sufi order, of which the Lebou form the bulk of the membership. The Lebou are a Senegalese ethnic group composed largely of fishermen (Gamble 1957). Early in this century, a fish-genie appeared to a Lebou fisherman named Guèye offering to him unlimited power, even prophethood, if he would meet certain conditions. The man refused, but told friends of the offer. The story goes that a man, who thereafter called himself Laye, heard of the offer, made an alliance with the fish-genie, and from this the Layenne order was born (Mercier and Balandier 1952:110). The Layennes numbered 21,000 in 1970 (IGN 1977) and some 35,000 today. Naturally, this is not the official version of the origins of the order, but it is an example of belief in the possibilities of esoteric power, and the personal choices available vis-à-vis this power.

Explanation and Preconditions

Well-being for self, family, clan, and community is dependent upon being in harmony with transcendent beings and forces. The harmony is based upon all entities of the cosmos filling their roles. Man, being merely human, frequently fails to adequately fill his role by either inadvertent or willful neglect. The resultant state of affairs is called *umute*, the state of misfortune that is the result of ceremonial disequilibrium. This state is the closest concept to sin found in the ATR of the Senegambia.

Interior Vision and Revelation. Certain persons are the designated interlocutors for the natural-supernatural dialogue that is essential to the maintenance of this harmony. They have the gift of interior vision which enables them to understand the true realities behind the visible reality. This understanding enables them to determine what steps need to be taken to reestablish harmony, that is, to remove *umute*.

The actions involving interior vision and the revelation of the prescriptions needed to restore harmony are shown in the first two columns of figure 19. Note that Islam and Islamo-traditional practices include relatively few kinds of explanatory elements and that traditional religion has many. The few kinds of explanatory elements does not mean that such practices are of limited usage in Islam. In fact, *listikar* and *xalwa* are very frequently employed, and are versatile and amenable to many different explanatory needs. What the limited number of procedures seems to mean is that because of the strictures of Islam and because Islamic terminology, cultural artifacts, or rites must be used to justify such rites as being considered Islamic, it is easier to employ a limited number of basic rites as Islamic, while maintaining many others that are known to be effective as a parallel set, outside the pale of Islam. This can be done as long as the system is accepted by the community. This might be seen by the outside observer as some sort of compromise with Islamic orthodoxy. Lamin Sanneh (1983:235–36), an African scholar of African religious history, explains the typical historical interaction between Islam and ATR in West Africa in the following terms:

In other places we can observe a similar process of Islam being assimilated into an existing religious world... In Sierra Leone Islam came upon a highly organised Poro society, and in the ensuing encounter it was definitely Islam that played second fiddle. The Muslim cleric was adopted into the Poro hierarchy and given a role which suited his familiarity with the sacred Arabic script. He used his knowledge of the science of magic squares *('ilm awfaq)*, the basis of Islamic talismans, to provide the Poro with powerful medicine for use against their enemies...

A study of Islam in the Middle Volta Basin in the pre-colonial Gold Coast gives many examples of the interaction between Islam and the traditional religions and customs. Islamic ritual was absorbed into the important Dangba festival where subordinate chiefs reaffirmed their tutelage under the Paramount Chief... The predilection for religious symbolism and for experimenting with spiritual power acts as a vortex into which Islam is sucked; the tolerance and adaptability which have trailed it through African communities emanated from this active centre.

The last two columns of figure 19 indicate whether the prescription is intended to benefit the individual or entity seeking the explanation, or whether it will cause another individual or entity harm, misfortune, or loss. In the first case the column is entitled self-increasing and in the second, other-decreasing. Each element is entered in the column that indicates its primary or most-typical purpose. Arrows (> > or < <) indicate secondary purposes.

Preconditions. The rites used to determine the causes of misfortune or to determine the hidden realities, with the concomitant revelation of the remedies required to achieve the ends desired by the client, often presuppose that certain steps of preparation will be necessary before revelation can be received from the transcendent forces and beings. These are basically steps that will bring the intermediary into a state of ritual purity. They may include ritual washings, fasting, refraining from sex, or other elements.

Incense is a much-used preparatory element. It is considered to be ritually purifying. Some spirits have preferred incenses, so the burning of the incense preferred by the spirit one desires to communicate with is a necessary overture to inciting it to be present and attentive to the request of the practitioner. Some of these incenses are very costly. Incenses have specific names, e.g., *safi* and *mustacat*. Knowing which incense attracts the particular

Metatheme 2: Peace Achieved by Means of Power 155

spirit with the power to carry out the desired operation is part of *siru* 'hidden knowledge'. People also just enjoy burning incense. Fired-clay burners are commonly sold items; consequently, the mere presence of incense in a house does not necessarily indicate that religious rites are being carried on.

Such preconditions are not included in figure 19 and are not further described in the essay, as they are not particularly relevant to the propositions under discussion. Note that these preconditions for EXPLANATION are different from the preconditions for CONTROL, which are treated below (and in figure 19 in the Prevenient Action column).

Elements of Explanation

Divination. An example of the search for explanation is provided by *listikar*, the practice in which the diviner purifies himself ritually and then passes the night in a state of readiness to receive through a vision the clarification of the esoteric state of affairs and the remedy required to effect the wishes of the client. It is considered to be Islamic, in contrast to the *tëddale*, which is a similar but traditional rite.

The Islamic content comes from the fact that *listikar* (from *istikhara*, A.), a form of Muslim prayer involving ritual prayer (*du'a*, A.) in the purification process, is based on Islamic traditions (*hadith*), and looks to Allah as the source of the inspiration. Throughout Islamic history, *istikhara* has been subject to practices not sanctioned by the orthodox traditions. One of these nonorthodox practices is seeking divine revelation through dreams (Gibb and Kramers 1965:187). This practice is exactly what is considered to be Islamic in the Senegambia.

Mystical retreat. A second example of a phenomenon used for explanation is *xalwa*. This is an Islamic mystical retreat that is based on a special *wird*, that is, a predetermined prayer litany consisting of words or phrases, especially the names of God, and which is repeated in addition to the prescribed five prayers of the day. The purpose of *xalwa* is to enter into communication with *jinns*, and then by use of certain of the names of Allah, obtain clarification of the realities of the hidden world, and to receive the request desired by the client.[37] *xalwa* was described in some detail under metatheme 1, subtheme 2-B: consequences of a breach.

---

[37] The "client" can be the person, male or female, carrying out the *xalwa* rite. That is, *xalwa* can be carried out for oneself as well as on behalf of others.

Elements of Prevenient Action

Prevenient action covers elements that relate to explanation and control, yet do not require special rites relating to interior vision to provide the desired explanations and prescriptions. These actions are part of what could be labeled the religious public domain. Some are known and used by average members of society. Others are used by specialists, but they use them without elaborate ritual, as it is known that the desired control will, or may, result from the prevenient action being taken. A simple example is prayer to divinity. Prayer has been ascertained to be a precondition for either a common believer or a designated intermediary being granted certain requests; in other words, to his exerting control over the destiny of some individual. The prayer does not exert the control, but the divinity will not move to exert it until the preconditions are met, that is, until the prevenient action is taken.

Another common example in the Senegambia is the repetition of a formula, a set sequence of specific words that inherently contain the power to effect certain ends. This could be the common use of the phrase *nelen kar*, which is believed to ward off the destructive effects of the evil tongue. Prevenient elements are shown in column 3 of figure 19.

Asking pardon. tuub is simply asking or entreating pardon for an offense committed, whether to Allah or to a person. It is considered to be Islamic as in traditional religion the concept of asking God for pardon for sins committed was rather unknown.

Fasting. koor is abstaining from food, and usually drink, including not even swallowing one's saliva. It is Islamic in that traditional religion included some ascetic elements, but only as part of particular rituals, not as prescribed general religious behavior (cf. Fürer-Haimendorf 1985:93). Muslim fasting is largely limited to the month of Ramadan, during daylight hours only.

Formulas. aar 'God protect us', is a general purpose formula for calling on God's help in any circumstance. *astafurlaa* 'forgive me God for...' is borrowed from the Arabic *astakhfirullah*. It is a request to Allah for pardon and purification (Moreau 1982:177). It is also used in the prayer litanies of the Tijani order, being repeated hundreds of times a day. *jébbalu* is the act of being put under the spiritual protection of another. In

Metatheme 2: Peace Achieved by Means of Power

the Mouride order it includes the formula, repeated as an oath in Wolof, "I submit my body and my soul to you. I will do everything you order me, and abstain from anything you forbid me" (Cruise O'Brien 1971:85).

subbóoxun 'may God protect me from you'. This formula is used when someone speaks, looks at, or touches another in a way that is perceived to involve evil intent. The formula has maximum potency when repeated orally immediately after an act. The person on the receiving end repeats the formula outside the hearing of the other person, who would be grossly offended at hearing the formula, which would indicate a very negative interpretation of the first person's behavior.

Intercession. rammu is intercession on behalf of another, for grace in this world or in the next. As Senegambian world view considers the office of intermediary to be largely limited to specially authorized individuals, the concept of *rammu* is largely limited to the mediation of Muhammad before Allah, and of the Muslim saints before Muhammad. The Prophet of Islam is the eternally approved intercessor for all faithful Muslims. Allah would be loathe to refuse his intercession for, after all, Allah chose him to be the intermediary between Himself and all those believers who are submitted to His will. Although there is frequent appeal for the prayers of Muslims on behalf of the dead at times of death, or at anniversaries of deaths, the requests seem more to involve prayers to Muhammad than to Allah. Such prayers on behalf of the dead serve more to increase the eternal merit of those offering the prayers than to achieve intercessory effect.

Holy work. In the Mouride order, *tarbiyu* 'holy work' is an exchange made with a marabout. It involves the giving of manual labor, usually farm work, in exchange for the marabout's benediction. *tarbiyu* means literally 'to serve'. With the *jébbalu* 'oath of allegiance' it forms the foundation of the Mouride marabout-disciple relationship. The *jébbalu* is not considered to be a sufficient basis for obtaining the marabout's *barke*. The disciple must also demonstrate genuine veneration through service. This is done on the basis of the *tarbiyu* (Sy 1969:172).

Taboos. Taboos *(tere* and *aaye)* are folk beliefs that are transmitted through the culture. They may have African, Arabic, or other ethnic or geographic origins. They are subject to adaptation under Islamic and modernizing influences. To most Senegambians, they are neither Islamic nor non-Islamic; they are simply accepted as part of existence. They are placed in figure 19 in the Islamo-traditional section.

The taboos given here are all currently spoken of. This is just a tiny sample of the hundreds of taboos one hears and reads about. Many are universally known and widely followed. Others are more limited to one area or ethnic group. Some are still widely followed while others are widely questioned. Modern scientific education and perceived derision from Western-educated people and foreigners have weakened many taboos, especially in the cities, but they are still somewhat feared, if not completely believed in. Particular taboos that are questioned are often followed just in case there may be something to them.

Certain taboos relate to an effect on personal destiny. The effect may be negative; that is, the effect of the nonobservance of a taboo will be self-decremental. Following are some well-known taboos; additional taboos are provided in appendix 6.

1. Upon leaving one's house in the morning, the first encounter with a man/woman/child will augur good or ill for the day. This taboo comes in several varieties. The common factor is that the first encounter of the day can augur good or ill. Whether the good or ill will result from an encounter with man, woman or child, depends upon the particular taboo one holds to. For a shopkeeper or vendor, the first sale of the day is important as an augury for that business day.
2. Never mend clothing while it is being worn. To do so is to risk becoming *rafle* 'to be without clothing'.
3. Do not buy salt at night, but if there is need to do so, call it *saf cin* 'cooking flavor'. If anyone pronounces the word salt at night either he or she will be trapped by *dëmm* 'soul-eaters, witches', or else will be identified as a *dëmm*, known to need condiments only at night.
4. Never wash clothes on Saturday. To do so is to risk being deprived of clothing.
5. If Tabaski or Korité (the two biggest Muslim annual holy days) falls on a Friday, and both the closing prayers of the feastday and the normal Friday noonday prayers are said, there is danger that the temporal power will fall.[38] Korité fell on Friday, April, 27, 1990. The national government of Senegal appeared to take this taboo very seriously as no noonday prayers were allowed in the central mosque in Dakar, although

---

[38] Closing prayers are in focus because they constitute the essential ritual elements of the two festivals.

no official reason for the closing of the mosque was given (Gningue 1990). The several Senegalese I talked to about the subject all had no doubt that the true reason was the taboo.
6. When sweeping the floor, do not sweep from one room to another; rather, collect the sweepings in each room. If the sweepings are swept out of a room, there is risk that whatever confidential things were said in the room will be let out.

The discussion of the elements shown in figure 19 that relate to control are taken next under theme two.

Theme 2: Knowledge of Future Destiny

It is possible and desirable to exercise control over one's destiny, over the events of life, and over the events of the community.

Theme 2 is focused on control. Explanation and prescription are means. Their goal is control of destiny: life, people, events, success, illnesses, the natural elements, the spirit world, community. In sum, everything in the world and out of the world. Any and all of these can be threatening if not kept in balance.

Control is aimed either to benefit the one seeking the explanation-prescription, or else to diminish the power and place of some targeted individual, group, or thing. The first are the self-increasing means of control shown in column four. The second are shown in column five as other-decreasing control. The practice of black magic, involved in the practices listed in column five, are implicitly condemned in the Qur'an (Ali 1983:37.15; 61.6), but are practiced by many Muslims in the Senegambia. A relatively mild, but very common, example is the magical use of Qur'anic verses in a ritual called *mbind,* which a number of Senegalese have told me is frequently used to ensure victory in a sports event.

Note that all columns of explanation and control contain elements of Islamic, Islamo-traditional and traditional religion alike. The basic underlying purpose of traditional religion has continued extant under Islam, although there have been many surface-level modifications.

CONTROL means that the powers of transempirical beings and/or forces are enlisted on behalf of the supplicant. Senegambians generally have a keen sense of needing extra-human help for a great many, if not most, of the events of life. This is evident from an examination of the two control columns of figure 19. Some of the elements for which help, that is control, may be desired are: protection, success, miracles, benediction, personal advantage or domination over others, and cursing or defeat of enemies.

Elements of Control: Self-increasing and Other-decreasing

A careful examination of the two control columns of figure 19 reveals that although Islamic elements include some procedures that may be aimed against others, most are aimed at self-advantage. In the Islamo-traditional and traditional sections the chart is replete with practices aimed against others. This probably reflects Islam's focus on paradise and its strictures against black magic.

Prayer. Extemporaneous prayer *(du'a)* is ordinarily spoken, not just formulated silently. Occasionally in the Senegambia, one sees two men standing on the street or in a market, facing each other, both with hands outstretched. One has his palms down touching the hand of the other whose palms are facing upwards. The one with palms up, symbolic of being open to receiving a benediction from Allah, is being prayed for. At the close of the prayer, the recipient will rub his face and touch his chest at the level of his heart with the palms of his hands, in gesture of transferring the benediction received to himself. He also pronounces the close of the prayer with the word *amiin*, meaning 'may God accept and grant the request'. This is one example of *du'a,* or more commonly in Wolof, *ñaan.* Typically, the recipient has asked the other for his benedictory prayer, for a general need, or for a specific request. The one requested to pray is ordinarily a marabout but may occasionally be someone of known blessing and uprightness. *du'a* can also be used as a prayer against another person.

ñaan-yàlla is a prayer for either protection for oneself or one's own, or for the malediction of others. It is probably more typically used for the latter. *tawféex* is a state of divine protection, an improved well-being, or even happiness. It can also refer to peace of body and mind.

Religion. The Wolofized Arabic word for Islam as a religion is *lislaam.* In general it refers to the practice of the five pillars of Islam. *lislaam* is thought of in terms of the concerns and provisions of paradise for the individual believer. This contrasts with the communal concepts of traditional religion. For instance the Diola, an ethnic group of southern Senegal and northern Guinea-Bissau who still hold to traditional religion, believe that the spirits of the dead of individual Diola villages live in a spirit community in the forests of Guinea-Bissau. Clairvoyant Diola can find the village of their related manes, and discreetly watch them from a distance, although this is dangerous activity as the manes do not wish to be disturbed (Boly 1990).

Miracles. The Arabic word for miracle, *karama,* is known but not much used in the Senegambia. It does not even have a Wolofized form. Two Wolof words are used for miracles. They relate to traditional religion as well as to Islam. They are *kawtef,* meaning something that originates in the beyond, with God, a miracle; and *kéeman* which refers to an event that is beyond human knowledge or intelligence, a mystery, a miracle. The concept of miracles and the miraculous is very well developed. Marabouts are credited with all kinds of miraculous powers. The hagiographies of leading marabouts are filled to the extreme with the miraculous. Although *karama* would be limited in orthodox Islam to miracles that benefit the Muslim, that is, the generous deeds of Allah (Gibb and Kramers 1965:216), *kawtef* and *kéeman* may involve miraculous acts against others. Such limitations on the usage of *karama* may explain why the word never achieved general usage in the area.

Benediction. The benediction of Allah *(barke)* is transmitted through Sufi saints, such as Amadou Bamba. It is a mystical power which can be obtained through direct or indirect physical contact, with the saint or through something directly related to him, such as by touching the grillwork surrounding the sarcophagus at his mausoleum. A saint's *barke* is transmitted hereditarily from him to descendents, but a disciple's received *barke* has a tendency to dissipate; hence, it needs to be renewed periodically, by such actions as making pilgrimage to the tombs of dead saints, visiting living saints, renewing the act of submission to a marabout, or presenting gifts to him. *barke* is also related to other contexts of submission: children to parents, wife to husband, citizens to authorities. From such submission to the established hierarchy *barke* is believed to flow as a general principle. *barke* is a fundamental concept in Senegambian world view.

Another kind of benediction is *tuyaaba.* It is ordinarily conceived to be something that is immediately repaid by Allah for a good act. In this sense a common expression is 'may God repay you for . . . (what you have done)'. *tuyaaba* may also refer to reward in paradise. In any case, it is something that is recorded on the divine ledger as a credit to the person committing a benevolent act.

Protector Spirits. A personal protector spirit is called *rawane*. Every human being is believed to have a spiritual double or shadow, and without which the physical human body could not continue to exist. The concept seems to be analogous to the widespread Muslim belief in the *qarina* (A.) 'the one united' (Musk 1984:50). Musk (1984:50) quotes Zwemer (1917:9) as to the meaning:

> By *Qarin* or *Qarina*, the Moslem understands the double of the individual, his companion, his mate, his familiar demon. In the case of males a female mate, and in the case of females a male.

When a marabout or shaman seeks to harm or diminish someone, he does it through an attack on the spiritual double of that person. The Mandinka of south-central Senegal believe that the spirit doubles of the people living in a village all live together in a parallel, invisible, spirit village nearby (Schaffer and Cooper 1980). In the Senegambia, there is a wide range of complex beliefs in personal spirits, differing from area to area, from clan to clan, and as to degree of Islamization.

Magical Texts. Qur'anic words and passages that have magical, mystical power to harm or bring misfortune on those against whom they are directed are called *mbind*. Such texts are considered to be especially potent. When they are directed against a person, and the marabout throws the *mbind* into the ocean, the person goes insane, with an insanity that is like the tides: it comes and it goes in intensity. Such a curse cannot be lifted as the *mbind* is lost in the ocean. Another common use is against a competing team in sports. The marabout writes out the *mbind* which is put under a heavy weight. The whole team against whom the *mbind* is directed will then not be able to play well, but will play as though they had heavy weights on their feet.

Malediction. The state of malediction that is the consequence of supernatural banishment or ostracism is called *toskare*. It results in social isolation and in being left without spiritual protection. *repp* is another condition of malediction, occurring to someone who persists in self-destructive behavior. It is thought the person has a cursed destiny and that he seemingly does everything possible to bring it to pass. For example, someone who is a drug addict or a habitual criminal may be described as *dafa repp* 'he has a rendezvous with death'. In other words, the person is marching in step with his accursed destiny.

This covers the Islamic elements of figure 19. Descriptions of the elements of Islamo-traditional and traditional religion are located in appendix two. Further detailed descriptions will only be given for two elements, amulets and talismans, and taboos. It is unnecessary to include more descriptions, as the goal has been to clarify the purposes and assumptions behind the elements which were summarized as explanation, prescription, and control. It seems clear that the Islamic elements quite naturally fit this classificatory scheme. A careful examination of the remainder of figure 19 will show that the neo-traditional and traditional elements fit even more naturally, if this is possible, into the system, which I presume is basically pre-Islamic.

The elements contained in the following two sections cannot be said to be Islamic, but they are part of life in Islamic Senegambia. They have not been proscribed by Islam, although there are a few orthodox Muslims who preach against them. As they are so much a part of daily life in the Senegambia, and as just remanding them to the glossary would hardly reveal their importance, they are taken up briefly here.

Theme 3: Protection through Esoteric Power

Humans should have protection through esoteric power at personal, family, and community levels, in order to: (a) be defended against destructive cosmic forces; (b) resist esoteric attacks set in motion by enemies; and (c) avoid or challenge chronic misfortune.

Beyond merely keeping and restoring balance, the Senegambian believes he or she has need for an effective defense against the machinations of others, whose interests at some points and times are sure to conflict with the interests of oneself or one's group. Hence, theme 3 speaks to the imperative of a good esoteric defense to guard the individual or the group against any and all kinds of attack or disequilibrium in the transcendent realm. Talismans are the most commonly used means of explicit protection.

Charmed Elements: Talismans and Amulets

Talismans and amulets are almost universally used in the Senegambia. About the only nonusers are a few orthodox Muslims, some Roman Catholics, and a high percentage of the few Protestant Christians in the region. Otherwise, it is typical for people to wear not just one but several amulets.

Talismans are used for the protection of people, animals, vehicles, houses, fields, and anything else of value. They can be other-decremental as well as self-incremental. In 1982 when we rented a house in a middle-class neighborhood of Dakar, we found over a dozen talismans in and around the house. Some were located high in the trees in the yard.

The difference between amulets and talismans is not well defined. French usage, very prominent in West Africa, separates the two on the basis of the amulet being an object with magical powers made to be worn on the body while a talisman is a more general term for any object that is given magical powers. Thus, an amulet is a special kind of talisman. But even in French usage the differences are not clear-cut (Rey and Rey-Debove 1988).

Wallis Budge (1961:14), from his extensive study of amulets and talismans through history and across cultures, concludes:

> The object of the talisman is quite different from that of the amulet. The amulet is supposed to exercise its protective powers on behalf of the individual or thing continually, whereas the talisman is only intended to perform one specific task. Thus a talisman may be placed in the ground with money or treasure, which it is expected to protect and do nothing else. But the line which divides the amulet from the talisman has rarely been observed by any people who regard such things as parts of the machinery of magic, and in modern times the use and meanings of the two objects are generally confounded, even by educated folk who are superstitious. And the experts are not agreed on the subject.

Talismans, used as the generic term, have a long history in both west Africa and among the Arabs. Monteil (1980:174) quotes Arabic literature as far back as the tenth century that refers to charms and amulets being used against the evil eye and other dangers, and containing Qur'anic verses. Historian Philip Curtin (1975:67), tracing the Islamization of the Senegambia, states:

Metatheme 2: Peace Achieved by Means of Power

All these [Islamic] forms of charm had close parallels in pre-Muslim practice. One common charm, for example, was the *aye*, made by writing verses from the Koran on a wooden plaque, then washing the plaque with water, which absorbed the spiritual power of the written words. The pre-Islamic conterpart in Bundu [on the present Senegal-Mali border] was a similar liquid made by mixing water with the ritually prepared bark or roots of certain trees. The *aye* thus drew its power from wood of the plaque as well as the words of the Koran.

Talismans come in the form of bracelets, necklaces, rings, small pouches, arm-, waist-, leg-, neck-, and ankle-bands, bones, animal horns, sheets of paper and other materials, and countless other forms. They may be made of iron, copper, silver, and other metals, or a combination of metals, leather, cotton, or other fibers. An agent of esoteric power is usually placed in the container, although in the case of metals the container itself may be inscribed with esoteric symbols which are given power through incantation. The most common agent is a piece of paper with Arabic writing on it, including cabalistic symbols. I visited one marabout's clinic and saw stacks of paper slips with such writing and symbols—stacks of photocopies. These were destined to be cut up, folded and sewn inside leather pouches.

Herbs, mineral matter, cowrie shells, animal horns, and other materials may also be used. The variety of materials and uses is almost infinite. Each talisman is prepared by a marabout or traditional specialist. Talismans can be prepared for defensive (protective) or offensive (against others) purposes. Many specialists can provide either Islamic or traditional amulets, depending on the needs of the client and the specifics of the need.

There is a highly developed talisman-amulet vocabulary, as one would expect. The industry is also doing well. Descriptive terms refer to various elements such as purpose, shape, material of construction, contents, origin, and where to be worn or placed. Each Senegambian language has its own set of terms. Figure 20 presents a small sample of the Wolof terms, with a short indication of the use, or esoteric focus, involved with each. The definitions should not be understood as precise; many variants exist, with different specialists combining or defining their products in a kaleidoscope of uses and meanings. The purpose of the chart is to give an idea of the breadth and complexity of the area of amulets and talismans as a commentary on the obviously felt need for peace and protection in all the dimensions of life.

Name	Particularity
gàllaaj	An object whose purpose is esoteric protection; can contain either traditional or written elements (generic name).
kàcciri	A necklace of braided leather.
laar	An animal hide or a cow's tail, used especially to ward off effects of the evil mouth.
lapatake	A charm serving for all kinds of hand combat.
maxtume	A relatively large boxlike talisman, made of leather or brass and worn on a cord or chain hung around the neck.
muslaay	A protective talisman, deriving from *muslu* 'to protect against'.
ndombo	An amulet constructed of sewn leather.
ndombo-tere	A traditional, i.e., non-Islamic, amulet.
ñiir	A protection for nursing babies.
sàmm kër	A talisman for protecting a house.
takk	A talisman that serves to bind the person(s) targeted in almost any sense desired, made of cotton twine, usually with eleven knots.
téeré	Talismans that use cabalistic lore, symbols, or arrangements.
wattal	A protective talisman for pregnant women.
xaatim	A talisman containing Qur'anic and cabalistic writing.
xàpp	A belt or waistband incorporating a talisman.
xonjom	A talisman whose power is based on traditional magic.
xoos	A principal house or village talisman, established by the first house owner or the village founder.

Fig. 20. Names and uses of Wolof talismans

The Prosperity Genie

A different kind of augury is provided by various mysterious beings. The most commonly spoken of is the *kuus,* the genie of prosperity. The *kuus* is very small and seems to be encountered only when a person is alone. People frequently claim to have encountered them, and tell many stories about them.

When a *kuus* is encountered, it is always aggressive, seeking to wrestle physically with humans. If the person wrestles the *kuus* to the ground, the

Metatheme 2: Peace Achieved by Means of Power

kuus will offer great riches in exchange for his liberty. This is the prosperity side. However, if the human loses the struggle, he (it seems that only men encounter *kuus*) may go insane, have his soul eaten, or suffer other negative consequences. Sometimes *kuus* cause a person to act in a certain way without ever being seen. There are many stories and many concepts connected with these fabulous beings.

The point of including a description of *kuus* is to show that virtually everything in life can be, and typically is, attributed to supernatural causes. Prosperity, fortune, misfortune, sickness, health, insanity, plagues of locusts, good rains, poor rains, intelligence, stupidity, insanity, beauty, ugliness—whatever the condition—all have spiritual explanations. Even when a scientific explanation is known, Senegambians have traditionally looked for the causative spiritual realities that they assume exist beneath the surface manifestations of those realities—even to the extent of believing in *kuus*. Individuals from the West find many Senegambian beliefs beyond belief, but I have heard many people insist on the veracity of some of their experiences.

Robin Horton (1971:93) asks what he considers to be the key question that "any interpretation of religious phenomena must tackle." This is "why *spiritual beings*" (italics his) are so prominent in African cosmologies. He considers that the anthropological symbolist approach proved itself barren in this regard. Likewise, comparative religionists have "offered little in the way of interpretation" (1971:94). Horton (1971:94) then defends his own approach:

> Disillusioned both with anthropological orthodoxy and with the comparative religionists, a number of philosophers and philosophically minded social scientists have recently been calling for a return to the intellectualist approach which takes systems of traditional religious belief *at their face value*—i.e., as theoretical systems intended for the explanation, prediction, and control of space-time events. [italics mine]

Taking traditional African belief at face value would surely go further than Horton proposes. It would include belief in *kuus*, for example. It would accept the possessing spirits of the *ndëpp* rituals as being real spirits, and on ad infinitum. Evidently this was so far from Horton's mind and so alien to his own nonsupernaturalist world view presuppositions that he equates a scheme for explaining beliefs with the beliefs and beings themselves.

So we are left with the question, why spiritual beings? The simplest answer is also the most difficult one and the one most anthropologists evidently refuse to consider: "Because they exist and have a power to act in the space-time world." Does such an answer include a belief in *kuus*? Not necessarily.

It is not within the scope of this study to argue for or against the validity of the Senegambian belief system. What is attempted is to determine its underpinning assumptions. Even within these limitations I think there is place for Horton's question. At least a footnote is in order to acknowlege one's relationship to the values of a people who have been willing to allow many of their most cherished beliefs to be probed in depth by a foreigner.

Having seen and talked in all seriousness with many Senegambians, I suggest a contrasting face-value answer to Horton's question: "Because the Senegambian interior world exists." After sifting through the recounting of countless experiences, I find there is a residue of problems that defies scientific, rational explanation. Yes, there are auto-suggestion, self-fulfillment of ideas, chicanery, illusion, delusion, reification of social structures, mechanisms of social control effected through the sorcery complex, and many other mechanisms in operation that have been proposed as learned explanations. But beyond all these there is an inexplicable residue.

This face-value approach is also economical, at least in a world view study. The participant observer can concentrate on the evidence and the deductions of the organizing principles and ontological meanings behind it. Nothing must, a priori, be rejected or explained away. This is not to say that everything is accepted at face value, or that careful scrutiny is not essential. It does mean not being a total skeptic, a position which gives ground for understanding and empathy that I believe are necessary prerequisites for deep-level cross-cultural understanding.

Is a minimal supernaturalism incompatible with objective science? I do not believe so. It may be *more* compatible than an a priori rejection of all supernaturalism. How can a position that rejects everything that is beyond empirical proof be more objective than one that does not thus dismiss the unknowable out of hand? Therefore the question of the *kuus* remains open. I have never seen one, but who knows, some day when I am out in the forest alone...

Esoteric Control over People

There is a potent supernatural power that a few marabouts are believed to possess. This esoteric gift *(xiirtal)* gives its possessor the power to control the will of another in order to make the person an abject follower.

Metatheme 2: Peace Achieved by Means of Power

The subject is rather hush-hush as the possession of this power is never openly admitted by those purported to possess it. This silence is a common characteristic of maraboutism, the common, corrupted misuse of popular Islam, and is a major basis for criticism of marabouts and their religious system—that it is obscurantist, exploitative, and retrograde, and not compatible with true Islam.

Severe criticisms are leveled against marabouts and maraboutism from time to time in Senegalese media. Maraboutism by definition is the misuse of real or feigned mystical power for personal gain. The criticisms are always carefully worded so that they never attack true marabouts but only the charlatans. Charlatans are defined as Satanically inspired marabouts who are out for personal gain and who introduce *bidda* to the faithful. *bidda* are teachings contrary to the Qur'an and the example of Muhammad. These marabouts are called self-proclaimed intermediaries between Allah and man (cf. B. Diop 1985, Faye 1987, Wade 1986). Sometimes commentaries are accompanied by humorous cartoons that are always careful not to go so far as to offend true marabouts (cf. B. Diop 1985).

xiirtal is here classified under Islam because that is where it is put by Senegalese Muslims. I have only heard it referred to in relation to marabouts, never to traditional healers or leaders, although in principle it is a magical practice that does not require its usage being limited to religious contexts.

As *xiirtal* is a veiled subject, it is especially difficult for the outsider to get detailed data and verify them by cross-checks with practitioners. Whenever I have asked marabouts directly about some of the more hidden, or powerful, or esoteric matters of their beliefs and practices, they have told me that they would not disclose such a matter to me, not even to confirm or deny it in principle. One said he did not disclose his most powerful practices and medicines even to his disciples, lest one use the power against him. One marabout did offer to teach me everything he knew, but at a price of several hundred U.S. dollars before any discussions or teaching even began. For a number of reasons I did not accept the offer. *xiirtal* is one of these concealed subjects, but the concept and accounts of its usage are widely discussed on the popular level.

Contemporary accounts of Bamba, taken from the official French government files, contain many indications of his charisma, including the following descriptions:

> [1907] He surrounds himself in a rigorous protocole. He has the Qur'an recited several times a day ... His private audiences constitute

rare favors, and when, by chance, he speaks, it is always in the name of Allah. He gives his blessing, spitting on the head and in the hands of the prostrate worshippers. The water of his personal ablutions is carefully collected, and the sand that absorbs any drops is sold by his disciples as amulets.

[1913] There is another marabout [Bamba], well known, very influential, who is believed to have the power to spellbind, to hypnotize, whoever approaches him. [Monteil 1966a:171]

Perhaps it is just natural that such exceptional leadership would foster the belief that Bamba's gift had supernatural origins, especially among a people who believe that nothing happens in this world without direct supernatural causes, and who above all attribute success and failure to the intervention of supernatural forces. In any case, Bamba is credited with having had *xiirtal*.

It is common for people today to say that Bamba learned the secret of a special *saafara* that would give him esoteric control over the wills of people to whom he directed it. This *saafara*, or magic potion, contained donkey milk as its key ingredient. Bamba is said to have learned this esoteric control while in exile in Mauritania, 1902–1907.

The Beydane, the Maure ruling caste on Senegal's northern border, are said to use the same potion to control members of their servile caste, the Haratine. The Haratines have been officially declared to be emancipated from slavery in recent decades, but their real status and roles "have changed little" (Curran and Schrock 1972:56). In 1989 it was reported that Haratines carried out bloody reprisals against Senegambian blacks, in accordance with their masters' political designs (Africa Confidential 1989). As currently as 1990, Senegal's Foreign Minister accused Mauritania before the Organization of African Unity of still practicing slavery (Sissouma 1990).

I have heard the story of a professional designer from Dakar who went to Touba, the Mouride headquarters city, to consult with top Mouride leaders about a professional job he was working on. He became a Mouride, abandoned his family in Dakar, married another wife at Touba, and now gives all of his income to his marabout (one of the top Mouride leaders).

Even the founder of the Senegalese branch of the Tijani order, El Hajj Malick, is said to have feared the power of Amadou Bamba to put people under his charismatic spell. Whenever Malick sent an envoy to Bamba, his contemporary, he warned the messenger not to let the latter hold on to his hand at the time of greeting and shaking hands, as he, Malick, had lost several envoys to Bamba's hypnotic powers, which could be exercised by means of prolonged touch. The envoys had become disciples of Bamba, abandoning the Tijani brotherhood.

Imposition of Will over Others

An extension of competition is seen in the concept of imposition and obtrusion of one person upon others, including their *nawle*. This is called in Wolof, *jiitu,* to impose oneself on others. Again a good starting point is a Wolof proverb: *juudù bu réy ndey ak baay, waaye faayda boroom* 'if noble blood comes from either father or mother, knowing how to impose or be dignified comes from oneself'. This means that in the highly stratified societies of the Wolof and other Senegambian peoples where social position is largely ascribed, although ancestry may give the individual a theoretically high place, the all-important qualities of dignity and esteem depend on the individual imposing himself or herself on others. Meekness is not of value.

The concept of imposition goes beyond the simple rivalry expressed in *wujj* and *nawle* to a frequent, studied attempt to put down others. It is not just attempting to get ahead but to cause setbacks to others, preferably by fair means, but it also often involves means considered foul even by society. These latter means are carried out on the sly, primarily through the use of magical arts, including black magic.

Success in Social Competition

The spirit of competition between peers is very great. Two frequently used words in Wolof express much of this spirit. The CLAD dictionary (1977) defines these as *wujj* 'co-wife, rival, competitor' and *nawle* 'person of the same condition or social rank'.

The spirit of competition *(wujj),* goes even beyond what Senegalese accept as fact, the notorious and universal rivalry that co-wives have between themselves and their children within a polygynous household. The term *wujj* also denotes any kind of competition or rivalry. Hence, one can assume the concept has been long present in the society.

The *nawle,* one's peer, is a friend or associate but competitor at the same time. A Wolof proverb says, *nit ku nekk ci adduna war na bàyyi xel ci nawleem* 'everyone in this world had better pay attention to his or her *nawle*'. Another states, *nawle nit rekk ka ko sonal* 'There is no one that causes so much trouble as a *nawle*'. This is understood to mean that the competition of the *nawle* forces a person to make uncomfortable or inconvenient efforts so as to not be left in an inferior position or fall behind in any way.

From childhood one is taught to keep up with one's *nawle*. A common reproach to children is *yées ci say nawle* 'do you want to be your *nawle's* garbage?' (Sylla 1978:175).

One must keep up with the *nawle* in everything from the trifling to the serious. Some examples of the effects of competition would even include the following: when a man buys a pair of trousers his *nawle* (singular or plural) will do everything possible to obtain a pair of equal or superior quality. Or, a mother will try to ensure that her children eat more, dress better, and get better grades in school, to keep ahead of her *nawle*. At the work place, in the office, or between friends in their homes, there is much effort not to let one's *nawle* get ahead.

Those, for example, who dress better, have more beautiful girl friends or wives, are more generous in gift giving (e.g., at a wedding), or have better furniture, are treated with more respect and honor than are others. Sarcasm, disdain, ridicule, and gossip are quickly and openly heaped on those who fall behind. These attitudes in society result in a great fear of losing one's dignity before one's peers. This is a serious state of affairs, even in an urban context, given the generally limited economic possibilities in the region.

This spirit of competition is widespread, if not almost universal, among all social groups and at all levels of society, to the point that some Senegalese say it is a major driving force of the dominant Wolof society. One of the consequences is that it provides a huge clientele for the marabouts, who offer access to supernatural powers which hold the hope of enabling one to keep up with the *nawle*. It also benefits the professional praise singers, who are called in for weddings and other occasions to eulogize their hosts and others present. Both marabouts and praise singers profit from the system, where both defensive and offensive control is sought. Many of the elements of figure 19 that appeal to transempirical powers are used in relation to this competition with peers.

The Transfer of Evil

One of the most pervasive subjects of Senegalese life is that of *cat* 'evil tongue'. A second Wolof word, *gémmiñ,* is used synonymously with *cat.* Literally, *cat* means 'tip' (of the tongue), and *gémmiñ* means 'mouth'. A third and related belief is *laal* 'evil touch', literally just meaning 'touch'. Yet

Metatheme 2: Peace Achieved by Means of Power

a fourth belief involves *bët* 'evil eye', with *bët* literally just meaning 'eye'. Beyond the literal meanings of these words lies a widespread complex of beliefs. I will use the term *cat* as the cover term, as this is by far the most-referred to and most-feared evil of this complex of evils.

In Serer, the evil tongue is called *donn* 'mouth'. In Pulaar it is *demngal* or *deemde* 'tongue' or 'tongues'. All the ethnic groups of the Senegambia I was able to research have active concepts, vocabulary, and counter-measures regarding the evil tongue.

In the worldwide survey of the evil eye reported by Clarence Maloney (1976), evil eye, evil mouth, hot mouth, evil breath, evil tongue, and evil touch are all considered to be related beliefs. Beliefs and practices concerning the evil eye were found to be much more widespread than those relating to the others. Maloney (1976b:vii-viii) reports the general conclusions:

> The common features found in the descriptions of the belief in the twelve world regions (or ethnic groups) described in this book seem to be limited to the following: (1) power emanates from the eye (or mouth) and strikes some object or person; (2) the stricken object is of value, and its destruction or injury is sudden; (3) the one casting the evil eye may not know he has the power; (4) the one affected may not be able to identify the source of the power; (5) the evil eye can be deflected or its effects modified or cured by particular devices, rituals, and symbols; (6) the belief helps to explain or rationalize sickness, misfortune, or loss of possessions such as animals or crops; and (7) in at least some functioning of the belief everywhere, envy is a factor.

All seven of these common features apply to the evil tongue complex in the Senegambia, with the following differences. Harm can overtake a victim slowly as well as suddenly (feature 2). The identity of the person(s) causing the misfortune is seldom in focus (feature 4). The operations of divination and retaliation reported for some areas do not seem to be at all present in the Senegambia (cf. Cosminsky 1976:168, Garrison and Arensberg 1976:292, 297, and Maloney 1976a:137). Yet there is some blame attributed to specific individuals. A typical case would be a university student telling a friend about his worry over an examination due to be taken the following day. If the friend says, "don't worry, you are intelligent and have studied diligently, so for sure you will do well tomorrow," and then if the student fails the exam, he will typically blame the friend (although not to his face) for causing his failure through the evil tongue.

The evil tongue is such a widespread concern that it is the subject of many taboos, proverbs, magical countermeasures, and strategies in everyday life. As would be expected, it is also reflected in the vocabularies of Senegambian languages, e.g., *ragal cat* is the 'fear of *cat*'. Other examples are contained in the following discussion.

A well-known Wolof proverb distills an ideology of life, of which *cat* is a major part: *ku ñépp tufli nga tooy* 'well-watered will be the person everyone spits upon'. This refers to words and actions towards others, and to one's own comportment in society. One should not speak or act against the opinions of others. An excess of ostentation is to be avoided. The breaking of the norms of society will result in "the curse that comes as a result of the convergence of (the power of) several tongues speaking (negatively) about one person" (Sylla 1978:100).

This complex is much more than the fear of gossip, or even of the social sanctions that gossip can produce. It involves the belief that one or more tongues speaking negatively about a person will engender or produce a force that will bring about the person's misfortune or downfall. It also includes the notion that the more tongues there are that speak negatively, the more power will be generated.

A common belief holds that as leaves of a tree can be caused to wither by *cat*, and everyone knows that humans are more fragile than trees, so humans need to be careful to avoid the dangers arising from people expressing *gëëmiñu* 'bad things from the mouth' against them.

The evil tongue is not an isolated concept. It accords with other folk beliefs in Senegambian society, and especially those that fall under metatheme 8, the beliefs related to the power of the uttered word (see appendix 3). Among these are the belief in the power of the recited Qur'an and, in Wolof society, the honor and importance ascribed to charismatic oratory and to other verbal arts.

People do not just want to be well-spoken of, or avoid being ill-spoken of. They assiduously want to live in such a way that others will not only think well of them, but no words will be spoken or uttered against them. Thoughts are much less severe than words spoken against someone.

Compliments are a very sensitive issue, and especially compliments that refer to a person's body. A person should only compliment his or her close friends; otherwise, compliments raise suspicions about one's motives. When a compliment is received from someone whose motives are not known, the custom is to repeat the defensive magical formula, *bul ma lekk*, 'do not eat me'. This most explicitly refers to witches *(dëmm)* who masquerade as normal people but who eat the souls of others. It also has wider application, in counteracting the power of *cat,* if present.

In Dakar, as in other Senegalese cities and towns, one commonly sees an old shoe or a cow's tail hanging from the back of a vehicle. These are considered to be impure objects and cancel the effect of impure tongues or impure eyes that might be directed against them. Mini-busses used in public transportation (*car rapides* F. and W.) frequently have formulas painted on them, such as *neleen kaar* 'say *kaar*', *kaar* being a magical word that neutralizes the effect of *cat.* Such defenses against *cat* are not merely decided upon by, say, the vehicle owner. They are a visible part of (esoteric) procedures requested of, and given by, various categories of ritual practitioners, including Muslim marabouts or clerics. Another formula is *manduleen ci man,* 'protect me from you', which means, 'protect me from your tongue by not saying anything about me or commenting about me with others'.

The fear of counting good things is another way *ragal cat,* 'the fear of *cat*' is expressed. It is not acceptable to ask a stranger how many children he or she has, or to bring attention to how many there are of any good thing. When newspapers report a large or small gathering, no attempt is made to count or estimate any precise number of participants. To do so would be to invite misfortune. When questions are asked by government census agents in taking the national census, or by others seeking statistical information, they need to do so very tactfully, or indirectly, if they are to succeed in their task. More is involved than the common belief that people are afraid of being taxed when they refuse to answer, or lie, or are evasive. The well-known Senegalese author, Ousmane Sembène, wrote a historical novel about the railway workers' strike of the 1940s (Ousmane 1960). The book is entitled *God's Bits of Wood* (in Wolof, *bant u maam yàlla*), referring to the term the strikers used of themselves. This term, God's bits of wood, was commonly used to refer to children in a family and people in any group. In recent times it has fallen out of use, but the fear behind its usage continues to be strong.

Examples of beliefs and practices concerning *cat* could be provided ad infinitum. What seems to be most important, however, is to find the basic concept or assumption behind *cat.* This is the principle of transfer. It will be taken up following a discussion of evil eye.

The Evil Eye. The evil eye is a recognized danger in the Senegambia, but does not have the importance accorded it in the Mediterranean area and in some other areas of the world, as described in Gilmore (1987), Maloney (1976), and Elworthy (1958). It is as though it had diffused south from the Mediterranean area, but only half-heartedly. Perhaps it came with the diffusion of Islam, but did not fully harmonize or meet a need in the belief system found here. It would seem that the beliefs and practices relating to the evil tongue encompass most of what would elsewhere be the domain of the evil eye, and so there was no extensive void in the belief system that needed to be filled with this belief. What need there was, was mostly subsumed under *cat*, the evil tongue.

Yet there are definite beliefs in, and fears related to, the evil eye. Two areas, especially, have been important. The first relates to eating. People fear eating heartily when someone without enough to eat could be watching (however a snack would not be a problem). This does not stem from pity for the person which the one eating may indeed have for the less fortunate, but from the fear of transfer of the misfortune of the underfed to the well-fed. Hence, people have traditionally sought to eat in private. Part of the fear is explained in the belief that food will become indigestible in the stomach and a person will begin to waste away and may even eventually die.

Sight is believed to have power, analogous to but less important than the power of the uttered word. The power can be positive or negative. Eyes of love *(bët u bëëgel)* and eyes of hate *(bët u baañ)* express the two poles of the power of sight which can be transmitted from one person to another.

The taboo against eating in view of people outside one's circle of confidence is breaking down, especially in urban areas. People eat in restaurants and at open-air restaurants called *tangana* that consist of tables and benches located outside a factory gate or hospital, where workers and others can be served coffee, bread, or a meal.

Another belief relates to night eyes *(bët u guddi)*. The complex of beliefs about witches *(dëmm)* also known as *nit u guddi* 'person of the night' includes ascribing to them the power of sight that penetrates both darkness and the human body. This ability of supernatural sight makes witches very powerful and much feared.

The Principle of Transfer. There is nothing inherently malevolent about words or looks. It is only under particular conditions or from certain people that they become dangerous. Above all, the problem arises when the will, or purpose, behind them has its origin in hate, jealousy, envy, cursing, or witchcraft; then the word or looks become troublesome. The

Metatheme 2: Peace Achieved by Means of Power

purpose or wish is called *yéene* 'wish'. It can be good *(yéene ju baax)* or bad *(yéene ju bon)*.

The principle can be called the principle of transfer. It is expressed in the concept of *topp* and *rewde* (P.), literally 'to follow', but meaning 'something that comes from or follows something from somewhere else'. Words that have an evil or destructive purpose can cause misfortune. It is something like a radio transmitter and radio receiver. A person with antisocial sentiment toward another sends out voice waves or sight waves that can be received by people, animals, or even objects, and which then immediately or over time cause misfortune, illness, or death. If the waves are sent with goodwill, they will be received as good sound or music, but if they are transmitted with ill will, the result will be static in the receiver, that is, misfortune. The good or the evil is transferred to the person or object.

Several strategies are used to remedy this state of affairs in which everyone finds himself or herself constantly subject to bombardment by destructive forces. The first is to do nothing to arouse the jealousy, hatred, or other kinds of ill will from others. At a place of employment, for example, it may be evidenced by an unwillingness to try to get ahead. With neighbors and family, it may take the form of living modestly and unostentatiously even if one has the means to live otherwise. Almost everyone is restrained from doing what he or she would prefer to do in some area of life because of this fear of arousing ill will, but there is also much ostentation, conspicuous spending, trying to outdo the Joneses in many areas of life. Other factors enter in to create this contradiction of values. Human action is complex and, even on the level of world view assumptions, various themes may be in competition with others.

A second strategy is to erect defenses against the destructive forces of the evil tongue and eye. These defenses can be general or specific. Given the widespread belief in and fear of these forces, the defense industry is well developed and prospering.

We have already mentioned some examples of defense: hanging up an old shoe or cow's tail, painting a magic formula on a vehicle, and repeating an effective magic formula upon being complimented. Defenses go far beyond such simple and seemingly benign practices.

The general term for an object used in an esoteric defense is *muslaay*, but there are specific terms that define more specific defenses: *kaar* is a spoken word or formula used to counteract the evil tongue; *lugg* is a formula, always used with the human touch of the healer, to counteract a broad class of poisons; *mocc* are formulas and touchings used for healing where there is pain. The ritual practices to which these terms refer are carried out by ritual specialists of the several kinds found in the society. These are discussed in the following recapitulation section.

The third category of defense is actually to go on the offensive. Various esoteric procedures are available offensively to preclude misfortune, gain good fortune for oneself, or achieve the misfortune of an enemy. As these procedures cover much more than a defense or an offense relating to *cat*, they were discussed earlier in this chapter.

All of these beliefs and practices are the warp and woof of a complex socioreligious system and the world view assumptions on which they are built. It is difficult to describe one part without referring to several other parts, as in the Senegambian social fabric the threads are not just two-dimensional, but multi-directional, with underlying threads or themes connecting all the major themes together in the complex fabric of culture.

That *cat* and similar beliefs are related to internal, personal peace hardly needs to be pointed out. Numbers of Senegambians I have approached about the subject have not even wanted to talk about it, as though the mere discussion of the topic might bring reprisal. *cat* is a constant worry for a high percentage of Senegambians, I would judge. Means are constantly employed for protection and for obtaining the peace of mind that they hope will be derived from it.

Recapitulation of Explanation, Prescription, and Control

Complementary Distribution of Practitioners

In this chapter we saw that the formula EXPLANATION, PRESCRIPTION, and CONTROL (EPC) clarified the purposes behind the basic religious phenomena, whether practiced under Islam, popular Islam, or traditional religion. It enabled us to understand much of how the quest for transcendent peace is carried out in its myriad facets and dimensions.

It still, however, may seem strange that Islam and ATR revealed so much in common. In this recapitulation, supplementary data reinforce the claim of the validity of the earlier analyses. At the same time, it reveals a relationship of complementary distribution between the functions of Islam on the one hand, ATR on the other, and popular or Sufi Islam between the two.

We saw in figure 19 the practices of the three subsystems of Senegambian religion. The analysis of the practices revealed the implicitly followed formula EPC. An examination of the practitioners involved reveals both confirming and contrasting facts. Figure 21 lists forty-nine types of religious practitioners that are active in eight different roles or specializations in the Senegambia. The types are organized by category of practice.

The confirming facts come from seeing more clearly the functions of the practitioners who carry on the particular classes of rites. In the previous discussion, only the many kinds of rites themselves were shown to follow the formula EPC. We now see the ritual process with additional information about who the practitioners are and the cosmic realities with which they are dealing. This information provides facts that confirm, or complement, our understanding of the system being analyzed. The contrasting facts are revealed in the different specializations present in the society, all being carried out by particular types of religious leaders within the EPC framework, forming a highly elaborated and complex ritual system.

To better understand the contrasting practices, we need to know what these practitioners do, what the core functions of each category are, and what the essential differences between them are, differences that will reveal the criteria used in considering them as separate types. These functions and distinctions are presented in figure 22. It shows, for example, that the essential function of a priest is to represent a regularly organized and permanent religious enterprise that has established norms, times, and places of religious practice. The essential distinction between priests and other practitioners is that priestly rites center on the lunar or solar calendar. In contrast, the essential function of a shaman is to receive personal communications from supernatural beings over which the shaman has some degree of control or mastery. The shaman's rites are performed at critical times and at decisive points in the ecological cycle. Priests and shamans do not usually function in the same system. If they are found in the same society they normally represent two different, or parallel, religious systems.

Next we need to know the metaphysical focus of each category of practitioner, so that we can get at the world view assumptions that are the bases of each, which will help us understand why each category is needed in the system from the viewpoint of Senegambian society. Metaphysical focus refers to the metaphysical reality or realities that a particular religious practitioner deals with. In other words, religions deal with beings and forces that constitute the complete cosmic spectrum or inventory of beings and forces believed to exist in the universe. Any one religion accepts or deals with only a limited part of this spectrum. For example, in much of the Christianity of the Western world, many of the beings and forces with which ATR deals are thought to be mere superstitions; hence, the doctrines and practices of many branches of Western Christianity have no metaphysical focuses in this area.

Priests

alim (W., A., pl. *ulema*)	doctor of Islamic law	Islam
imam	leader of Muslim ritual prayers; mosque leader	Islam
jàngkat	leader of Sufi chanting rites	Islam
kilifa	authority in a Sufi order	Islam
làbbe	Christian (Roman Catholic) priest	Christian
muqàddam	authority in the Tijani or Qadri Sufi order	Islam
séex	chief of a Sufi order	Islam
sëriñ daara	orthodox Muslim leader	Islam
tamsir	marabout with superior training	Islam
xaali	Islamic judge	Islam
xalif	head of a Sufi order	Islam
yelimaan	imam, leader of ritual prayers	Islam

Prophets

boroom jamano	spiritual guide of an age or a people	Islam
waarkat	preacher	Islam
wàlliyu	Sufi saint, a friend of Allah	Islam
wasilah	intermediary between Allah and man	Islam
yonent	prophet, a messenger of Allah	Islam

Shamans

jaraaf	community chief, (necessarily) with esoteric, ceremonial powers (largely archaic category)	ATR
saltige	shaman chief	ATR
selbe	chief of initiation rites	ATR
sëriñ tariax	marabout, shaman of esoteric sciences	ATR

Mediums

boroomi xam-xamu baatin	practitioner of hidden knowledge	Islam/ATR
ndëppkat	leader of healing/possession rites	ATR
ñàng	person with esoteric powers	ATR
woykat	leader of traditional religious music	ATR

(continued)

Magicians

boroomi xam-xam bu ñuul	practitioner of black magic	ATR
boroomi xam-xamu diine	practitioner of Islamic magic	Islam
jibarkat	practitioner of black magic	ATR
luggkat	pronouncer of magic/esoteric formulas	ATR/neutral*
luxuskat	conjurer	ATR
tàkkaan	magician, fire-eater (pejorative term)	ATR/neutral

Diviners

gisaanekat	clairvoyant	neutral
giskat	person with interior vision	neutral
seetkat	traditional or Islamic clairvoyant	Islam/ATR
sëriñ xaatim	maker of amulets or talismans	ATR
tanikat	diviner who uses cowrie shells	ATR

Healers

boroomi reen	herbalist	neutral
mocckat	pronouncer of magic/esoteric formulas, accompanied by touchings	ATR/neutral

Auto-practitioners

boroomi xàmb	individual, male or female, who maintains a traditional altar (to a spirit or spirits)	ATR
boroomi xérém	pagan	ATR
dëmm	witch/wizard, devourer of souls	ATR/neutral
gurmet	Christian	Christian
jullit	Muslim believer	Islam
nazraani	Christian	Christian
sëriñ	traditional or Islamic religious guide	Islam/ATR
soxna	saintly woman	Islam/neutral
taalibe	disciple of a marabout	Islam
xérémkat	person who practices traditional religious rites	ATR
xaritu jinné	friend of the devil/genie	ATR

* neutral indicates a practice that is neither particularly Islamic nor of ATR, but that is based on cosmic realities.

Fig. 21. Ritual practitioners in the Senegambia: Roles and religious affiliations

Category	Essential Function	Essential Distinction
priest	represents a regularly organized and permanent enterprise with established norms, times, and places	rites follow calendrical cycle
prophet	delivers a message received in a personal call; achieves or is ascribed extraordinary powers	prophet has a personal call, priest does not
shaman	receives personal communication from a supernatural being, over which he/she has control or mastery	rites are performed at critical junctures and in ecological cycle; priest and shaman do not usually function in the same system
medium	serves as a vehicle through which transhuman beings communicate with humans	medium is a subtype of shaman, with less or no control over supernatural beings
magician	manipulates impersonal, ritual power; licit and illicit magic typically found in same society	results depend upon error-free procedure and formulas and absence of stronger counter-magic
diviner	diagnoses immediate causes of personal, medical, or social problems	a prophet type who is solely concerned with individuals and small groups
healer or doctor	provides therapy, i.e., curing of illness, by natural means, including psychosomatic factors	the separate roles of diviner and healer are often combined in one person
auto-practitioner	practices on behalf of self or restricted kin group	requisites for access to the transempirical have been met

Note: The criteria used to construct this figure have been largely adapted from E. B. Idowu 1973, S. F. Nadel 1954, M. Titiev 1965, V. Turner 1985, and C. Von Furer-Haimendorf 1985.

Fig. 22. General categories of ritual practitioners

Similarly, the various categories of Islamic and ATR practitioners accept or deal only with limited kinds of beings and forces. For example, within the category of magician, the *jibarkat* practices black magic while the *luggkat* is the practitioner of choice for the person with a fish bone lodged in his throat. They each deal with a different part of the cosmic spectrum; that is, they have different metaphysical focuses.

Metatheme 2: Peace Achieved by Means of Power

Cosmic Domain	Beings and Forces		
The supernatural, extraterrestrial world: the invisible world of spirits UPPER ZONE	God	*allah*	2.107; 20.8
	archangels	*malaika*	2.97; 81.19
	angels	*malaika*	3.39; 8.9
	Satan	*iblis/shaytan*	3.155; 4.117
	devils	*shayatin*	
The transempirical in this world: the supernatural world acting in the visible world MIDDLE ZONE	auguries, omens	*taair*	7.131; 27.47
	blessings	*baraka, yubarik*	7.95; 25.1,10
	curses	*lamat*	11.60; 24.23
	demon possession	*majnun, jinatu*	23.70; 51.52
	destiny, fate	*ajal*	7.34; 16.61
	divination, soothsaying	*kahin*	52.29; 69.42
	evil spirits, devils, demons	*shaytan*	15.17; 37.7
	jinn		55.15; 72.1
	magic, sorcery, witchcraft	*sihr*	21.3; 51.52
	miracles, signs	*ayat*	3.49; 10.1
	misfortune	*musibah*	4.62
	Qur'an		20.2; 29.47
	visions	*ruya*	17.60; 37.105
The natural world: the visible, material world LOWER ZONE	humans with special access to the middle or upper zones:		
	Muhammad		7.158; 33.40
	saints	*awliya,* sg. *wali*	10.62
	marabouts (for Sufi Islam)		
	Muslims		2.128; 7.126
	People of the Book	*ahlul kitab*	2.101; 3.199
	pagans	*ishrak*	2.105; 9.5
	polytheists	*mushrikun*	22.17; 98.6

Note: All italicized terms are Arabic; Qur'anic references are to Ali 1983.

Fig. 23. The beings and forces in the cosmography of Islam

In figures 23 and 24 the beings and forces that are accepted as components of the universe are listed. The lists include most of the beings and forces thought to exist in the cosmographies of Islam and of ATR, respectively. They are categorized by their principal locus of existence.

Cosmic Domain		Beings and Forces
The supernatural, extraterrestrial world: the invisible world of spirits **UPPER ZONE**	the Supreme Being gods divinities	*yàlla*
The transempirical in this world: the invisible world acting in the visible world **MIDDLE ZONE**	ancestors	*maam*
	auguries, omens	*gaaf*
	blessings	*tuyaaba, barke, texe*
	conjurings	*luxus*
	curses	*móolu, ñaan-yàlla, xala, xër*
	demons	*seytaane, njuuma*
	destinies	*àtte, àtte yàlla, reefo, ndogal*
	divine chastisements	*mbugël*
	divinations	*gisaane, listikar*
	evil tongue, eye, touch	*cat, bët, laal*
	fixations, charms	*wooj, xürtal, noob*
	formulas	*léemu*
	hallucinations of spirits	*jommi*
	hypnotic powers	*nibiniiki, noobi*
	invocations of spirits	*léemu*
	invulnerability	*tul*
	jinn, believing and unbelieving	*jinne jii tuubna*, and *jinne jii tuubul*
	luck, fortune	*jig, wërsëg*
	magic, black	*jibar; xam xam bu ñuul*
	magic, ceremonial or white	*xam-xamu baatin*
	magic, personal	*xarbaax*
	malediction	*toskare*
	medicine	*sunguf*
	miracles	*kawteef, kéeman*
	misfortune	*kort, umute*
	oracles	e.g., *guy jàng*
	possession, spirit	*njuuma, ndëpp*
	prosperity genie	*kuus*
	protection	*ñag, yiir*
	rainmaking	*baaw-naan*
	sacred forest	*lël*

(continued)

Cosmic Domain		Beings and Forces
	sorcery	*liggéey, xalwa*
	spirits, protector, family	*rab, rawane*
	spirits, territorial	e.g., *kumba lamba*[39]
	talismans, amulets	*gàllaaj, mbind, muslaay, ndongo-tere*
	totems	*mbañ, tuur*
	transfer	*topp*
	witchcraft	*ndëmm*
The natural world: the visible, material world LOWER ZONE	earth residents with special access to the middle and/or upper zones:	
	pals of the devil	*xaritu jinne*
	shamans	e.g., *sëriñ tariax* and *ndëppkat*
	mediums	e.g., *ñàng* and *ndëppkat*
	diviners	e.g., *gisaanekat; seetkat*
	humans with incarnated souls	*noonoh*, (Sf.)
	human beings	*nit*
	animals	*mala*
	plants	*garab*
	earth/minerals	*suuf*
	the visible world	*saxiir*

Fig. 24. The beings and forces in the cosmography of African Traditional Religion and Popular Islam

First, there is the domain of supernatural and extraterrestrial beings. This domain is the invisible world of spirits. It is called the UPPER ZONE.

The next level is that of the transempirical in this world, that is, of the beings and forces of the invisible world which act in the visible world. It is called the MIDDLE ZONE.

---

[39]*kumba lamba* is the chief, or protector, spirit of the Senegalese city Rufisque. Most, or perhaps all, Senegalese cities, towns, and villages have such spirits who are known by name and to whom offerings are made. The spirits appear to certain people at certain times, assuming totemic form. For example, *kumba lamba* always appears in the form of a black cat.

At the third and lowest level is the natural world, that is, the visible, material world known to the senses—the LOWER ZONE. Each of the eight categories of ritual practitioners found in the society, given in figure 22, has a distinct interest, knowledge, and set of practices regarding the beings and forces in the cosmographies it accepts as part of its religious system and which are listed in figures 23 and 24. None of the ritual specialists deals with the full range of beings and forces recognized by the specific culture.

The terms upper, middle and lower, as referring to these cosmic levels, are taken from anthropologist-missiologist Paul Hiebert. He (1982:39) develops what he calls "an analytical framework for the analysis of religious systems." In discussing the middle level, which is his main concern, Hiebert (1982:44) states that for most religions it is the level at which the "questions of the uncertainty of the future, the crises of the present life and the unknowns of the past" are dealt with. His claim for this level certainly holds true for the Senegambia.

Note how well-populated the middle level is in ATR (figure 24). The supernatural powers in this zone are accepted as normal components of the universe. They are of critical, daily importance to most people. Consequently, the practitioners who have, or claim to have, knowledge of and at least some control over these matters receive primary attention by members of society.

Note also that Islam recognizes the existence of a wide variety of supernatural powers in the middle zone, but the recognition does not translate into practice. The importance of the middle level is acknowledged, but orthodox Islam sanctions practices and practitioners only with a metaphysical focus in the upper zone. Hence, we can state that the practitioners of ATR, with an almost total focus on the middle zone, play essential roles in the Senegambian religious system: dealing with the beings and forces recognized by Islam as relevant, but only slightly and ambiguously, and without instructions as to how to relate to them. (By comparison, the Qur'an is very detailed in instructions about prayer and other forms of cultus relating to the upper zone, which are principally directed to Allah.)

Islam, in the Qur'an, does include a number of strictures against the good Muslim straying from Allah's right guidance in following illicit practices. Teachings against such practices include the following taken from Ali 1983:

> They followed what the evil ones gave out (falsely) against the power of Solomon: the blasphemers were, not Solomon, but the

Metatheme 2: Peace Achieved by Means of Power

> evil ones, teaching men magic, and such things as came down at Babylon. [2.102]
>
> O ye who believe! Intoxicants and gambling, (dedication of) stones, and (divination by) arrows, are an abomination—of Satan's handiwork: eschew such (abomination), that ye may prosper. [5.90]
>
> It was not God who instituted (superstitions like those of) a slit-ear she-camel let loose for free pasture.... It is blasphemers who invent a lie agaist God; but most of them lack wisdom. [5.103]
>
> O ye who believe! Guard your own souls: If ye follow (right) guidance, no hurt can come to you from those who stray. [5.105]
>
> When they had had their throw, Moses said: "What ye have brought is sorcery: God will surely make it of no effect: for God prospereth not the work of those who make mischief." [10.81]
>
> For to God belong the Forces of the heavens and the earth; and God is exalted in Power, full of Wisdom. [48.7]

In spite of these condemnations and reminders that Allah is most powerful, there is no provision for confronting or addressing the extra-human, threatening powers retained by the residents of the middle zone. Their powers may be less than those of Allah, but they are considerable, nonetheless, with the potential of carrying out malevolent actions toward mankind. In the Senegambia, dealing with such powers is of primary importance to the daily pursuit of life, success, happiness, and above all, to the realization of peace.

We see that the formula EPC does indeed have high explanatory power for the religious phenomena of both Islam and ATR, and for the overlapping zone between them. This discussion has served to demonstrate that the Wolof proverb quoted in chapter two indeed fits the socioreligious realities of the Senegambia: *liggéey yall àddina ba mu meel ni doto dee, liggéey yall àllaaxira ba mu meel ni suba ngay dee* 'work for the world as if you were not going to die; work for the future life as if you were to die tomorrow'. The meaning is elliptical, as it is in most Wolof philosophical discourse, but it is an incitement to two kinds of work *(liggéey):* (1) work for this life (including working to interact positively with the supernatural and the esoteric that determine the outcome of life), and (2) work for the future life (viz., paradise). The first relates to the concerns that ATR deals with; the second relates to the eschatological concerns of Islam. In simplified form, it means that ATR provides the EPC for the concerns of this life while Islam provides for those of the future life.

If Muslims employed only the orthodox practitioners of Islamic ritual, the result would be a major phenomenological vacuum. What we have anthropologically defined as priests and prophets, those specialists who address the upper zone, would be all there was. Except for the limited permitted use of magic, such as in seeking mystical guidance in making decisions (*istikhara,* A.; *listikar,* Wolof) (Gibb and Kramers 1965:186–187), the omission would entirely leave out shamans, magicians, mediums, and diviners. Fundamental premises of the belief system would be denied fulfillment; for example, that the spirit world is real and powerful and impinges upon mankind, and that man is destined to initiate actions to reestablish cosmic balance. The pursuit of transcendent peace would be disallowed in many of its forms, or at least the mechanisms for its pursuit would be absent. It would not seem possible to suppress these practices without major changes occurring at the world view level of culture.

Seen in these terms it becomes clear that, from a world view position, it is essential to have available in the society the practitioners of ATR alongside those of orthodox Islam. Throughout most of its history such a coexistence with folk religion has been characteristic of Islam. The historical perspective on all forms of magic (*sihr,* A.) is provided by Gibb and Kramers (1965:545):

> Islam is a system of frank supernaturalism; for it there is our material world of the senses and behind that a world of spirits, into relation with which we can enter by means of either magic or religion. From the Islamic point of view, the question is whether the intercourse with the world of spirits may affect man's relation to Allah and imperil his eternal salvation.

Gibb and Kramers (1965:547) conclude their discussion of the ambivalent nature of the historical place of magic in Islam in these words:

> Thus in Kur'an and *hadith,* in orthodox theology, in mystical theology of all phases stretching to pantheistic theosophy, in philosophy and natural science of all kinds from almost experimental psychology to the speculations of the pseudo-Ibn Sina, in primitive animistic devotion, the existence of magic as a reality, though it may be a dangerous one, has been perpetuated.

It is clear that this general statement perfectly fits the realities of Islam in the Sengambia. Our discussion has provided two explanatory rationales to help the reader understand why this should be so: (1) the people's beliefs in the beings and forces of the middle zone and their corresponding assumption that man's well-being depends upon placating them, and (2) the complementary distribution of the metaphysical focuses of the two systems, that is, that Islam addresses the powers of the upper zone and ATR those of the middle zone.

Religious Symbiosis

Besides the complementary distribution of the practitioners of Islam and ATR, and of their metaphysical focuses, there is in the region an ethnic complementary distribution, to which I apply the term RELIGIOUS SYMBIOSIS.

The seven types of ritual practitioners identified for Senegambian society are not distributed geographically in direct proportion to local population densities (autopractitioners are not included as they are outside the scope of this discussion because they do not provide ritual services to others). Rather, they are distributed according to ethnic group, which is in part a reflection of the degree of Islamization of that ethnic group.

In ideal terms, all ritual practitioners among the Wolof and other highly Islamized ethnic groups should be Islamic, that is, they all should be either priests or prophets (noting that the distribution of the latter is extremely limited in Islam). An exception are the Lebou, who are not ethnically Wolof but have adopted the language. They are Muslims who follow a widely recognized syncretistic form of Islam and therefore, in practice, hardly discriminate between Islam and ATR. Healers can be found among the Wolof, but they basically use techniques that are areligious, and therefore neither Islamic nor non-Islamic. Diviners are found among Wolof and non-Wolof, as Islam allows for the practice of orthodox forms of divination.

Shamans, mediums, and magicians are found predominantly in non-Wolof, non-Muslim ethnic groups (see figure 22 for an outline of these categories of practitioners). These are the heavy duty practitioners, those who deal with the more difficult esoteric practices which require greater powers and training on the part of the practitioner and who confront the more serious and dangerous matters of human-transhuman relationships. Such practitioners are found especially among the Serer, Mancagne, and

Manjak ethnic groups. The practitioners live in their traditional ethnic homelands, or, increasingly, they may live near or among the Wolof, in which case their services are readily available when needed. There are many exceptions to this general ethnic distribution of practitioners. A Wolof, for example, could be a medium. The man might have grown up in a Serer compound, or might be married to a Diola. But in general I have observed there seems to be some excuse in people's minds that explains such an anomaly to the ideal.

Even a rough statistical figure for the ethnic distribution of the various classes of ritualists is very difficult to obtain. J. Trincaz (1981:127), citing a study by A. Zempléni, gives a ratio of one Muslim ritual practitioner (shaman, medium, magician, diviner) for every 150 Muslims in Senegal. With an estimated population in 1988 of 7,100,000 that is ninety-two percent Muslim, there would be 4,355 Muslim ritual practitioners for the country, beside those that are not Muslim. So in this study involving only a tiny sample, any statement referring to the distribution and types of ritualists must be very tentative.

Since the beginning of colonialism, virtually all Wolof have consciously identified themselves as Muslims (Clarke 1982: 202ff). As Wolof have learned to be more and more orthodox, they have tended to discard many traditional African religious practices. This is on the ideal level, but it is widely believed to be actual fact. At the beginning of my research I repeatedly sought to verify what I was being told, that traditional practices had disappeared from Wolof society. I received the uniform response, "They are no longer found among the Wolof." But after I had learned some Wolof terms and knew details of some of the rituals used by non-Wolof, and then asked more precise questions, people confirmed that these non- or pre-Islamic practices were indeed still practiced by at least some Wolof, but virtually in secret. To what extent Wolof continue traditional practices, even in Islamized form, and especially in rural villages, is extremely difficult to judge. At a more conscious level, people really believe these things have disappeared because the Wolof are good Muslims and by definition good Muslims are not involved with non-Muslim ritualists. This is also probably believed because the practitioners from other ethnic groups seem to be much more common and renowned for their spiritual powers and welcoming of outside business.

The best way to describe the situation is that it is a kind of symbiosis. I would call it RELIGIOUS SYMBIOSIS. John Honigmann (1959:270) describes symbiosis as a relationship in which

Metatheme 2: Peace Achieved by Means of Power

> two or more communities [develop] into a state of complex interdependence... Each culture becomes specialized in a different direction but finds itself dependent on the roles or services provided in the other.

Beals and Hoijer (1965:462) apply the phrase "symbiotic trade relations" to a situation where

> two more or less independent societies establish a special trading relationship whereby a larger and economically more advanced society is linked by trade to a society that has no internal division of labor and is unable, without the aid of its trading partner, to produce an exchangeable surplus.

In the Senegambia the trading relationship is built upon commerce in ritual practices. On the one hand, banning un-Islamic kinds of ritual practitioners from Wolof society can assure Wolof and others that they are indeed true Muslims. On the other hand, the society can benefit from the services rendered and the power that coheres to these other practitioners, by allowing them to exist in less orthodox and non-Muslim societies. So there is an interdependence, a symbiosis, or a symbiotic religious relationship.

The Wolof are the largest and most economically advanced society of the area. They also represent the great tradition (Redfield 1969) of Islam. This provides Wolof religious practitioners with an aura of Islamic respectability that is reinforced by separation from pagan practices of the little traditions of the non-Muslim peoples.

Each side provides valuable, mutual services to the other. The Wolof provide clientele for the Muslim ritualists. This clientele provides cash, the most obvious benefit. But, implicitly, the peoples of the smaller, non-Islamized groups gain a recognition of their spiritual power and of their importance. And since the long-term physical, cultural, and religious survival of the smaller groups is threatened, to be needed for ritual purposes is insurance against disappearance. Also, in face of the overwhelmingly numerous and culturally aggressive Wolof, the smaller groups have an identity crisis. The demand for their traditional ritual services is positive reinforcement of their identity.

The two major benefits that accrue to the Wolof are their ability to maintain their prestige as good Muslims with the many personal and collective benefits that this prestige brings. Secondly, they preserve their access to the spiritual and ritual power they still believe in, especially when they are faced with personal or family crises.

So a symbiotic religious relationship exists between the Wolof and the smaller ethnic groups. Many of these practitioners are actually living in cities, towns, and villages away from their autochthonous areas, and so are of easy access to their Wolof clientele. They are a functional part of Wolof society even when they reside spatially separated from the Wolof. Many practitioners of wide repute still live within the confines of their ethnic groups. It is very common for people of Dakar, for example, to travel to various kinds of specialists in the interior of the country, for treatment of illness or for any other need concerning which one or another specialist is known to have particular powers.

A very humorous and socially relevant case is described in the play *Xala*, written by the well-known Senegalese playwright Sembéne Ousmane (1973). It has been made into an internationally known film. *xala* means 'curse of impotency' in Wolof. The storyline is about a wealthy Senegalese who takes a fourth wife but is impotent with the beautiful young bride. Among other adventures, he travels around the interior in his Mercedes Benz attempting to find a cure with Serer ritual practitioners. In Senegal, the plot is accepted as a typical problem with a typical search for a cure, even if it is social commentary and comedy at the same time. It also provides evidence for what is here called religious symbiosis.

5
Pilgrimage to Touba, the Sacred City of Senegal

World View in Real Life

If the world view propositions that have been proposed in this essay represent the fundamental and pervasive facts of the culture, they should be identifiable in all major real life events. This is not to say they should be obvious to the man on the street but, if the basic assumptions of the deep-level belief system do not project up into the realities of life from which they were supposedly derived, they are invalidly formulated propositions. The man on the street will act on the assumptions even though he cannot verbalize them.

The major event of the year in the Senegambian region is the annual pilgrimage to the city of Touba in central Senegal. By the major event is meant that, more than any other normal event, it involves the most people, receives the most media coverage, is best known inside and outside the area, affects nonparticipants more, involves very large sums of money, plus other superlatives that could be adduced.

All eight metathemes can be identified in substantial ways in the Magal, as the pilgrimage is known in the media.[40] This leads to a hypothesis that is proposed and will be tested with the Magal: all of the deep-level assumptions of a culture will underlie its most celebrated events. Terms that may be substituted for "underlie" in this statement are "project up

---

[40]In the official Wolof orthography it is written *Màggal*.

into" or "support." This hypothesis has a corollary: the more deep-level assumptions that project up into an event, the more meaningful that event will be to the people of the culture. Finding evidence for the accurate formulation of the metathemes will serve partly to validate the propositions but especially will show more clearly how world view assumptions operate in the culture.

This approach may appear to be little more than circular reasoning: world view is deduced from culture, then world view assumptions are validated by identifying them in the culture. What is being considered here is not so simple. World view propositions are deduced from the full breadth of the culture—from cultural ideas about cosmology, social organization, interpersonal relations, the code of morality, the phenomena of nature, illness, emotions—from every domain possible. In consideration of as much of this cultural breadth as possible, propositions are formulated that state the fewest possible underlying principles that the culture bearers use to create order from the limitless profusion of impressions and experiences that constitute the unordered raw material of daily life. These principles are intuitively used to give meaning to the people's cultural universe. In mathematical terms, they are those few factors of the culture upon which all cultural products are built. But, as in mathematics, not all the discovered factors in a mathematical system are present in any particular product, so in world view not all the assumptions of a culture are necessarily operative in any particular behavior.[41]

What the hypothesis states is that, although the world view propositions were derived from the full breadth of cultural domains in each of which a limited set of world view themes may have been operative, in the really significant events of the culture all (or most) of the propositions will project (one cannot say the propositions will be present) up to the event. Such a concentration of themes intensifies the event and makes it a microcosm of the cultural macrocosm. This intensification is satisfying to the culture bearers and raises the event from the perfunctory to the celebratory, and from marginality to centrality in the culture.

---

[41]As a clarification consider this analogy: two and three are factors of the product six. Two and four are factors of the product eight. So, even in these two examples not all the factors are present in all the products. In world view terms, the factors are the world view propositions or cultural building blocks. The products are cultural domains. The Magal is a major cultural event we are examining to see if most or all the factors/propositions are present at a deep level of the culture.

Pilgrimage in Sufi Islam

The following sections first review the place pilgrimages hold in Sufi Islam, then provide a brief background to the pre-Islamic institutions for which pilgrimages substituted as functional equivalents. The main section is a description of the Magal, followed by a world view analysis.

Trimingham, in his classic work on the Sufi orders of Islam, distinguishes between pilgrimage and visitation. He (1971:26) limits usage of the former to one of the five orthodox pillars (i.e., the pilgrimage to Mecca), while he calls the rites carried out at tombs of Sufi saints VISITATION. In the Senegambia such visitation is far more an integral part of Islam than is the pilgrimage to Mecca. It also replaces and serves explicitly as a religious substitute for the orthodox pilgrimage. Consequently, in this study the term pilgrimage is used for rites carried out at Touba and elsewhere in the Senegambia, as well as for the rite at Mecca.

Michael Gilsenan (1973:47), in his study of Sufi Islam, identified four major categories of Sufi "visitation festivals" in Egypt: (1) large public occasions, such as commemorating the birth of Muhammad; (2) large public ceremonies originating with the saint of a particular order, but having become a general religious celebration in which any or all Muslims participate; (3) celebrations of a regional character, mostly limited to the adherents of a particular order; and (4) festivals associated mainly with kinship, political, or other ascriptive groupings.

Many of the characteristics of these "Saints' Days," as Gilsenan terms them, apply to the pilgrimages of the Senegambia. The following description fits almost perfectly:

> A good deal... of religious merit, is attached to [this] kind of group endeavor. Here the range of persons attending and their social relations with each other are critical and often of local-level political importance. Such occasions give an opportunity for establishing, renewing, or severing social ties before an audience of significant others. Groups may publicly define their interrelations within the framework of the spectacle of the day of the Saint, part of whose religious constituency they claim to be... They have a very strong element of the medieval fair and people from all over the country... attend... Official estimates of the attendance at the 1964 Tanta *mulid* for example were one and a quarter million people. [Gilsenan 1973:48]

Gilsenan's work provides a valuable basis for comparison with saints' days in the Senegambia. There is much in common between the rites in the two countries, but there are also significant differences. The major difference is that in the Senegambia there is really only one major category of saint's day, with one subcategory. Senegambian pilgrimages are a mixture of Gilsenan's (1) and (2), in that they are large public occasions, and those of the majority Tijani order commemorate the Prophet's birth. They also originate with the saint of a particular order, but no Senegambian pilgrimage has become a general, non-sectarian Muslim gathering. To suggest the idea of a non-sectarian pilgrimage would be, I suspect, a non sequitur, dimly analogous to the idea of paying homage to someone else's grandfather; possible, but not very meaningful. Each pilgrimage is organized and carried out by one particular order for its adherents. Other Muslims are free to attend, but their participation would be extremely limited and marginal.

The one sub-type of pilgrimage is also limited to a particular order. It is comparable to a family gathering but, in some cases a family of many thousands of adherents. Branches of orders organize these regional pilgrimages where those who owe allegiance to the branch's leader or saint gather together at set times of religious commemoration. Such adherents attend the main annual pilgrimages and those of their branch. These secondary gatherings correspond in part to Gilsenan's category four.

These differences in expression of the same Islamic institution in Egypt and the Senegambia reveal important elements of Senegambian world view and reflect an essential quality of the Islam found there. Islam is very personalized. The people want to relate to an authority figure, even if Islam has no official clergy. They want to maintain a community of kin, even if Islam stresses the universality of the faith and of believerhood. And they also want a religious hierarchy even if Islamic doctrine teaches equality and individual responsibility of the faithful before Allah. In stating what the people want does not means that they consciously seek that in Islam. What is meant is that their world view calls for strong elements of social hierarchy and the ideal of living in community, so that Senegambians will respond to those possibilities in Islam that allow for expression in these directions, or else they will adapt Islamic institutions until there is a better fit with their world view, wherever this is allowed.

Trimingham's insights are especially apropos, although in the Senegambia the Islamization of traditional religion did not always follow what he describes as having been the pattern in sub-Saharan Africa.

> With the adoption of Islam kinship loses its religious basis,[42] yet it is not weakened but maintains an autonomy of its own. Black African societies have a guaranteed structure of social stability so long as they remain agricultural and maintain customary institutions, and, if... the social structure is not upset. We have shown how when Islam is adopted by whole communities, family or village, the group remains a unity, distinguished by its own pattern of culture and a social life ruled primarily by custom, often in contradiction to the abstract rules of Islam.
>
> One primary consideration rules people's adoption of the sociological elements of Islam—the maintenance of family or clan solidarity based on custom; anything that might menace or undermine the group is barred. Islamic law has definite individualistic elements and against the introduction of these all the forces of African conservatism are arrayed. [1980:87–88]

Contrary to what Trimingham describes, kinship did not everywhere lose its religious basis; in the Senegambia it was subsumed under the tariqas (religious orders) of Sufi Islam. The same comment applies to his footnote. The ancestor cult was greatly modified under the tariqas, but was maintained in spirit in the saint, and in the saint's communication with Muhammad, with the angels, and with *jinn*. The saint substituted for the clan progenitor. A nickname given to Amadou Bamba is *banba*, meaning 'that clay there'. This refers to the belief held by some Mourides that at the moment of the creation of Adam, Bamba was at God's side and was told, "Hand me that clay there," which was then used in creating the first human. Bamba is indeed an ancestral figure.

Even the concept of baraka, which is transmitted through the saints' descendants and therefore is available to the saints' spiritual heirs, relates to traditional concepts of the reincarnated souls of the dead and the continued presence of the ancestors in human society.

And finally, social stability is not tied to agricultural societies. Senegambian Sufi orders have adapted to and are prospering in urban environments.

Elsewhere, Trimingham describes the place of *ziara* (A.) or *siyaare* (Wolof) as visitation or pilgrimage across the Islamic world. These comments apply very well to the Senegambia and show that although the meaning of

---

[42]Trimingham's footnote is as follows: "We have mentioned previously... the rapid decline and then elimination of the ancestor cult" (1980:156).

pilgrimage has been adapted to a particular world view, the form is part of the universe of Islam. Visitation is carried out:

> for the purpose of *muraqaba* (spiritual communion) with the saint, finding in the material symbol an aid to meditation. But the popular belief is that the saint's soul lingers about his tomb and places *(maqams)* specially associated with him whilst he was on earth or at which he had manifested himself. At such places his intercession can be sought. [Trimingham 1971:26]

> The *qubba* (domed tomb) of the founder is the focal point of the organization, a centre of veneration to which visitations *(ziyarat)* are made. Offerings in money and kind are made regularly and are associated with requests for the intercession of the *wali* or a thanksgiving for benefits received. The sanctuary and its territory are sacred *(haram* or *hurm)* where refugees from vengeance or justice can seek sanctuary. [1971:179]

A relationship with a saint can be established or renewed, and his baraka be received during pilgrimage:

> The simplest form is to stand in front of the tomb and recite the Fatiha, which [the baraka] is caught by the symbolic act of raising the hands, palms upwards, during the recitation and then transferred by passing them down upon the face. There are many procedures for intercession to God through the saint. [1971:180]

The description of the Magal will show that all these standard elements of pilgrimage are present at Touba. Often one reads that Islam in Africa is substandard and different in a way found in few other parts of the world. Quinn's (1972:57) comment would be typical, if mild. "Islam came to the Senegambia in what orthodox scholars consider a contaminated form." The differences between Islam in Africa and the Islamic heartland are emphasized. The present study shows that, in form, the Magal conforms to orthodox Sufism even if the content is very much a religious and cultural synthesis, as explained so well by Benjamin Ray (1976:176):

> The history of Islam south of the Sahara is therefore a history of several phases and types of religion. It is a history of developing orthodoxy and of developing synthesis in which Islam both strengthened and blended with local communal and ritual values and permanently widened the African religious and social world.

The result was not a confused syncretism, but a variety of new religious and cultural syntheses which bear the unique character of sub-Saharan Islam.

Pilgrimage in the Senegambia

Traditional religion in the Senegambia has always sacralized time and space. Commemorations at auspicious times and in sacred places have served to refresh and restore the spirit, to facilitate communion with and renew bonds with the supernatural, and to renew the bonds of kinship and community. They also served to reinforce the common faith, in joy and fraternity with others. A major part of religion was to maintain equilibrium in all the established relationships, man ↔ transempirical beings and forces, man ↔ man, and man ↔ nature. This was religion in the present tense. I. M. Lewis (1980:59) points out how this contrasts with Islam, which has so much of its focus in the future tense. The exuberant nature of traditional religious events also contrasts with the infestivity of those of orthodox Islam.

Traditional society had many celebrations at consecrated places. One of the most important was the complex of rites and beliefs centered around initiation into adulthood of both male and female adolescents.[43] The Wolof institutions and terminology are typical of West Africa, but their pristine forms are now largely known only in history. These involve the sacred forest where young men were instructed in tribal ideology, lore and history *(lël)*, and where circumcision *(njong)* took place. The *kasag* were the special chants and dances learned by the participants. Each initiation class *(njuli,* S.) was under the charge of a *selbe*, but the whole village followed the proceedings with great interest, large quantities of food, much singing and dancing, and much moral support.

Camara Laye (1954:93–107), in *The African Child*, his classical autobiographical description of African life, describes the educational and celebratory nature of the circumcision rites in personal and social terms:

> It was not without misgivings that I approached this transition from childhood to manhood ... I knew perfectly well that I was going to be hurt, but I wanted to be a man and it seemed to me that nothing could be too painful if, by enduring it, I was to come to a

---

[43]It still is in some ethnic groups but largely has disappeared or continues only in much impoverished form in most.

man's estate. My companions felt the same; like myself, they were prepared to pay for it with their blood.

For the great feast of the circumcision is the occasion of a great banquet attended by numerous guests; a banquet so enormous that, despite the number of guests, there is enough for days and days before the end is reached. Obviously this entails great expense. So, whoever is a friend of the family of the boy to be circumcised, or is bound to the family by bonds of obligation, makes it a point of honour to contribute to the banquet; and he will help both those who are in need of help and those who are not. That is why, at each circumcision, there is this sudden abundance of gifts and good things...

The teaching we received in the bush [the sacred forest], far from all prying eyes, had nothing very mysterious about it... These lessons, the same as had been taught to all those who had gone before us, confined themselves to outlining the sort of conduct befitting a man... And we had to tell nothing of what we learned, either to women or to the uninitiated; neither had we to reveal any of the secret rites of circumcision. That is the custom. Women, too, are not allowed to tell anything about the rites of excision.

The importance of social integration in these ritual celebrations is especially discernible in the initiation ceremonies. Among the Serer, the just-circumcised youth is ritually and individually devoured by the *maam* (S.), the supreme tutelary divinity of circumcision rites, who is also the Serer founding ancestor spirit. Thus, the initiate dies at the same time he is born into manhood. The symbolic birth-death serves to anchor the just-born man in the living community and clan and, at the same time, aligns him with the ancestors. His ritual death means he is already an ancestor, reintegrated, or reincarnated, into the living community. He is, and therefore all initiated males are, symbolically ancestral and normal human at the same time (Woronoff 1978:244–245, Kane 1978).[44]

Many other rituals were part of traditional life. The *baaw-naan*, especially among the Lebou, was and still is a large public ceremony organized when the rains do not begin at the normal time of year. Mercier and Balandier describe its present form as a mixture of the pre-Islamic with the

---

[44]The anthropological literature contains many accounts of African initiation and celebration. See for example Gibbs 1965, Hamer 1973, Sangree 1965, Schaffer and Cooper 1980, Vansina 1973, Watkins 1943.

Islamic. All the men gather in the local mosque on a Friday night to pray and recite the Qur'an. The women perform the traditional ritual, with the older women putting on men's clothes and dancing in circles around the praise singers, to the accompaniment of much drumming. Special chants are employed which honor the spirits (Mercier and Balandier 1952:94–95, Marone 1970:157). Thus the men are interceding for the grace of Allah, and the women are imploring the favor of the community protector spirits, in rites that are required to be public, community-wide, and commemorative of the community's allegiance to divinity.

Other community socioreligious gatherings were or are: *bère*, the traditional form of wrestling, in large part to celebrate a successful harvest just past and it is accompanied by such activities as drumming, chants, sacrifices, prayers for victory, praises, and magical potions to give strength; *miis* (Sf.) is the ceremonial hunting of game and plants that auspicates the approaching rainy season and it is a community affair, carried out under the guidance of the head shaman, that reveals the community's spiritual condition (the actual state of cosmos-mundane equilibrium) and the quality of the coming rains; and *xooy* (S.) is the gathering of several villages under the charge of shamans-in-chief, that functions similarly to the *miis*.

The last public calendric celebration to be mentioned is the one that has been most carried over into Senegambian Islam. This is the *gàmmu*. Even the name has been appropriated by Islam in that the Tijani order calls their main annual pilgrimage to Tivaouane in central-western Senegal by the name Gamou (F.), as well as calling their lesser pilgrimages to other centers by the same name.

Traditional *gàmmu* were major annual events organized by Wolof and Serer kingdoms to honor deceased kings. They were closely tied to religious beliefs and veneration of ancestors.

gàmmu are of many different forms. David Boilat (1984:361–63), writing in 1853, describes the Wolof *gammou* of northern Senegal as an eight-day public celebration of drumming, dancing, political, and moral renewal.

I. Marone (1970:156) writes of the Lebou *gàmmu* of the Dakar region as primarily occasions to make vows, especially to Ndek Dawur, the patron spirit of Dakar. Dancing and chanting are held in the precincts of a Lebou mosque. A Lebou ethnic official presides. He is a Muslim and also a faithful devotee of the spirits of the ancestors. Although the ritual appears relaxed and merely folkloric, the purpose is very seriously an appeal for protection by esoteric forces.

One traditional *gàmmu* that is still celebrated is held each year at Kahone, near the Senegalese city of Kaolack. It is held just before the expected onset of the rains. Its purpose is to chant the honors of all the deceased kings of the old Serer monarchy. Ancient battles are reenacted, with blood descendants of the kings chanting the histories of the battles. Special drums (*junjung*, S.) are used that are brought out only once a year for the *gàmmu*. Dancers and chorus visit certain baobab trees and other sacred places. Everyone partakes of a meal together. Finally, all participants assemble around the ancient royal palace to sing the praises of the kings. Ancient artifacts, especially rifles, are brought out for designated individuals to inspect. Chanting and dancing continue all night. In the morning, before dispersing, the nearby village of an illustrious queen mother is visited (Dione 1990).

Dione's account corresponds with the sketches of ancient *gàmmu* glimpsed in the oral history of Waalo, the northern Wolof kingdom. The griot historian, Amadou Wade, recounted the activities of the *gàmmu*: various games, wrestling, drumming, games of ball, and drinking brandy. The celebrations lasted a whole week. The Waalo *gàmmu* were very important to the king, as the lords of the realm were required to be present, on pain of death or at least destitution, and to pay their annual tribute. One-third went to the king, one-third to the princely assembly, and one-third to finance the *gàmmu* (Wade 1964:462–482).

With these rites there is also a strong concept of group force. This means that the group has a role in the cosmic order that no other entity can fill. Marcel Cardaire (1954:14) very clearly summarizes this aspect of African, and Senegambian, world view:

> The traditional religions of Black Africa are characterized by the participation of all creatures in the equilibrium of the Creation... The individual is a 'force' and the sum of individual forces makes up the group force. The totality of these collective 'forces' itself constitutes the 'Force' that moves the world. Each family received, at Creation, its place in the world order, and each family and each group has its correspondent in the animal, vegetable and even mineral, realm. These are related to human groups by totemism; thus, all are tied to the maintenance of equilibrium. Every society, from smallest to largest, has its special place in the order of the universe. Together all are bound together in multiple interobligations and every infraction calls into question the equilibrium of the Creation.

Cardaire touches on the importance of cosmic equilibrium, on the ideal of interdependency and integration at all levels of the cosmos, on the essentiality of all sizes and compositions of human groups, and on the ties between human, animal, vegetable, and mineral kingdoms. In a very few lines he has outlined a considerable part of Senegambian world view. He applies his characterization to Black Africa, but I have studiously avoided applying Senegambian facts and inferences beyond the area. If my findings apply to the Senegambia, at least some obviously apply beyond its borders. As I present little supporting data, I cannot make such applications.

Amadou Bamba, the Saint

The dominant personality of the Senegambian region for the entire post-conquest period, 1886 to the present, is Amadou Bamba. Many details of his life are seen to be important to the analysis of world view themes, even though at surface level they seem to be inconsequential. His life as a whole is presented here, even though some facts have been referred to under prior discussions.

Amadou Bamba's great-grandfather and great-grandmother came from the Futa region of the central Senegal River valley. They were of a Tukulor line celebrated for its Islamic teachers, judges, and counsellors. The Poular-speaking Tukulor had adopted Islam in the 11th century (A.-B. Diop 1965:13ff). Bamba's father became the chief Muslim judge (*xaali*, from *kadi*, A.) of the court of Lat Dior, the last Wolof king (d. 1886) of Kajoor, which was the last Wolof kingdom to resist the French. He married a niece of Lat Dior and after the latter's decease married one of the king's ex-wives. He also married into several other leading Wolof maraboutic families.

Bamba's father was also closely associated with Maba Diakhou, the mid-19th-century Muslim cleric, leader of successful military jihads and rebellions against the French in central Senegal and the Gambia, where he had conquered the kingdom of Badibu. Maba was a disciple of the legendary El-Hajj Oumar Tall, a dominant figure in West African military jihads and the principal founder of the Tijani order in West Afica.

When Bamba's father died, Lat Dior offered the chief judgship to Bamba, then only thirty years old. Bamba rejected it as being too worldly, but he remained a principal advisor to the king.

Bamba's religious training began under the tutelage of his father, who maintained one of the most prestigious schools of Muslim learning in the area. The training followed the Qadri order with which his father was affiliated. After his father died in 1880, Bamba moved to St. Louis, Senegal, and was formally initiated into the Qadri. He then went to study in Mauretania under Cheikh Sidia, the most renowned teacher-marabout of the time in West Africa, who was also Qadri. At the end of several years of study, Bamba was made caliph for the Wolof people. He then returned to central Senegal where he established a new rural settlement. Numbers of his relatives and many of his father's former disciples joined him in this Muslim school-agricultural community.

This was not long before the final defeat by the French of King Lat Dior. The day before the last battle in 1886, Lat Dior went to see Bamba to ask for his blessing on the military action Dior expected to carry out the next day against a French contingent.

> They had a long meeting. Lat Dior said he had come to say good-bye because "I want to put an end to the white men today, whatever the cost." Amadou Bamba promised to pray for him so that peace would return. Lat Dior persisted, asking only for God's eternal blessing. The marabout then gave him a [white] percale robe, spat some verses of the Qur'an into his hands and let him leave. [E.-H. Samb 1981:58]

Wolof society, by far the dominant one in the Senegambia, collapsed politically, socially, and economically upon the defeat and death of Lat Dior. The French gained total control of the country. In the process they uprooted and even set fire to villages deemed rebellious, killed and maimed Senegalese (Clarke 1982:204), dismantled Wolof and other kingdoms, chose new chiefs on the basis of their submissiveness, forced surrender of local armies and their redeployment as agricultural workers on lands where cash crops were of primary interest to the French, and introduced a foreign language, foreign ideas, and a radically different educational system. Even the moral order was in crisis as traditional values were called into question. The basic institutions and values were being replaced by others which were very foreign.

The people were shocked, humiliated, and subjugated. In the decades before the collapse of the Wolof kingdoms, the common people had felt themselves betrayed and oppressed by their kings, the royal families, and the *céddo*, the powerful warrior-slaves of royalty. The latter had become very powerful, ruthless, and self-serving. Islam and ATR had struggled for centuries to gain, regain, or maintain the ascendancy. Kings and marabouts were often directly involved in power struggles. The people had long been

Muslim in at least a superficial sense, but most of royalty had remained ambiguous about Islam (Colvin 1974). As bad as traditional political rule had become, the colonial conquest was much worse.

For one thing, Kajoor, the central coastal Wolof kingdom, had sacrificed much over the centuries, first to gain and then to maintain its independence from other Wolof kingdoms. Much regional and individual identity was tied to being independent. Now, losing independence to an alien power that conquered and governed by competely different rules, Wolof society experienced a sense of defeat, shame, and dishonor. It perceived itself to be close to moral annihilation.

> The sense of honor, *jom*, among [the Wolof] constitutes the highest and most fundamental quality, and upon which all other moral qualities are grafted. This jom dictates to the Wolof in all circumstances the refusal to accept shame... [A. Sylla 1978:177]

The defeat by the French was far more crushing than the defeats suffered in interethnic and interkingdom wars. In the wars between Senegambians there were, of course, many personal and family tragedies, losses, and enslavements. But in spite of these evils, people could keep their identity, society could reestablish itself, with everyone (even those freshly enslaved during raiding forays) being given a legal status, and all members and levels of society being consciously integrated into a complex web of social hierarchies, each with rights and duties toward all the others, and mutually receiving respect.

The French conquest was different. It sought total domination, control, and maximization of benefit to itself. Society was not integrated, but divided. Senegambians were trained as soldiers and as administrators to act as agents of domination, setting brother against brother.

The French had totally alien ideas about education, about the use of time (no traditional days or nights of celebration, ritual or dancing, as work output would be diminished), enforced labor (to take people when and where the colonizer pleased), and so on. In sum, much of what the Senegambians held most dear was being destroyed. The shame was felt profoundly. It would even have been less humiliating if the French had offered to share their obviously superior knowledge and power, even though it would have come with the strange and uncomfortable way of life of the French. But the French did not offer to share their power and knowledge, so there was little hope for the people, just abject domination in a totally unequal relationship.

Had a partnership been offered, it is very conceivable, although of course conjectural, that Senegambian society would have willingly adopted much of the foreign culture, as it had overwhelming power, material goods, a place in the world, and other much admired and much desired elements. The Wolof have been described by many observers as a very adaptable people who have shown themselves ready to adapt when they are convinced it is to their advantage (Gamble 1957:79, Gorer 1935:41). But this was not an option, except for a small educated elite who were allowed to gain partial access to this foreign world by largely cutting itself off from its own people, taking the role of colonial administrator, that is, foreign agent, and thus becoming despised in the process.

This discussion has gone into some historical detail, not to recount the history, but to provide a minimum background for understanding Senegambian world view. These historical facts are burned into the collective and individual memories of the people. Many of their basic assumptions about themselves, others, and the world were molded by the colonial experience.[45]

People turned to Bamba. He rejected armed resistance (even the military jihads that had been advocated and practiced by most of his co-religionists) to the superior power. He early realized he had an even more potent weapon: cultural resistance that would be immune to armed aggression and would serve to maintain core values and preserve Senegambian identity. Given the history of the widespread jihad movement of West African Islam for the previous several centuries, Bamba's ideas were revolutionary. As Cruise O'Brien (1971:290) states, "He was the first *marabout* not to carry a gun, only the Koran." The *nasraani* (meaning 'Nazarene' or 'Christian') religion and culture were contadictory to all Senegambian sacred traditions, trampling what was most dear. For example, it forbade singing, dancing, and drumming all night in the observance of important traditional rites, as then people would be less able to carry on productive work the next day. The invaders must be rejected, even if armed resistance was ruled out. Islam was the way to preserve self-identity; nothing stronger was available. He became the de facto leader of traditional Wolof society. Up to this point in history, Wolof society had been but partially Islamized. It now turned totally to Islam.

---

[45]Many books and papers have been written on the history of the region. The résumé above has been synthesized from C. Coulon 1981, A.-B. Diop 1965, M. Diop 1981, E. LeRoy 1982, M. Magassouba 1985, V. Monteil 1966a, 1966b, and 1980, A. Samb 1969, C. Sy 1969, J. Trimingham 1971, among others, as well as from personal discussions with Senegambians.

In the process of supporting the people and society, Bamba founded a new Muslim Sufi order of the dispossessed, with remnants of the aristocracy and other, lower, classes. People flocked to him by the thousands. They were mostly Wolof, but many Serer also joined the Mourides, as the order was named.

The French colonial authorities became alarmed at the masses gathering around Bamba. They exiled him to Gabon from 1895 to 1902. This only served to increase his following. Fantastic legends about Bamba developed during this period, increasing his prestige and renown more and more. One of the most popular legends, still told and believed by many today, concerned the voyage to Gabon. The captain of the ship carrying Bamba is said to have refused him permission to perform the ritual prayers. Bamba rejected man's authority in such a matter and jumped overboard, laid his mat upon the ocean and said his prayers in peace, while the French crew watched in astonishment (Cruise O'Brien 1971:43).

Upon his return, he settled in a village deep in the interior of central Senegal, where his following rapidly swelled in numbers and in devotion. The French again became alarmed and exiled him to Mauritania from 1902 to 1907. He was then allowed to return but was kept under administrative surveillance. French policy then changed from opposing Bamba and the Mourides, to a successful cooperation with the order in expanding the production of the peanut cash crop and in other endeavors. Bamba died in 1927. His genius was to merge and reinterpret traditional political and religious systems, and to mount a successful resistance to the French, not on the basis of military or political power but on the basis of moral, cultural, and religious renewal.

The power of traditional Senegambian rulers had been established on four pillars: proper hereditary ascendency, personal moral superiority, political power, and religious power. All were essential to supreme leadership. The religious role, historically typical in West Africa, has been called fetish-king, priest-king, and sacred king (Ray 1976:119ff). Such priest-kings were those rulers whose authority rested on two bases. They were expected and required by their peoples to possess personal qualities of leadership but also a reputation for, if not demonstrations of, spiritual or esoteric powers; both were considered essential to paramount leadership. D. Gilliland (1986:133–34) defines this role of priest-king:

> He was the embodiment of both judicial and religious elements of community life. He was a type of primitive leader whose right to rule derived directly from his contact with the source of religious

power. It was of highest political importance that the ruler was a master of the spiritual forces available to him. He knew he could institute change only if political factors were in a state of flux and if the religious institutions were also in a period of readjustment. The sensitive role of the religious factors has always been of fundamental importance to politics.

The traditional relationship and alliance, people ↔ priest-king, now became people ↔ marabout. Bamba's new kingdom had ideological, social, and political bases. His fundamental principal was social solidarity. He took in all castes and made them one society, the Mouride order. He liberated and ennobled the lower strata of society. He accepted the discredited warrior-slaves *(céddo)* and organized them into the Mouride suborder, called Bay Fall. These became the servants but also the avant-garde and defenders of the order against detractors and enemies. He taught Muslim egalitarianism to all. He taught the rudiments of the Islamic faith, including the Qur'an. He gave them all work and security in establishing a vast network of new farms on the eastern frontier. He created a revolution. The Mourides were like a phoenix rising from the ashes of political, religious, and cultural collapse. Bamba became the symbol of resistance to colonialism and its spiritual refuge. Mouridism became the reinterpreter, continuator, and depository of traditional values.

René Moreau, long a student of Islam in West Africa, believes the early successes of Mouridism were closely related to Bamba's teachings that contained psychological messages offering much-needed dignity. This is expressed, for example, in the following quotations from the early writings of Bamba:

> Through Islam you can put an end to the shame of those living in humiliation. Nothing hinders you from benefitting from my teaching, from I who am black. The noblest person in the sight of my God is without doubt the one who is pious. [Moreau 1982:166]

Even today, a hundred years later, all Senegalese, whether Mouride or even Muslim or not, speak with deep feeling of what Amadou Bamba did for the people in the aftermath of defeat and in the midst of despair and uncertainty.

But Mouridism provided much more than an initial and continuing psychological uplift. It provided work, which to a great extent meant peanut farming. In its theology it explicitly raised work to the status of a holy activity, along with prayer and religious instruction (Cruise O'Brien

1971:90). It also provided a new belief system, a (syncretistic) variety of Islam to replace the discredited traditions of the Wolof priest-kings.

Mouridism was comfortable and understandable to the masses. It spread peanut farming to virgin areas by organizing collective farms *(daaras)* where young people could work in traditional-type age grades, undergoing great hardships as a revised form of traditional initiation into adulthood. Mouridism also provided a new noble class, the descendants of Bamba or of his innermost circle of lieutenants. It also corrected some of the structural imbalances of traditional stratified society. An example was the integration of people from all castes into the *daaras*. Under the teachings of Islamic equality, people from the various castes worked and lived together, doing manual farm labor, now a sacralized activity. Sy (1969:143) succinctly summarizes this cultural dimension:

> It is in this effort of the reconstruction of a coherent whole, with the preservation and reinterpretation of essential features of traditional life in harmony with the needs of the time, that the Mouridism of Amadou Bamba appears to us as an original phenomenon, capable of 'reviving' and invigorating populations that were threatened with disappearance under colonialism.

Mourides grew from their founding in 1886 to 100,000 at Bamba's death to some 1,600,000 today (Cruise O'Brien 1975:157, my extrapolation to 1990). Even today the Mouride leaders constitute a vital political force that especially benefits the Senegambian rural masses whose interests would otherwise be less important to the successors to colonial government, to the urban elite, and to the leaders of the modern nation-state. Mercier (1965:166) describes this role in the following terms:

> The power and influence of the traditional political chiefs has to a large extent been transferred to the *khalifas* of the great Islamic sects; the latter represent today the principle force capable of resisting the modernist elite, and the one with which the latter and the political movements identified with it must to some extent come to terms.

It is certainly valid that Mourides and other Senegalese consider Bamba to be the master figure of their society and of their Islamic faith. His achievements would not seem to need the embellishments of hagiography. Yet it is comprehensible that his reputation be ever added to, and for many of his followers to make him into not just the ideal Senegalese man but also a semi-divine ancestral figure, given the world view context of the

Senegambia. The great pilgrimage to the city Bamba founded, Touba, is as much a celebration of the man and what he accomplished for his people, as it is of Senegambian Islam.

The Magal, or Pilgrimage

Introduction

The Mouride Sufi brotherhood and its Magal, or great annual pilgrimage to their sacred city Touba, are well known to both popular and anthropological literature. (See, for example, Kirtley and Kirtley 1985, D. Cruise O'Brien 1971, Sy 1969.) Martin Klein (1972:157) states that the Mourides "have probably been studied more intensively than any other twentieth-century African Moslem movement."

I attended the Magal in October 1986 with two Senegalese friends. One had lived and worked for three years at Touba, so he was able to serve as a knowledgeable guide.

The overwhelming impression was the vastness of the crowds. The Kirtleys (1985:229) estimated the pilgrims to be half a million in 1984, Boudin (1985:106) at one-and-a-half million in 1985. According to the sampling system I used, along with the observation of the countless trucks, buses, and cars still clogging highways in their bumper-to-bumper approach from several directions, and the many thousands of people lining streets and filling most courtyards, the number was at least a million.

Theoretical Framework and Thesis

The theoretical approach used in this study of the Magal is that suggested by Abdul Hamid el-Zein (1977:251) in his critique of several anthropological approaches to Islam and to Sufism in particular:

> I have shown that the saint may be profitably viewed as a symbol, not in the sense of being a vehicle for meaning, but as a relational construct in which the dimension of purity/impurity, defilement and sacralization are articulated with a broad and variable range of content, including political, economic, and otherwise pragmatic aspects of life. The saint thus symbolically embodies fundamental properties of a system of classification in the matrix of which all institutions (politics, economics, etc.) and institutionally related

behavior (manipulation of power, disposition of resources, etc.) are necessarily framed.

In more practical terms this means that, again quoting el-Zein (1977:252):

> 'Islam', without referring it to the facets of a system of which it is part, does not exist. Put another way, the utility of the concept 'Islam' as a predefined religion with its supreme 'truth' is extremely limited in anthropological analysis. Even the dichotomy of folk Islam/elite Islam is infertile and fruitless.

I agree completely with el-Zein. If his remarks are valid for Egypt, his country of origin, there is no doubt they are at least as applicable for the Senegambia. Islam is largely a set of forms, as has been discussed at several points. These forms are filled with locally adapted contents. This is only true in relative terms, as certainly there are specific contents that cannot be accepted into Islam; nevertheless, the contents can be so varied that el-Zein is correct in saying, at least anthropologically, the word Islam, as the term used to designate a religion, has little meaning of itself. As has also been demonstrated at countless points, the dichotomy folk-orthodox Islam is almost meaningless in the Senegambia, again, from the anthropological approach of studying man in his culture.

In this section, therefore, the Islam in question is described as a system of life or a complex of beliefs, symbols, and activities and not just a religion that can be adequately described in terms of theology and praxis. As we are looking at just the major phenomenon of one Sufi brotherhood, the scope of this paper is very limited. Nevertheless, the goal is to describe the pilgrimage and then show how it is the ritual expression of a complex way of life.

The thesis of the section is derived from the theoretical approach: the Magal, as a phenomenon of Mouride Sufi Islam, cannot be adequately understood as a mere religious event but as a symbol of a complex underlying matrix of religious, political, economic, cultural, psychological, nationalistic, social, and historical elements.

Description of the Magal

The Magal is an annual commemoration of the founder and chief saint of the Mouride brotherhood, Amadou Bamba MBacké. It consists of a pilgrimage to Touba, the Mouride sacred city founded by Bamba. It was instituted in 1928, the year after Bamba's death and is held on the eighteenth day of the lunar month Safar, date of the return of Bamba to

Senegal in 1902 after seven years of French-imposed exile in Gabon (Monteil 1966a:187).

The pilgrimage involves several obligations and options which do not have to be carried out in any particular sequence:

1. pay respects to the Caliph General
2. visit the great mosque
3. meditate at the tombs of Bamba and his deceased successors
4. visit the grand marabout of one's branch of allegiance
5. visit the Sacred Baobab tree in the cemetery (Bourlon 1962:60–61)
6. participate in various optional elements

With the vast hordes of pilgrims now crowding Touba at each Magal, not everyone can visit the Caliph or spend time meditating in the mosque or at the tombs of the saints or visit the cemetery. Just to enter the mosque and pass by the tomb of Bamba one faces continuously long lines day and night. The police exert strict control and almost force the pilgrims to enter the mosque and pass the tombs on the run.

Each step of the pilgrimage is now briefly described.

1. The journalistic description by the Kirtleys (1985:231) gives the facts and the flavor:

> Past straining disciples, we were escorted through the palace gates to the sanctum. There we were warned to remove our shoes, avoid movement, and not to approach the caliph. An old man, he was seated behind the bars of a protective wooden cage on the other side of the room. He was corpulent and swaddled in deep folds of indigo cloth.
>
> His gaze fastened on a little window to the outside world, past which filed his talibés. Each brought a gift—often money, or a goat or hen—which he slipped through the aperture; the caliph then chanted the briefest of prayers and spat into his disciple's upturned hands, as a sign of blessing.
>
> I was spellbound by the burning hope in each talibé's eyes as he lingered to touch the old man's hands, stealing an extra half second with the divine. Then a policeman would shove him aside. Again and again the ritual was repeated. The silence and sanctity mesmerized me. I scarcely knew I was being ushered

out of the room. Without speaking a word, I was assured, we had received the caliph's blessing!

2. The great mosque is a huge complex structure, large enough to accommodate 4,000 praying faithful at one time. Its five minarets dominate the city and the plains for miles around. It is one of the largest in sub-Saharan Africa. It is richly appointed throughout its vast interior. At the time of the great Magal, the tombs of the founder and his three deceased successors are the objects of most of the attention, although one sees people praying, meditating, reading, and chanting throughout the many chambers. At the entrance to each tomb many importunate disciples beg for alms.

3. The tomb of Bamba is inside the mosque, in a chamber lavishly decorated in arabesque. The vault itself is protected by an artistic steel grill, and is covered on all sides with a dark green tapestry on which are affixed poems written by Bamba in Arabic. The Arabic characters are made of pure gold, a mosque guide informed me.

As pilgrims enter the sacred chamber they touch the door frame or the steel grillwork and then rub their hands over their foreheads, hair and face, as though spreading over their bodies the essence of the spiritual force their hands received at touching the sacred enclosure. This essence is of course baraka, well-known throughout the Sufi world. It is the

> mystical power (of divine origin), which can be transmitted by physical contact, direct or indirect. To eat food which the (saint) has left, to touch his clothes, to receive his saliva upon the body, or even to walk barefoot on the sand of Touba is to benefit from this form of grace, which is believed not only to have spiritual value, but also to bring success in worldly enterprise. [D. Cruise O'Brien 1971:97]

4. Each quarter of the city contains the residence of its reigning grand marabout. The residences are occupied by these saints only occasionally or at special times as most of them have their permanent residences elsewhere. Such saints are exclusively of the MBacké family (direct descendants of Amadou Bamba) although a very few are direct descendants of Bamba's Prime Minister Ibra Fall. Each of these men has a following, in most cases large and in some cases immense. There is a great deal of (usually) hidden rivalry between these leaders and their clans.

Each residence overflows with pilgrims who claim allegiance to each particular living saint. They pay homage and bring gifts. There are religious chants at night, with loudspeakers installed in the spacious courtyards. It is easy to identify these residences because of the crowds, the people camped out in the nearby streets, the commotion, and the chanting.

5. The last step of the pilgrimage is a visit to the cemetery and in particular to the Sacred Baobab tree. It was under this tree in about 1891 that the angel Gabriel gave Bamba a vision indicating it was here he should someday construct a mosque. This scene would seem to be symbolic of the appearance of the angel Gabriel to Muhammad near the Lote-tree, described in Surah 53.14ff (Ali 1983:1444–45). Women pilgrims visit the tombs of Bamba's most prominent wife and the wives of other Mouride notables (Bourlon 1962:61, Coulon 1981:86).

6. There are several optional elements that constitute important activities although they are secondary to the elements already described.

    One is visiting the grand marabouts and the sub-Magal of the Bay Fall, a sub-sect of the Mourides, at Mbaké, its central town located seven kilometers from Touba. Many pilgrims walk to Mbaké as part of their pilgrimage. The Bay Fall are well-known for their all-night religious chants and many other practices, some of which involve the esoteric.

    A second is taking part in chants. There are several large temporary shelters put up, mostly near the great mosque. At night and all night long, these are the scenes of religious chants where famous name chanters lead the chants, usually praise poems in Arabic written in honor of Bamba or poems written by Bamba himself. Such chanting typically leads to states of ecstasy.

    A third is promenading. Throughout the city, countless vendors set up simple-to-elaborate stalls, selling food, drinks, and wares of endless variety. Many kinds of holy relics are also for sale. Performances of all sorts attract crowds: Islamic preachers, chanters, magicians, snake handlers, and others in infinite variety.

    Yet other elements are drinking water from the spring, named Zamzam, that is said to have been miraculously provided to Bamba in this semi-desert area. Baraka is imparted through the water. Similarly, sand is available for pilgrims to take by pinches, to be kept as a powerful talisman. This sand is available from a pail kept by a disciple at Bamba's tomb; it supposedly comes from Bamba's tomb. I did not observe this, but it is reported by A. Samb (1969:740).

The last day is Official Day. The President of Senegal sends a delegation of high officials out from Dakar to present his greetings. Speeches are made before a great public by the Caliph General and by the President's official representative. These are carried nationwide on radio and television. The Magal is then officially over but it is several days before all the pilgrims leave town.

The Matrix

Is the great Mouride Magal a religious event? Entirely? Primarily? Only superficially? Senegal's major daily newspaper called the Magal "the major event of the nation's spiritual life" (Le Soleil 1986).

El-Zein (1977:252) was quoted above as saying " 'Islam' as a predefined religion... is extremely limited in anthropological analysis." One of my strongest impressions at the Magal was how complex and multifaceted it was. Although the major observable events could be largely explained in religious terms, there is much more to the Magal that is of fundamental significance than the observable religious elements. A description limited to the religious aspects would leave out a great amount of anthropologically significant information. The religious phenomena comprise a complex symbol of an even more complex underlying matrix.

The major components of the matrix are described in the following paragraphs.

Religious. There is no doubt that the Magal is a religious event. Even if it is more than religious, it remains profoundly that. This was my greatest surprise in attending the Magal. I had previously talked to many people about it, including Mourides, and had read much about it, so I knew the basic facts. But this did not tell me of the fervor I would see lighting up the faces of many pilgrims. At one point I was drinking a Coke in a little shelter and was looking out on a crowd of men and women, mostly in their teens and twenties. Chanting was coming from the next booth. The expressions on the young peoples' faces were rapturous. I wondered how a tiny booth could hold a group as large as the one being listened to. I then realized someone in the booth was playing a cassette and the growing crowd had just stopped because of this tape recording.

Such fervor was seen over and over. There were countless groups of performers with thick circles of pilgrims crushing in around them. Generally they were singing praises to Amadou Bamba. Every time Bamba's name was mentioned in the chant a rousing shout went up, with each pilgrim raising the right arm high in salute. People believe in their saint. He is truly a saint to them. The Magal affects them at a profound religious level.

The religious content of Mouridism and the Magal was clearly stated to all. There were some forty large cloth banners fastened to the high mosque fence and along prominent streets in the center of the city. The cloth was dark green with lettering in Arabic and in French translation. On each banner was written a quotation from the writings of Bamba. They were very instructive. Those that best distilled key Mouride doctrines were:

> Anyone who gives himself to us is protected from distress now and on the day of judgment.

> The Creator absolutely gave to me the guidance of all men of my time. God will honor all requests that I address to him.

> God ordered me to proclaim that I am a refuge and a sanctuary. Whoever wants happiness in this world and in the next should seek it with me.

Political. The thesis that religion and politics are inseparable in Islam has been often stated by scholars. One recent statement is apropos to our discussion:

> "Religion" and "politics" are *not* separable and contrasting entities or social arenas in Islamic life. The political institutions are profoundly "religious," at least in principle, while the religious institutions often perform or participate in "political" functions. [Voll 1986:175]

The Official Day ceremonies are primarily political. The Mourides control hundreds of thousands of votes, and they represent law and order for a major part of the country. The high-level delegation from the capital represents all the Sengalese people—Muslim, Christian, and animist alike. The President's representative reiterates the value and importance of the Magal (and by implication, the Mourides) to the nation. The Caliph General thanks the President for his support and financial aid and reiterates his confidence in the President, his policies and the way he is leading the country (Niasse 1986, Gning 1986). These speeches are carefully listened to and talked about throughout the country. Cassette recordings of past speeches are sold in urban markets. People look for open and hidden meanings. They scrutinize the smiles, frowns, and gestures of the participants, as relations between the state and Mourides are of supreme importance to the body politic. Relations have not always been cordial in the past, and when they are not, the fact is reflected in the drama enacted on Official Day.

Economic. The Mouride movement has involved a very large economic component since its founding. The initial attraction and expansion of Mouridism was based on peanut farming, historically Senegal's major economic product. The Mourides were estimated to provide twenty-five per cent of national peanut production in 1957 to 1958, or some 200,000 to 300,000 tons per year. Other estimates claim from one-third to three-quarters of national production comes from Mouride land (D. Cruise O'Brien 1971:215–216). In any case, he (1971:214) says:

> The large annual contribution of Mouride cultivators to Senegal's [peanut] harvest has secured the brotherhood an important place in the national economy, all the more important in recent years as the [Mouride leaders] and their followers have also become increasingly active in urban commerce and investment.

One final quotation should remove any possible lingering doubt about the inseparability of economic factors from the Mouride religion:

> Since independence in 1960, the Government of the Republic of Senegal has continued the colonial policy of giving economic aid and assistance to the religious leader, and the volume of assistance has even risen sharply, as the Government relies heavily on the political support of the *marabouts*. The [Caliph]-General, notably, has benefitted from a series of loans for "agricultural improvements," which he has not been under great pressure to repay... President Senghor, addressing the [Caliph]-General at a ceremony in Touba in 1963, accomplished the following feat of definition— "Once more, what is Socialism if not, essentially, the socio-economic system which gives primacy and priority to work? And who has done this better than Amadou Bamba and his successors." [Cruise O'Brien 1971:219]

Cultural and Psychological. The founding and rapid expansion of Mouridism coincided with the final defeat of the last Wolof king and the implantation of French colonial rule. It was at this time, too, that the

Wolof masses converted to Islam.[46] The old Wolof social and moral order had collapsed. The bases of the culture and old ways of life were threatened with extinction. Bamba's teaching and example provided both hope and a practical strategy for living under changed and foreign conditions. Bamba offered dignity and a new way of life based upon traditional principles. He offered a part in a universal brotherhood of man, Islam. Even if Islam was not as powerful militarily as the Europeans, it was available and it had a greater place and power than traditional political and belief systems that had been demonstrated to be entirely inadequate in the changing Senegambian world. Lastly, Bamba offered a guarantee of entry into paradise.

When Mouride pilgrims go to the Magal, I believe even the masses are keenly aware of the importance Bamba played in their cultural and psychological survival after military defeat and the onset of the colonial night. Their feelings seem to be in part similar to what a person would feel toward another who had rescued him from drowning. People seem to be much less aware of the restructuring and reinterpretation of Wolof society along cultural norms, but these latter characteristics are the stuff of scholars, not of the average man or woman.

Social. A large part of the three days spent at the Magal is devoted to visiting with close and distant kin and friends and making new acquaintances. The Magal is a special time of renewing and building relationships. There is a great tradition of hospitality at Touba, with people opening their homes and courtyards to pilgrims—relatives, friends, and guests. Throughout the Magal people spend much more time with friends than with their religious observances. This was also one of my surprises, to see how the social factors were so important. I was invited to a number of compounds, just to talk, to share meals, to drink tea, and even to spend the night (usually on a mat in the courtyard). Even though I was not a Muslim, I was received cordially and hospitably.

I was struck by the relaxed nature of the Magal. Religious duties can be carried out in any order. There is no printed program, no schedule of events, no set times. The only fixed items are the official speeches on the final day and even then the hour is not specified.

---

[46]It should be noted that Mouridism started among the Wolof and has remained largely limited to them, although more recently many Serer, a large neighboring ethnic group, have converted from animism to Mouride Islam. Monteil (1980:369) estimates that one-third of Wolof and one-eighth of all Senegalese are Mourides.

Nationalistic. Mouridism is a SENEGALESE Islamic movement. This is very important. Bamba emphasized that his brotherhood was Senegalese and African. This was seen, for example, on the banner which said, "Our Prophet (Mohammed) granted me the favor of acceding to independence, guiding with me the community of the faithful. This is surely one of his marvelous deeds." Samb (1969:734), a Senegalese Islamic scholar, calls the Magal the "Senegalese Mecca." By this he means more than just a comparison. For many Mourides, Touba and the Magal are more central to their Islamic beliefs and practices than is the Mecca of Saudi Arabia.

This contrasts with being Arabic and, of course, European. Mouridism can be Senegalese because both God and Mohammed commissioned Bamba to establish Mouridism and Touba, and to serve as a guide to paradise. So it bypasses the Arabs, with whom most Senegalese Muslims are always in tension.

René Lake (1985), a Senegalese Christian journalist, wrote in an editorial in Senegal's national daily:

> There are justifications for a Christian Senegalese to be interested in everything that concerns Islam and that justifies his presence at the great Magal at Touba. [Among these reasons] ... is the historical role Islam played in the fight against colonialism ... [and] the cultural resistance that preserved our national identity from destruction.
>
> There in the architectural monument that is the Touba mosque, there where the founder of Mouridism reposes, I mixed my ardor with that of the thousands of my Muslim brothers who with open emotion had come to meditate and pray.

Historical. Many historical factors have already been given under the elements above. This is not ancient history to Senegalese. They only gained their independence in 1960 and still feel they are dominated by France and the West in many ways. They also feel religiously and culturally threatened by the Arab Muslim heartland. Thus, there is a strong identification with Bamba and a frequent retelling of stories of the ways he stood up to the French governors, and refused to submit. Bamba is revered for this, and the Magal brings each Senegalese present, whether Mouride or not, a little closer to his or her ideal historical Senegalese figure.

Analysis of the Magal as Ritual and Symbol

The Magal is a phenomenon of Sufi Islam. That is, it contains the major elements characteristic of Sufism and Sufi pilgrimages: veneration of saints, renewal of baraka, belief in the efficacy of intercession by the saints, renewal of expressions of loyalty, recalling the hagiography, and presenting gifts (Shenk 1983). These were the ritual elements covered in the description of the Magal.

I believe that what was called the matrix, above, are elements of which the Magal is the symbol. When people talk about the Magal, they do so largely in terms of the religious ritual elements, but they frequently add comments about the social aspects, recognizing them as an integral part of the whole. The other elements symbolized in the pilgrimage constitute a popularly undefined background on which the Magal is enacted. The people enact the symbols without being explicitly conscious of them.

A political symbol, for example, is attendance at the Magal which is a vote for Mouridism, accompanied by the favoritism the government shows it and the personal advantages that accrue therefrom. As an economic symbol, an immense attendance demonstrates the weight of Mouridism in the economic affairs of the country. As a cultural symbol, it makes statements about being a Senegalese celebration, carried out entirely under the leadership, financing, and organization of Senegalese in a Senegalese manner. It also proclaims the force of Senegalese Islam vis-à-vis Arabic Islam. It is even a symbol of Senegalese ability to compete with the pilgrimage to Mecca in ideology and in number of celebrants. And the saint, as symbol of all the other symbols, stands above the Magal and Mouridism as the central figure in both the religion and the ritual.

As this is not a comparative study, we cannot answer questions that are raised by el-Zein (1977) in his critique of other discussions of Islam. Such questions could be phrased for our study as "Is the Magal a true expression of Islam?" or "Is there a single true Islam of which Mouridism is a part?" But we have seen that the Magal is a religious event, and much more. We have seen that the saint is the symbol of all the other symbols. We have also seen that, however much it is truly or typically Islamic, Mouridism and the Magal cannot be understood as "Islamic," in el-Zein's words, "without referring it to the facets of a system" (1977:252). That is, without reference to the underlying system, the Magal loses much of its intrinsic meaning. The form of pilgrimage, universal in Sufi Islam, has only a vague meaning unless it is considered in its local context. The form is universal; the meaning is determined locally.

Some Observations about the Magal

The Magal is culturally AFRICAN. Even though Islam and Arabic culture have been present for centuries and Arabic is accepted as the sacred language, there is still strong, explicit desire to be African rather than Arabic or European. Africans want a culturally comfortable religion, and their expression of Islam meets that criterion.

The Magal is national. Its leaders are all Senegalese, not Arabs or Europeans.

The Magal is a symbol of social and economic solidarity and support. Such a mutual-support system is quintessentially African. Western culture is too often perceived as materialistic and individualistic, which are repugnant traits. Hospitality is very important. My experience showed that even fervent Mourides cordially welcomed me to their holy city and holy commemoration. All households consciously cook a surplus of food, so they can be hospitable to strangers.

The Magal is a collective rite. Even though ostensibly religious, much more time is spent socializing than carrying out strictly religious duties.

The Magal is musically African. The musical idiom, observed in the all-night chants and other musical elements of the Magal, has been around for centuries. It is far more African and appreciated than European religious music played on European instruments as found in Christian missions and churches in the Senegambia.

The Magal involves the miraculous. Amadou Bamba and other saints are credited with many miracles.

The Magal is mystical. Senegalese greatly appreciate and desire mystical experiences and meaningful ritual observances.

The Magal and Senegambian World View

This chapter on the Magal was introduced with the thesis that if the world view propositions formulated in this essay represent the fundamental and pervasive facts of the culture, they should be identifiable in all major real life events.

The Magal, the order of Mourides and Amadou Bamba, their founder, as well as the cultural matrix in which these are embedded, have now all been described in some detail. A rather general analysis has been provided. What remains is to identify where world view assumptions fit into this complex of beliefs and practices. In the concluding section the explanatory power of such a particular kind of anthropological analysis is examined.

This identification is carried out in a very straightforward manner. Each of the eight metathemes deduced for the Senegambian culture is discussed in turn, showing how each one, with its most relevant themes and subthemes, is implicated in the Magal. The full list of metathemes, themes and subthemes is provided in appendix 3.

Metatheme 1

> *Senegambians seek to have a personal transcendent peace, which is experienced through a moral conscience, a spirit of personal peace, and social peace.*

The major part of the religious elements of the Magal are related to this metatheme. More precisely, I suggest that the elements are generated by, or that there is a causal relationship between, the culture's world view assumptions and Magal ideology and praxis. I return to this question of causal-generational relationships in the conclusions.

Although not obvious, the Magal is certainly a part of the Senegambian search for transcendent peace. Peace is above all dependent upon establishing effective alliances with transcendent beings and forces, through designated intermediaries. For Mourides, Amadou Bamba is the supremely designated individual with amply demonstrated access to the interior world. His accomplishments—resistance and ultimate success—over the active opposition of the most powerful secular force in the world, that of European civilization, is proof to Mourides that Bamba had spiritual power that exceeded European secular power. His ultimate victory is taken as a major proof of this spiritual power and his exalted position in the cosmic order. Therefore, to make and to renew one's alliance with him and with his supernaturally endowed and designated successors and heirs is to take the surest path to peace and prosperity. It means being aligned on the side of real, cosmic power, whatever the circumstances and problems of the moment.

Man's role is to initiate and execute appropriate actions (cults and ceremonies) that serve to maintain communion between man and transempirical beings and forces. The Magal is cultus: paying homage to Allah, Muhammad, and Bamba, the supreme beings of the universe. Generous offerings are made of means, time, and effort. Prayers for divine protection and blessing are explicitly and implicitly made. Chanting praises, partaking of sacred water, recharging baraka, meditating, renewing allegiances, and more, are elements of the cultus. They are defined and prescribed by Bamba's successors as appropriate, and incumbent upon all Mourides to fulfill, just as pilgrimage to Mecca is incumbent on all orthodox Muslims (but neglected, if not rejected outright by Mourides).

Peace is achieved in the human soul when there is cosmic balance and cosmic laws are obeyed. The Magal is an act of obedience to the divinely ordained rules of religion and of life. Fullness of the soul, soul memory, soul restoration, soul awakening, and soul attachment all enter into play at the Magal. Past events of one's self, one's kin, of African history, of Amadou Bamba, and much more, are relived. Emotions are high. The symbols are lived as practical reality. The million other true believers involved in the Magal only serve to heighten emotions and deepen the profundity of the experience.

Metatheme 2

Peace, happiness, and success are achieved by means of power granted by supernatural forces of the transempirical world.

Metatheme 2 is an extension of Metatheme 1. This metatheme speaks especially to success and (esoteric) protection. Mourides believe their order provides both, and that participation in the Magal renews that provision. Amadou Bamba was successful in life, in spiritual revelations, in cosmic position, in political power, in attracting a following of multitudes, and in material rewards. His agricultural innovations were so successful that the French rallied to his cause when it became clear that they could benefit economically from the massive peanut production he could ensure for the colony. After Bamba's death Mouride successes continued, with Senegalese governments heavily endowing the order and its economic projects. Mourides have also successfully moved into urban and even international business. Politically they are much catered to by all levels of government. (See M.-C. Diop 1981, one of the countless studies of Mouride economic power.) Mouride success is, to the disciple, primarily a spiritual matter. Bamba and the Mourides have had success because it was and continues to be so ordained and favored by Allah. By adhering to and maintaining active status in the Mouride order, a disciple is both identifying with this success and voting himself a share in it. Participation in the Magal as a religious duty is inextricable from a background of desire for material well-being.

The protective aspects of the Magal can easily be seen in two prominent features. Mention has already been made of the large banners on display around the center of the city. These are official banners in the sense that they are prepared and displayed by the Mouride organizers of the Magal. They contain quotations from Bamba's voluminous writings. Many speak of success and protection for Mourides. Three of these are:

> Whoever puts confidence in us will be kept from trouble in this world and on the Day of Judgment.
>
> Any disciple that puts his confidence in us will be happy and kept from all evil.
>
> The Eternal has excluded the power of Satan from, and directed the resources of all the continents toward, my dwelling [Touba].

Although many Mourides would look to other power nodes for additional, specific protection, participation in the Magal includes this element.

The second feature is the sale of Mouride posters by many vendors at the Magal. The posters are photographs or drawings of Mouride saints, from Amadou Bamba, to his successors, to any Mouride notable, singly or in combination. A common poster is a sketch of a literal tree, with bust portraits of Mouride saints placed on the various branches, forming a family tree. I purchased a large poster that included the pictures of over 150 Mouride saints, from Bamba to many lesser figures. I have not yet found anyone who can identify for me all these saints.

The posters are good business. They are hung prominently in homes, offices, businesses, and vehicles. One gets the impression that most Mourides own and display such posters. Tijanis and adherents of other orders do the same with their saints. They serve as talismans and identify the order to which the individual or family adheres. They certainly serve as a statement of faith, allegiance, and dependence.

Metatheme 3

Humans should live in interdependent community,

This is a summary statement of Metatheme 3. COMMUNITY is a very large part of what the Magal is all about. There are no hotels in the city. Impersonal hotels would violate the spirit of personal hospitality and community that are made available to all as a sacred trust. The three days of the Magal are lived as a utopian ideal community, with sharing of faith, food, shelter, water, shade (Touba is in very hot, dry, and sub-Saharan Africa), friendship, peace and prosperity, history—each Mouride esteeming and honoring the other.

I had told the two Senegalese friends who accompanied me that I wanted to go to the Magal not just to experience it but to try to understand it. Of all the details they might have pointed out to me, the one they emphasized was the fact of community of the Magal. That, above all, was what they thought a European would least understand, yet it was the most important factor after the religious aspects.

To the casual Western observer the lack of hotels and other guest facilities, even portable toilets, the seeming haphazard organization, the lack of a program or timetable of events, the forced dependence on the relatively few city residents, the interminable time spent preparing meals, eating, and then drinking sweet mint-flavored green tea, and the idleness of spending hours just talking while resting on mats under the countless shade trees—all this looks like either mismanagement or a gross waste of time. To Senegambians it is an ultimate expression of the ideal community.

In describing the process of religious change from traditional religion to Islam among the Hausa, Trimingham makes a point that is doubly relevant to the Magal and other *siyaare* in the Senegambia. He (1959b:38–39) writes:

> Communal worship of spirits is not abandoned, but becomes confined to a mediating group of initiates *('yan bori),* which means a change in the whole conception of relationship with spirits. Individual offerings, it is true, go on everywhere and *bokaye* (medicine men) as well as *'yan bori* offer sacrifices to conciliate spirits causing illness, but the significant thing is that the communal cults are broken and can never again rule village life.

In applying these comments to the Senegambia, we see that true pre-Islamic community cultus has disappeared from the thoroughly Islamized peoples. Vestiges remain. Modified forms continue, but community-wide blood sacrifices, dancing, drumming, initiation, and such activities are indeed broken.

Although agreeing that purely traditional rites have ceased to be practiced, I believe a strong case can be made that they continue as functional substitutes in the *siyaare* (pilgrimage) such as the Magal. A major reason why the Senegambian *siyaare* are not openly Islamic as we have seen in Egypt and Morocco is that they are "communal cults," in Trimingham's terms. The communal aspect prevails over the Islamic aspect; therefore, each order organizes its own *siyaare*.

As Trimingham describes for the Hausa, the veneration of spirits has largely been confined to the several classes of religious practitioners. Such veneration is indeed largely individualized. But contrary to his categorical statement, community cultus does live on under Islam, and even rules, albeit in a very modified form.

Metatheme 4

> *Social peace is achieved through an integrated community life.*

The Magal is three days of living in peace and integrated community with one million others! It is sharing material goods. Several times I was invited to share a meal by more than one family, even though a non-Muslim and a white. Once while eating dinner with one family the whole courtyard at another house waited for me, not beginning until their foreign guest arrived (for his second meal that he could hardly do justice to).

The Magal has traditions and institutions that are followed, that guard the peace and serve the common interest. They are a reflection of the institutional nature of Senegambian community life everywhere. The Mouride hierarchy and organization is one. The suborder of the Bay Fall is another. These are followers of Bamba's first disciple, Ibra Fall. They have prominent peacekeeping and ceremonial roles that serve to integrate the Magal just as they served from the origins of Mouridism to integrate all strata of society into the order.

Peaceful values are to be lived out in multiple relationships. Although the Magal is too short to demonstrate this to any great degree, the extensive and intensive networking that goes on is meant to forge and renew social bonds at all possible levels and as extensively as possible. Such bonds are maintained very explicitly throughout the year and throughout life. This is an essential part of being Senegambian. These bonds have

Pilgrimage to Touba, the Sacred City of Senegal

many values. For one, they are utilitarian. The more friends one has, the greater the possibility of being able to solve a problem. This may be help from a strategically placed friend in government when something needs to be done. It may be financial help, or employment, or any of the countless events of life where society functions on the basis of personal relationships and not especially by established rules. The situation Suad Joseph (1978:63) describes for Lebanon doubtlessly applies to the Senegambia where "the state and the non-governmental institutions have been weak and poorly developed... Individuals have... to obtain services and resources through informal personal networks."

But far from last and least, Senegambians live for human relationships and friendships. They just plain enjoy meeting, knowing, and talking with people.

Metatheme 5

> *Man lives in symbiosis with nature, which is for him his source of physical life and survival.*

The application of this proposition to the Magal is far from obvious. The relationships between man and nature are ones that Islam universally minimizes, while in ATR they are of primary importance. As reverence for nature and cultus towards it typically involve fetishes, material symbols, and abodes of transempirical beings or forces, such practices receive the early condemnation of Islam:

> Islam is strongly opposed to the materialization of the spiritual and where its attack and rooting out is most effective is against 'idol worship', that is, cult of spirits symbolized by fetishes like Yoruba statuettes, Mande *boli* or *dyo*, Temne stones *(a-boro mesar)* symbolizing culture heros or ancestors, cones of clay, sacred animals symbolizing earth and water, or masks of mystery cults. [Trimingham 1959b:104]

Under the pressure of Islam and urbanization, this world view theme is of less overall relevance to the culture than was formerly the case. It remains very visible and relevant among more traditional Senegambian ethnic groups and subgroups.

Whether for these or other reasons, the Wolof have long seemed to be less concerned with nature than any of the other ethnic groups of the region. Among the Wolof there has for centuries been a strong national interest in politics, military affairs, trade, and other forms of activities focused externally. There has been a weakening of interest in and concern for nature. This has been noted by the social geographer Paul Pélissier (1966:101), who characterizes the Wolof in the following terms:

> The traditional Wolof country is remarkable for the richness of its politico-military history and the poverty of its agrarian traditions. It is, in this sense, completely antithetic to those rural civilizations that are called paleo-negritic, of which we encounter a remarkable example in the rice-cultivating Diola of the Lower Casamance [in southern Senegal], and, to a certain extent, the Serer peasants. All their past demonstrates that the Wolof have been, since their constitution as a distinct ethnic entity, engaged in building political structures, organizing a hierarchical and structured society, and that the rural masses, of heterogeneous origins, have always been submitted to the feudal-military demands of the warrior class that they served. They have never constituted a peasantry that was its own master and responsible for its own destiny.

This may appear to be a very long quotation for a very minor point, but it speaks to several relevant factors. One is that the weakness of the man-nature relationship among the Wolof is exceptional in the area. Another is that the Wolof were originators of the Mouride order and still constitute its overwhelming majority. Consequently, we see in this quotation from Pélissier, that the man-nature relationship would be expected to be especially weak in the Islamic Mouride order. But more importantly, although of less relevance to this particular discussion of the man-nature relationship, we see the connection between the founding and development of the Wolof-based Mourides and the historic Wolof commitment to "building political structures, organizing a hierarchical and structured society" and organizing the rural masses. Although this is not a world view matter that is applicable to the entire Senegambia, it is clearly one that involves the particularities of Wolof world view: it is part of the Wolof fundamental conceptual system, their self-identity, and their view of where they fit into the established cosmic order.

Another quotation from Pélissier (1966:213), describing the Serer who are more typically Senegambian, speaks to the importance of the man-nature relationship:

> How greatly Serer beliefs would remain incomprehensible to whoever imagines that their daily comportment, and above all, their work as peasants, is directed exclusively by secular concerns! The earth itself is life. In the eyes of the Serer 'the Earth is the

body of a living woman, desirable and fertile. They have given her a feminine name, Kumba Ndiaye; the rain is the seed that permits her to produce her fruit'. [quoting H. Gravrand 1961]

Returning to the discussion of nature in the Magal, we can observe several secondary traits that relate to it. The site of Touba, the Magal, the cemetery, the sacred baobab tree, the spring Zamzam—all strongly relate to man's symbiosis with nature. When Bamba first visited the region, it was an uninhabited forest. Through the guidance of the angel Gabriel, while resting in the shade of a baobab during a forty day retreat, he was directed to build a mosque and found a city. These constitute a very powerful set of traditional elements.

Senegalese oral history and origin myths are replete with traditions of settling virgin country and the complex of activities, rights, and obligations that appertain to the founders and their descendants. Concepts of customary law are still well-known from Senegambian tradition, such as fire rights, axe rights, and land use rights, which were held respectively by *boroom daay* 'fire owner', *boroom sémmiñ* 'axe owner', and *laman* 'master of the land, lord'. The central figures in this legal system are the founding ancestors, but these ancestors always moved and acted in dependence upon their guiding and protective spirits and totems. The lighting of the first fire and extent of burning in a virgin area, the first step in clearing the land, was carried out under the guidance of the spirits and in explicit recognition of dependence on nature. This pattern of dependence continued with cutting the trees, using the land, and building of settlements. Senegambian man did not proceed autonomously (Reverdy 1967).

When a founding father and his scouts went out in search of a more favorable site on which to settle, they did so by following the father's protecting spirit, which often temporarily took the form of a bird, flying ahead to indicate the way. When the bird settled in a tree, the founding father remained in that place (El-H. Samb 1981:14). The baobab was universally the tree of choice for spirit residence. Upon building a settlement and establishing an altar, the spirit reverted to its normal totemic form.

Saafi[47] tradition states that if the guiding bird remained three days in one tree it indicated that this was the spot where the founder was to settle. The tree and grove where the bird took residence were left uncut and

---

[47]The Saafi are an ethnic group numbering some 80,000, located 80 to 160 kilometers east and southeast of Dakar. They have maintained their language and traditions in spite of the conversion of the large majority to Islam and a few to Roman Catholicism.

became the sacred grove of that village, where many of the most important and sacred rites would take place, such as those of initiation-circumcision (Mbaye Ndiaye 1990).

Previously noted was the centrality of these rites and this grove to the concepts of birth, death, reincorporation, reincarnation, and integration of the individual into the community.

Thus we see that guidance by the spirits, the sacred groves and their traditions, ancestors (present in the cemetery and at the saints' tombs), the direct provision of nature (the spring water), divine guidance in the implantation of a settlement, the primordial role of clan founder, annual rededication and renewal rites at a sacred site—all these and more are present in the Magal.

To these traditional and African elements can be added several that are Arabic and Islamic: the appearance of the angel Gabriel and the prophet Muhammad to Bamba,[48] building a mosque on a divinely indicated site and following orthodox Islamic practices in it, establishing a seat of Islamic learning, carrying out all activities in the name of Allah, and all the traditions of Sufi Islam.

Metatheme 6

Man is defined in terms of kinship and in relation to the cosmos.

The themes under this metatheme relate to moral rectitude, transmitted values, ascribed social roles, and comportment toward non-kin.

Above all, the Magal is a symbol for all Mourides of the cosmic role of their saint, Amadou Bamba. He is the supreme ancestral figure. As Mourides they are part of his neo-kin. Their identity in Senegal, in the Senegambia, in Africa, in the Muslim world, and even in the eternal plan of Allah is part and parcel tied to being Mouride.

Bamba was the ideal, moral man, approved by Allah along with Muhammad to the extent of being granted his every desire and his every intercession on behalf of Mourides.

Mention has been made of the efforts that the residents of Touba and the pilgrims themselves make on behalf of non-kin. I saw that this was applied to me, a non-Mouride, non-African, non-Muslim, non-kin. In

---

[48]These are not described in this essay, but both of these foundational figures are believed to have appeared personally and made revelations to Bamba.

theory at least this duty applies, not just at the time of the Magal, but throughout the year and wherever Mourides are living.

Bamba and the Mouride leaders who are his successors, and Mouride rites have become the functional substitutes for the traditional complex of ancestor beings, beliefs, and practices. The great Mouride marabouts and their followers of allegiance have become neo-clans. Ties with and to these clans are made and renewed at the Magal and at the many other, lesser Mouride pilgrimages. Ties are also built and maintained through Mouride agricultural colonies *(darou)*, through urban as well as rural religio-social associations of Mouride adepts *(daayira)*, and through other institutions established by the dynamic Mouride movement.

Metatheme 7

> *The unique nature of being Black-African man, and of being Senegambian man in particular, has profound implications on thought patterns, on comportment, and on the emotions.*

This metatheme speaks to a very important yet veiled subject. I was able to lift the veil somewhat only after establishing close relations with some Senegambians. Since discovering this guarded subject, I have cautiously tried out some of my findings on more casual acquaintances. Their reaction is always one of surprise that I know of and have some understanding of this subject, but also agreement that the subject is really there and important to an understanding of Senegambian self-identity and world view. In fact, there is a vast literature, not anthropological, that deals with or at least touches upon the subject of what now acceptably is included in the term Africanity.[49]

The three themes under this metatheme provide an adequate summary of the dynamics of what it means to be a Senegambian in this world. (1) Having a black skin implies a heavy burden that can be manifested in attitudes such as defeatism, fatalism, submission, inferiority, and dejection. (2) The Black-African has been long oppressed in the world. (3) Solidarity between Black-African peoples is of great importance in confronting the historical discrimination that persists in the world today.

---

[49]See Cartey 1970, Cesaire 1939, Kesteloot 1987 and 1988, LeVine 1970, Nyang 1984, Paton 1948, and Senghor 1964, as a small sample of some relevant literature.

Bamba's writings contained implicit and explicit references to the African condition. I previously quoted two of his direct appeals to black Senegalese:

> Through Islam you can put an end to the shame of those living in humiliation.
>
> Nothing hinders you from benefitting from my teaching, from I who am black. The noblest person in the sight of my God is without doubt the one who is pious. [Moreau 1982:166]

Mouridism, with its substitution of the Magal for the hajj to Mecca, its nationalism, its speeches made in the Wolof language, its minimization of the importance of the Arabic language and Qur'an in its expression of Islam—is implicitly anti-Arabic in stance. Although Bamba's writings are all in Arabic, even these are part of what I would call the carefully drawn fine line between accepting the universality and orthodoxy of Arabic on the one hand, and Black-African-Senegambian nationalism on the other. Arabic is used to the extent needed to prove orthodoxy and capability in use and understanding of the language, but no more. It is little used in teaching, for example. There are easily identified reasons for anti-Arabicism. Although the Arabs brought the religion practiced by Mourides, there is deep resentment against the aggression, domination, slave raiding, and perceived attitudes of arrogance, superiority, and prejudices of Arabs against blacks, that they see as continuing to be held today.

Bypassing Arabic and the Arabs has been made possible, if not implicitly sanctioned, by the fact that Bamba received his revelations directly from the angel Gabriel and the prophet Muhammad. Certainly this is a clear, as well as subtle, augmentation of the valuation of the black race, and an assertion of equality with Arabs. And it was a valuation that was ordained by Allah himself.

Mouride Islamic self-assurance strongly contrasts with what Michael Lambek (1990:25) found among Muslims of the off-coastal regions of East Africa, where

> the people of Mayotte view themselves as far from the centers of Islamic learning and authority and hence are vulnerable to the influence of outsiders deemed to represent that authority... Their self-consciousness about knowledge was combined with a perceived need to learn more about their religion, a craving for accessible yet authoritative knowledge. As a result, they tended to give

precedence to versions of Islam that came from the outside; the more Swahili or Arab a man looked and acted, and the stronger his claims to such a background, the more respect he would be granted in religious contexts, at least initially and overtly.

Mouride self-assurance is apparently true to such an extent that one may wonder if my claim for the vexations of Africanity really apply to the Senegambia or at least to Mourides. I would answer by asserting that this is additional evidence that Bamba's movement is a remarkable achievement for meeting many of the religious, cultural, and psychological needs of the Wolof and other Senegambian peoples. They not only embraced Mouridism, they needed it for the extra-religious needs it met, as well as for those that were religious.

The Magal also celebrates Bamba's successful resistance to the economically and militarily more powerful white race. He and his successors proved that their culture and religion could successfully resist and ultimately win the retreat of the Europeans from the land. These are all subjects for profound meditation at the Magal.

Metatheme 8

> *The uttered word has inherent power that can be set in action through its proper formulation.*

The uttered human word can be very powerful, according to the Senegambian belief system. Léopold Senghor (1964:209), philosopher and former president of Senegal, expresses this reification of uttered speech in this way:

> *The spoken word, the Word,* is the ideal expression of the Vital Force, of the *being* in its completeness. God created the world by the *Word* ... With the existing being the word is the living breath that gives life to the *utterer*; it possesses magical virtue, it acts through the law of participation and creates the *object named* by its intrinsic virtue.

The evil tongue is one of the most-feared and most-defended against evils. Figure 19 listed the execratory elements of the evil tongue or mouth *(cat)*, the evil eye *(bët)*, and the evil touch *(laal)*, as well as the principle of the transfer of evil *(topp)*. These concepts represent a complex of beliefs, central to which is the concept that evil or misfortune can be transferred from a person who has evil intent onto the person against whom the evil intent is directed. Of this complex of beliefs, the one by far the most feared is the evil tongue. Through the power of transfer, words that are spoken against another person can cause misfortune, sickness, loss of goods, even death. I have had informants tell me that a person standing in front of a mirror, if he or she utters negative words, can bring harm on himself or herself.[50] Plants can be caused to wither and die from being spoken against, as can animals. Typically, large admirable rams, as well as other domestic animals of considerable value, wear collars to which amulets are attached. These amulets are obtained primarily for protection against the evil tongue. Virtually all ethnic groups of the Senegambia actively hold to these beliefs today.[51] This is but one example of Senegambian belief in the power of the human word, used destructively.

Makhily Gassama (1978:27–28), a Senegalese professor of literature, characterizes his civilization as one in which "words or the Word [constitute] the magic of the act of speaking."

The magic or power can be positive as well as negative. If the intent is positive and the conditions are propitious, the hearers of the human word properly uttered, and even those beyond hearing distance, can receive benediction and prosperity. A prime example is the widespread use of the uttered Qur'an. From mosque loudspeakers, from cassette players in stores, on radio and television, and especially at organized recitations, the Qur'an is broadcast. The belief is that the mere oral recitation of the sacred text is beneficial, whether or not a word of the Arabic is understood. The presence of a printed Qur'an does not have such power, i.e., magical effect; it is released in recitation.

Such magical use of the Qur'an concords exactly with the concept of the uttered word in ATR as is clearly brought out by Nyang (1984:15 quoting Jahn 1961 and Wauthier 1967):

> One of the touchstones of traditional African culture is the "magic power of the word"... In African metaphysics, as Jahn explains them, "all transformations, creation and procreation is [sic] made by the word"... The truth about this formulation of Jahn is not

---

[50]Just where the negative intent is involved in such cases, supposedly a prerequisite for nefarious results, I have been unable to determine.

[51]See Gilmore 1987, Maloney 1976, Reminick 1985, among the many who have researched the evil eye and associated complex of beliefs.

widely disputed, for as Wauthier himself noted, the word is all-powerful in Africa.

In his discussion of the concepts and uses of magic, especially in the Islamic world, Earl Grant (1987:525 quoting Newbigin 1966) defines magic as

> the exercise and [manipulation of] power through the use of a magic formula, a spoken or acted ritual. "Pagan magic may or may not invoke a manual act, but it always involves the use of words."

This is the magical use of the Qur'an—far more important for its magical qualities, in talismans and in unintelligible recitation, than it is for doctrinal instruction. Senegambian culture includes many elements of magical utterance. The most prominent and common form is what I call provenient formulas. In figure 19 these are found as elements of all three religious expressions: Islamic, Islamo-traditional, and traditional. Note that I have even placed Qur'anic words in the category of an Islamic formula.

In the Magal the uttered word plays an important part. Bamba's poetry is chanted in all-night chants—an essential part of the Magal as well as a part of all the high events of Mouride religious life throughout the year. In significant ways these recited poems hold a place equivalent to the recited or chanted Qur'an for their religious and magical qualities.

Mention has been made of oratory at the Magal. Oratory overlaps with hagiography. It almost seems to the non-Mouride observer that oratory and hagiography are combined and performed in the belief that the power of the uttered word creates the fact; that is, if an unbelievable feat is attributed orally to Amadou Bamba it must be true. Utterance, and especially so at the holy time of the Magal, makes it true and believable.

Mention has also been made of one of the central events of the Magal, the speeches of Official Day. The discourse of the Caliph General, the supreme living head and saint of the order, is waited for expectantly and followed very carefully. This is not just because of the political and economic implications it necessarily contains. It is, above all, the religious, oratorical, and even inspired contents that make it so important and that generate interest in and listening to Official Day oratory past or present.

I would go so far as to apply to the Caliph General's Magal speeches something of the importance that René Bravmann (1983:16, quoting Geertz 1976) and Clifford Geertz evoke for the Qur'an:

The Quran (which means neither 'testament' nor 'teaching' nor 'book', but 'recitation') differs from the other major scriptures of the world in that it contains not reports about God by a prophet or his disciples, but His direct speech, the syllables, words, and sentences of Allah. Like Allah, it is eternal and uncreated, one of His attributes, like Mercy and Omnipotence, not one of his creatures, like man or the earth... he who chants Quranic verses... chants not words about God, but of Him, and indeed, as those words are his essence chants God himself.

Popular Mouride belief holds that all essential knowledge is contained in Bamba's writings called *qasa'id* (A.): all the secrets of Allah and of the prophets, all instructions, and all the prayers that the disciple needs. This is a major reason why these poems are sung in all-night chants. They constitute the veritable Qur'an of Mouridism.

An idea of how Amadou Bamba, Mouridism, and the Magal are assimilated into Islam, both implicitly and explicitly, is provided by the analogy drawn by the Caliph General, Sëriñ Falilou, in his Magal speech of 1964, a recording of which I bought in a Dakar market in 1989. In it he calls the departure to exile of Amadou Bamba in 1895 a second Tabaski, with Sëriñ Amadou Bamba symbolizing the sacrificial lamb, like Ishmael (Mbacké 1964).[52]

The utterance of Bamba's successor and inheritor of charisma is at least a symbol, or current representation on earth, of these qualities of divine speech. It is inspired and connected with divinity, and it contains and imparts to the hearers some of the essence of these saints and of Allah himself.

Conclusions

This essay started with several goals. A primary goal, as stated in the Introduction, was to test the hypothesis: in Senegambian Muslim society, orthodox Islam, Sufi Islam, and African traditional religion constitute one coherent religious system, rather than three separate or parallel systems. The relationships between Islam, Sufi Islam, and ATR were described and analyzed on many pages of the study. These were major focuses of chapters three and four where the relationships were examined in considerable detail. The conclusion is that these three strands of religious praxis

---

[52]Tabaski (*íd al-Kabir*, A.) is the annual Islamic Sheep Feast. See entry in the Glossary.

and belief constitute one coherent system, yet their origins and Senegambian modifications are largely identifiable, traceable, and understandable. The understanding was provided in large part through an examination of the culture in terms of its basic premises, or world view.

Another primary goal was to study world view in the Senegambia, in societies where Islam and African traditional religion have long coexisted and mixed. The purpose was to ascertain whether or not a deep-level world view approach would lead to an analysis with a relatively high degree of explanatory power, revealing the rules for living and the organizing principles upon which these societies are based. In other words, to gain an understanding of Muslim society in the Senegambia as it is lived rather than assuming or accepting as fact a priori definitions as typically found in idealized studies of Islam.

The purpose was to avoid applying standard definitions to Senegambian Muslims, whether classical definitions of the past (and present) or even of the few, recent, revisionist definitions of folk Islam or African Islam. My approach to Senegambian beliefs and practices has sought to avoid the pitfalls of looking at Senegambians merely as orthodox Muslims, or folk Muslims or traditionalists or syncretists, but rather to seek to understand the intentionality of actions and the meanings these actions hold for the people themselves. Islam is a system of life and can be understood in only real life contexts. Universal or orthodox Islamic practices are particularly subject to local, culturally influenced meanings.

In examining Muslim life and practice in the Senegambia, this study has amply confirmed the remarks made by Earl Grant (1987:678) concerning the nature of Islamic society:

> Beneath its simplicity of design and the sublime confidence of its devotees, we have found a sub-surface world of realities with which its formal expressions... are unable to cope. Upon exploring this world we encountered a complex variegated mass of beliefs and practices that are as diverse in their origin as the various cultures... in which Islam has taken root.

Transcendent peace was found to be the dominant theme, and the world view analysis focused on it. Since a large number of themes were identified in the study, only those that dealt with transcendent peace were examined in detail. Had they all been examined exhaustively on their three levels, the result would have been more exhausting than revealing, to borrow a phrase from Berreman (1972). However, the full gamut of metathemes was examined in the context of the Magal, the major ceremonial event of the region. A complete listing of the themes is provided in appendix three.

The dominant Senegambian theme, transcendent peace, was seen to have great explanatory power, being directly related to and able to explain the bases for many personal and ritual behaviors observed in the Senegambian culture. It is not claimed, however, that transcendent peace explains such a wide range of behaviors as George Foster (1965 and 1972) claims for his limited good concept, referred to in the discussion in chapter three.

A further goal was to contribute to the development of a more comprehensive model of world view than has been available as an anthropological paradigm. The eight-level model, described in chapter two, was the result. The essential features of the model were the generalizations from culture carried out in two directions: toward ultimate relationships, giving metathemes, and toward ultimate causes, giving ontological absolutes. These generalizations are constructed inductively from cultural behavior, without appeal to psychological theories. The second major feature was the positing of an essential full range of relationships for what could be defined as complete world view studies. The scope of analyzed relationships was called the thematic range.

After formulating a more comprehensive model of world view, and after detailed examination of a specific Muslim culture, a major goal was to re-examine a significant real-life event from that culture, in light of its world view. This was done in chapter five for the Magal, the pilgrimage to Touba.

The hypothesis that a world view analysis would have greater explanatory power to better reveal and explain emic culture-bearing behavior than would a more conventional anthropological analysis was tested in chapter five. The Magal was first analyzed in what could be characterized as being a symbolic anthropological approach. Then a second world view analysis was provided. The second analysis was shown to better reveal the causes relating to behavior.

These goals have not been fully realized. All that is claimed is that attention has been given to each one in the preceding pages. It is hoped that some contribution has been made in each of these areas. I have attempted to build upon the work of many anthropologists and Islamic specialists. The essay should be considered in the sense expressed by Clifford Geertz (1973:25):

> A study is an advance if it is more incisive—whatever that may mean—than those that preceded it; but it stands less on their shoulders than, challenged and challenging, runs by their side.

Appendix 1
Pronunciation Guide for Wolof

Letter	Approximate English Equivalent	Example	Gloss
a	far	*nas*	a project
à	car	*sàkk*	to create
b	same as English	*bakkan*	nose
c	chain	*cosaan*	origins
d	same as English	*pëdd*	egg yolk
e	fell	*tell*	to be shallow
é	gay (approximate)	*yéene*	to declare
ë	focus (approximate)	*kër*	house, family
f	same as English	*fég*	to finish
g	go	*xajog*	squirrel
i	field	*lim*	to count
j	same as English	*julli*	Muslim prayer
k	same as English	*lekk*	to eat
l	same as English	*let*	to sharpen
m	same as English	*may*	divine grace
n	same as English	*meen*	maternal line
ñ	canyon	*ñaar*	two
ng	marking	*ngaw*	to sew
o	horn	*kort*	to cast lots
ó	go	*sóob*	to submerge
p	same as English	*pepp*	grain of millet
q	curl (but guttural)	*muqat*	coward

r	flap r as in Spanish	*tawreet*	Old Testament
s	same as English	*sopp*	to love
t	same as English	*tal*	to have time for
u	**u**se	*bukki*	hyena
w	same as English	*waaw*	yes
x	**acc**ount, (but guttural and raspy)	*tax*	to cause
y	same as English	*yitt*	to hit

Appendix 2
Glossary of Senegambian Words

All italicized terms are Wolof unless otherwise indicated. Abbreviations used are A. Arabic; D. Diola; E. English; F. French; P. Pulaar; S. Serer; Sf. Saafi. (Lebou is not given as the Lebou are Wolof speakers.)

aar: protection
addiya: alms of submission due the chief of a Sufi order
aj (hajj, A.): Muslim pilgrimage to Mecca
àllaaxira: paradise
asaka (zakat, A.): legal Muslim alms
astafurlaa: formula meaning 'God pardon me for...'
baatin: the hidden world, as contrasted with *saxiir,* the visible world
baaw-naan: rainmaking rites, especially as practiced by the Lebou
bakkan: breath of life, life, soul; nose
baraka (A.): see *barke*
barke (baraka, A.): divine benediction, implying spiritual and material prosperity
bëre: traditional wrestling, normally performed as a postharvest rite
bët: evil eye
biddaa: idolatry
bëciin (D.): spirit, altar, or cult of spirits
boroom: master, lord, owner
boroom jamano (qutb al-zaman, A.): master of the time, age, or people
cat: evil tongue or mouth
ceddo: caste of warrior-slaves attached to Wolof kings
cosaan: traditions; origins; the past

daara: Qur'anic school

daayira (dahira, F.): an association of men or women formed under the auspices of a Sufi order for purposes of spiritual and social well-being and the promotion of the order

deddale: incantations to cause the friendship of two persons to be broken, usually accomplished through the effects of a negative talisman

déeba-déeb: magico-religious practice, e.g., drinking a magic potion

dëmm: a witch, who feeds on the souls of the living

du'a (A.): Muslim extemporaneous prayer

fas: amulet in the form of a knotted cord

gaaf: an augury, omen; *aay gaaf:* bad omen; *baax gaaf:* good omen

gàllaaj: occult protection; amulet (generic term)

gàmmu: commemoration of the birth of the prophet Muhammad

géwél: member of the caste of praise singers

gis: interior vision; to see

gisaane: divination

giskat: diviner, person with interior vision

griot (F.): a *géwél*

hadith (A., W.): an authoritative tradition of the prophet Muhammad

hajj (A.): see *aj*

ijjasa (ijaza, A.): license or diploma

jàmm: peace, tranquility of spirit

jàng: organized religious event of chanting sacred texts, usually held at night

jat: recitation of magic formulas to render a dangerous animal inoffensive

jébbal: oath of allegiance Mouride disciples swear to their marabout

jébbalu: to put oneself under the spiritual protection of another

jibar: black magic

jig: to be benefic, auspicious

jiitu: to impose oneself on others

jinn (A.): see *jinne*

jinne: genie, spirit; supernatural beings, some of which are good and some of which are evil

joolaa: a cluster of ethnic groups in southwestern Senegambia—the English rendering is usually Diola

julli: the formal Muslim prayer or recitation; *salat* (A.)

juddu bu tuuti: badly born

juddu bu réy: wellborn

kaar: an uttered formula to counter the effect of *cat* 'evil tongue'

karama (A.): miracle performed by or through the power of Allah

Glossary of Senegambian Words

kasag: chants used in circumcision rites
kàttan: force, power; energy
kawteef: miracle; something originating in the transempirical world
kémaan: miracle; something that is beyond human intelligence to comprehend; a mystery
kilifa: caliph; a religious authority
kiss: magic potion to open the intelligence or understanding
koor: fast; Ramadan, the ninth month of the Muslim year which is the month of fasting (cf. *woor*)
kort: misfortune that is cast at a distance, especially death or insanity
kuf: interjection used as protection against maleficence
kuus: prosperity genie
làyene: a Senegalese Sufi order whose members are largely of the Lebou ethnic group
laal: evil touch
laax: millet porridge
lébu: an ethnic group that is found in the coastal area around Dakar who speak Wolof—their name is usually rendered *Lébou* in French, and Lebou in English
léemu: to recite traditional protective prayers; to bless
lël: rites of initiation into manhood and ethnic lore
liggéey: rites involving the casting of malefic forces toward or upon someone; black magic
lislam: Wolofized French expression meaning Islam; control of destiny in the hereafter
listikar: Islamic divination by means of dreams
lugg: to conjure poison by means of uttered magical formulas
luxuskat: magician who practices on a personal, rather than on a ceremonial, basis; includes those considered to be charlatans as well as those to whom real esoteric powers are attributed
maam (W., S.): grandparent; ancestor; the Serer circumcision-initiation divinity; the Serer founding ancestor spirit
maandu ci: formula used against *cat,* meaning 'protect me from your tongue'.
màggal (F.: *Magal*): annual pilgrimage of the Mouride order to Touba, their sacred city in Senegal
malaaka: angel (from A. *malika*)
marabout (F., E.): leader in a Sufi order; Muslim cleric
mbañ: totem, totemic animal; taboo
mbind: text, usually Qur'anic, with magical, malefic power

mbubb: long shirt, typically reaching to the ankles or ground, ideally made of fine material and elaborately embroidered
miis (Sf.): ritual hunting expedition carried out for purposes of divination
mocc: to conjure pain by means of uttered magical formulas
móolu: to curse; magical formulas for any kind of occult protection
mucc: salvation (in the sense of ritual equilibrium, the sine qua non of individual and community peace and prosperity)
muqàddam: an official of the Tijani or Qadiri Sufi order, authorized to initiate new disciples
murit: a Sufi order founded by Amadou Bamba (d. 1927), spelled Mouride in English and French
muslaay: a talisman (general term for a defense against occult forces)
nangu: maraboutic yoke
nawle: person, male or female, of the same condition or social rank; competitor
ndëmm: witchcraft; symbolic cannibalism (that of the soul, not of the flesh, of humans)
ndëpp: rite of spirit possession which has a therapeutic purpose
ngénte: ceremony of name-giving held eight days after birth, often called baptism
ngistal: ostentation, living for appearances
njong: rite of circumcision
njulli (S.): participant in a circumcision-initiation class
noo: breath; soul
noob: to cast a spell on someone or something
noot nit ki: to exercise control over other(s)
ñaan: extemporaneous uttered prayer to divinity (*duá*, A.)
ñaan-yàlla: Islamic prayer for protection or for malefic action against someone
ñag: occult protection or fence
ñàng: to be endowed with occult power
qadri: a Sufi order
qasa'id (A.): religious laudatory poem, frequently chanted
rab: spirit, spirits
rammu: intercession on behalf of someone, especially that of Muhammad on behalf of Muslims
rawane: Islamic personal protector spirit
repp: to fulfill one's ill-fated destiny
róonu: to make a cross on the forehead with lampblack, as a sign of protection

ruu: vital force; soul; spirit
rus: ashamed
saafara: Muslim magical water used to attain healing, success, or some other desired purpose
saafi: an ethnic group of central western Senegal, often referred to by the Wolof and other outsiders as Safen
salat (A.): see *julli*
saltige: a chief shaman
sang bi: master; the prophet Muhammad
sàngara: alcoholic drink
sàngat: a traditional purification which involves a ritual bath
sarax: a sacrifice; offering; the voluntary Muslim alms (from *sadaqah*, A.)
saxiir: the visible world, as contrasted with *baatin*, the hidden world (from *zahir*, A.)
sas: in the Mouride order, an exceptional levy required of disciples
sawm (A.): see *woor* and *koor*
séeréer: a major ethnic group of central-west Senegal, usually spelled Serer in English
séex: an official of the Mouride or Qadiri order, authorized to initiate new disciples
selbe: official in charge of initiation of boys being circumcised
serif: person who can trace ancestry back to the prophet Muhammad
sëriñ: religious teacher; spiritual leader; husband
sëriñ tariax: ritual practitioner who employs *xonjom* in religious or magical rites
seytaane: devil, demon; Satan (from *shaitan*, A.)
sikar: chanted prayer litany (from *dhikr*, A.)
silsila (W., A.): spiritual pedigree; a chain or lineage of spiritual descent
sirku: idolatry; the sin of associating someone or something with Allah (from *shirk*, A.)
siru: secret lore which is transmitted by initiation
siyaare (*ziara*, A.): pilgrimage to the tomb of a Sufi saint
subbóoxun: interjection used to conjure maleficence, meaning 'God protect me from you' (a gross insult if overheard by the person feared)
sunna (W., A.): practice or example modeled by Muhammad
taalibe (*talibé*, F.): disciple of a marabout
tabaski (*id al-Kabir*, A.): the annual sheep feast that commemorates Abraham's offering of Ishmael and of Allah supplying the substitutionary ram

tani: divination by means of cowrie shells
tarbiyu: to work for a marabout in exchange for his benediction
tariixa (*tariqa*, A.): Sufi order
tawféex: well-being; divine protection
tëddale: divination through dreams
téeré: an amulet or talisman derived from *xaatim*
teraanga: hospitality; mark of honor
tere: prohibitions, taboos, superstitions
texe: to be blessed, saved, in a religious sense, and by extension, materially
tierno (P.): same as *marabout*
tijani: a Sufi order, the largest in the Senegambia
topp: principle of transfer, especially of evil
toqental: magical potion put in a newborn's mouth before any nourishment
toolu àllarba: Wednesday field, whose labor is donated to a particular marabout
toorobbe (P.): a Muslim clerical caste of traditional Islamic Tukolor leaders, of heterogeneous ethnic origins
toskare: consequence of malediction
tubaab: a European or white person
tubbi: apostasy from Islam
tul: magical potion that provides invulnerability against all arms, used during warfare
tukulóor: a major ethnic group of northern Senegambia, usually spelled Tukolor in English and *Toucouleur* in French
tuub: to request pardon
tuur: traditional altar dedicated to cultus of spirits; the spirits attached to an altar; totem
tuur deret: a blood sacrifice
tuuru: to pour out libations at a spirit's altar
tuyaaba: divine benediction; reward given by God for good deeds
tyamaba: cultus of the river deity; the river deity
ulama (plural, A.; singular: *alim*): collective doctors of the law of Islamic society
umma (W., A.): universal community of Muslims, that is, without the restrictions of political borders
umute: sin, occult uncleanness; maleficence
waalo: the first established Wolof kingdom, located in the Senegal River delta area
wàlliyu (*wali*, A.): a Sufi saint; friend of Allah

Glossary of Senegambian Words

wasifa: a chanted supplementary prayer rite of the Tijani order
wasila: an intermediary between Allah and man; the marabout to whom one has given allegiance
weexal: payment for the performance of an occult rite
wird: a formula of prayer recitation carried out in addition to the five daily orthodox prayers
wooj: to cause (someone) to return, by occult means
wujj: co-wife; rival, competitor
woor: to fast; *sawm* (A.)(cf. *koor*)
xaatim: amulet containing Qur'anic and cabalistic writing
xaaw (khahf, A.): cotton cord; amulet made with cotton cord
xala: to cast impotence upon a man through *liggéey*
xalif: caliph; head of a Sufi order or major branch of an order
xam-xamu baatin: ceremonial magic; esoteric knowledge
xalwa (khalwa, A.): Islamic esoteric retreat requiring use of a special *wird*
xàmb: place, altar, established and maintained for the cultus to a personal protector spirit
xarbaax: personal magic
xel: intelligence, reason, mind; spirit
xel mu dal: interior peace
xérém: objects of traditional cultus; idols
xër-lo: to render someone insane by occult means
xiirtal: to bring someone to a state of subjection to another
xol: the human heart, soul
xonjom: occult science; traditional (non-Islamic) amulet; objects that have been embued with occult power
xor: an honorarium given to a healer
xooy (S.): village rites carried out before the rainy season to assess the community's spiritual condition and to predict the coming rains
yéene: to make a vow (for good or evil purpose)
yëg: to be awakened to occult knowledge, often in terms of *umu* 'bad auspice' or *wërsëg* 'good auspice'
yelimaan (imam, A.): Imam, leader of Muslim cultus
yàlla: God, Allah, the Creator
yiir: to be protected by divine or occult means
zakat (A.): see *asaka*
ziara (A.): see *siyaare*

Appendix 3
Senegambian World View Propositions

Metatheme 1

Senegambians seek to have a personal transcendent peace, which is experienced through a moral conscience, a spirit of personal peace, and social peace.

Theme 1

To possess peace, human beings need to establish alliances with the forces and beings that govern the world.

Subtheme 1-A. Peace in this world must be sought in accordance with the fundamental, superior, and unchangeable laws of the transempirical world.

Subtheme 1-B. Man's role is to initiate and execute appropriate, specific actions (cults and ceremonies) that can serve to reestablish and maintain communion with the beings and forces that operate in the world of man.

Subtheme 1-C. The beings and forces of the transempirical world confer on initiated individuals a consciousness awakened to the supernatural realm that makes them masters of the laws of the seen and the unseen.

Theme 2

Peace in the human spirit is the consequence of a condition of harmony between human beings and transempirical beings and forces.

Subtheme 2-A. When a person has the interior radiance of peace, it is manifested through coherence of thought and interior harmony, which together enable the person to counterbalance the ascendancy of transcendent forces over him or her.

Subtheme 2-B. When there is a breach in the relationship to transempirical beings and/or forces, man suffers disastrous consequences (such as insanity, chronic bad luck, and failure in life).

Theme 3

Peace in the human soul is the result of living in harmony with the laws established by the transempirical beings and forces.

Subtheme 3-A. The state of personal peace is measured by the fullness of the soul *(dënn bu yaa)*.

Subtheme 3-B. The condition of personal peace is experienced in terms of a spiritual revelation based on:

- (a) Soul memory *(xol du fàtte)*, which is the reservoir and the sum of all the experiences of life.
- (b) Soul restoration *(dund ag yeegu xol)*, which is the re-creating in an individual of a state of readiness to receive the miracle of communication with the transempirical world.
- (c) Soul awakening *(fit wu yee wu)*, which originates with initiation into the verities hidden behind the visible and sensible reality perceived by the uninitiated.
- (d) The attachment of the soul *(nooy ci mbir)* to the objects and symbols of transempirical forces, which is the result of soul awakening.

Senegambian World View Propositions

Theme 4

Transcendent peace results in spiritual and material blessing *(barke)*, social supremacy *(daraja)*, and a high place in the social hierarchy *(martaba)*.

Theme 5

Transcendent peace is a consequence of meeting the demands of the laws of cosmic balance. These laws emanate from the normal functioning of transempirical forces. Their purpose is to effect corrective action, when needed, that will lead to superior justice in interhuman relations.

Metatheme 2

Peace, happiness, and success are achieved by means of power granted by supernatural forces of the transempirical world.

Theme 1

It is possible to obtain knowledge about one's personal destiny, to understand the origins and causes of the events of life, and to obtain prescriptions for improving or altering future events in one's favor. The same principles and processes apply to community destinies and events.

Theme 2

It is possible and desirable to exercise control over one's destiny, over the events of life, and over the events of the community.

Theme 3

Humans should have protection(s) through esoteric power at personal, family, and community levels, in order to: (a) be defended against destructive cosmic forces; (b) resist occult attacks set in motion by enemies; and (c) avoid or challenge chronic misfortune.

Metatheme 3

Humans should live in interdependent community.

Theme 1

Humans should share material goods and nonmaterial values.

Subtheme 1-A. Sharing is defined on the basis of religious principles.

Subtheme 1-B. Sharing has moral, ideological, and philosophical content; it is not merely a personal or cultural choice.

Theme 2

Humans should work together.

Subtheme 2-A. The proper ways of life of mankind have their bases in historical fact.

Subtheme 2-B. The specific way of life of a people determines the quality of their whole culture and civilization.

Theme 3

Humans should esteem one another.

Subtheme 3-A. By following specific traditional wisdom members of society achieve mutual esteem.

Subtheme 3-B. Mutual esteem is incumbent upon everyone in society.

Metatheme 4

Social peace is achieved through an integrated community life.

Theme 1

Every community requires institutions that serve to guard the peace.

Subtheme 1-A. Social peace should be founded and maintained through established structures (e.g., *pénc*, committees of elders; mosques, *daayira*, religious-based associations; etc.).

Subtheme 1-B. The laws regulating social peace are customary, informal, and flexible (including joking relations, *kal*).

Subtheme 1-C. Humans need to be indulgent toward the faults of others.

Subtheme 1-D. Proverbs, and other forms of preserved wisdom, constitute a socially inherited reservoir of traditional values that especially serve the interests of social peace.

Theme 2

Peaceful values are to be lived out in daily life through multiple relationships as senior citizens/youth, husbands/wives, chiefs/commoners, citizens/citizens.

Subtheme 2-A. People of age are owed respect.

Subtheme 2-B. People should readily ask pardon of each other in cases of social breach *(baal ma àg)*.

Subtheme 2-C. Social isolation is to be avoided (at almost any price).

Subtheme 2-D. Physical aggression is prohibited except in cases of extreme provocation (e.g., to defend one's honor).

Metatheme 5

Man lives in symbiosis with nature, which is for him his source of physical life and survival.

Theme 1

The apprenticeship in the laws of nature is mediated through Senegambian traditional religion.

Subtheme 1-A. Man needs to have a mystical understanding of the animal, vegetable, and mineral realms.

Subtheme 1-B. Man needs to respect the taboos related to his position in the functioning of nature.

Theme 2

Man relates to the transempirical world by means of participation with and intervention in the operation of the natural phenomena through which the world is governed.

Subtheme 2-A. Certain individuals or castes have been designated for initiation into the esoteric knowledge and practices related to the *flora*, that they then exercise on behalf of society.

Subtheme 2-B. idem: *fauna.*

Subtheme 2-C. idem: *minerals, ores and metals.*

Subtheme 2-D. idem: *rain.*

Subtheme 2-E. idem: *the cosmos.*

Metatheme 6

Man is defined in terms of kinship and in relation to the cosmos.

Theme 1

The significance of man (*nit*, integral man, i.e., body, soul, and spirit) is measured by his moral rectitude.

Theme 2

The character of man is built upon the foundation of values transmitted by family and society.

Theme 3

Man's social status and position are defined in terms of kinship.

Theme 4

The comportment prescribed for a man toward non-kin is determined by respective social position.

Metatheme 7

The unique nature of being Black-African man, and of being Senegambian man in particular, has profound implications on thought patterns, on comportment, and on the emotions.

Theme 1

Having a black skin implies a heavy burden that can be manifested in attitudes such as defeatism, fatalism, submission, and dejection.

Theme 2

The Black-African has been long oppressed in the world.

Theme 3

Solidarity between Black-African peoples is of great importance in confronting the historical discrimination that persists in the world today.

Metatheme 8

The uttered word has inherent power that can be set in action through its proper formulation.

Theme 1

Sacred texts, both oral and written, and rhythms can serve to discharge mystical power through adequate formulations.

Theme 2

There is an elite number of inspired men who know the secrets of mystical and powerful speech.

Theme 3

There are magic formulas that have a capacity to cause supernatural mutation of, mastery of, or subjection of visible matter or invisible entities.

Theme 4

The speech of man can have power to transfer secret intent, either beneficial or harmful.

Appendix 4
Resumé of Senegambian World View

A summary formulation of all Senegambian world view themes is given below:

The universe is one unit. All created and uncreated beings, forces, and objects are part of that living, functioning, interdependent unit. All these beings, forces, and objects have established purposes and roles they are destined to fill.

Man exists as part of the universe. For him to realize his destiny and live a full life he must properly relate to the other elements of the universe, thus filling his prescribed role. Man's well-being is tied to his fulfillment of this destiny.

Man is in essence a spiritual being. That is, the universe is above all a spiritual unity, and man's nature is to be in communion and harmony with its component parts. African man seeks spiritual knowledge and spiritual sentiments as the highest values.

Transcendent peace is the highest value and state that man can achieve. It comes from a proper balance being established in relationships:

> man ↔ transempirical forces and beings
> man ↔ man
> man ↔ nature

It is achieved through paying due respect to transempirical beings, living a moral life, living in harmonious community with fellowman, and living in appreciation of nature.

Man has been assigned a central role in the established cosmic order. He is the ceremonial center, and his actions can cause imbalance or serve to initiate the reestablishment of balance. Man's destiny is to live in symbiosis with all the cosmic order.

Black-African man longs for balance, participation, goodness, happiness, and fulfillment, by fulfilling his ascribed role and by knowing he is accepted as a worthy participant by his society and also by the wider, world society.

When the established order is out of balance, as it is now and has been since the arrival of Arab and European peoples and especially of Western secular values, there is a profound sense of imbalance, misunderstanding, injustice, and lostness.

A deep sense of confusion of values, a serious loss of identity and self-esteem, and a certain crippling social and personal dysfunction may be the final result of the imbalance that now prevails.

Appendix 5
Ontological Absolutes

The ontological absolutes (ultimate causes or metacauses) that have been identified for Senegambian culture are:

1. *God.* God *(yàlla)* is transcendent, remote, and little concerned with, or at least little involved in, the daily affairs of his creation. (Additive statement for Sufi Muslims: although God *(Allah,* A.) is transcendent, the divine reality can be experienced through proper action.)

2. *Universe.* The universe is composed of both visible and invisible reality (to man), but the invisible is of greater ontological and causal significance than the visible.

3. *Peace.* Peace is the ideal state, and harmony is the ideal relationship of the universe. The states and relationships of peace provide the sine qua non of well-being in human existence.

4. *Integration.* At all levels of the universe, the ideal condition is integration. That is, all parts need to be brought together through interdependence, so that each will be able to play its predestined function.

5. *Destiny.* Every being and part of the universe has an assigned role that needs to be filled for the satisfactory functioning of the whole. (Additive statement for Muslims: submitting to divine law will provide assurance of approval on the Day of Judgment).

6. *Hierarchy.* The universe is organized on the basis of hierarchies of position and power at every level and within pre-established domains. Each position bears assigned responsibilities.

7. *Power.* The universe is administered through the exercise of both inherent and derived power.

8. *Reality.* All reality has two aspects: exterior and interior. This forces man both to accept and overcome his ambiguous position in a dichotomized cosmic structure.

9. *Human Beings.* Man is the ceremonial center of the universe; therefore, much initiatory responsibility rests upon him.

10. *Transfer.* All spiritual good or evil, and abstract qualities are transmitted through the principle of transfer, by means of the mechanism of intent.

Appendix 6
Selected Senegambian Taboos

The following were selected as representative of a corpus of taboos collected in January 1989 from town elders in the rural-like suburbs of Dakar, who were asked to provide currently followed taboos.

1. Always throw to the ground a little food or drink that you are consuming to protect yourself from the evil eye and the spirits.

2. Never throw hot water to the ground for fear of burning your ancestors.

3. Never call out in a loud voice someone's name at night, because the spirits may grab the person named and bind or destroy the soul—causing insanity, trouble, ill health, or even death. Instead of calling the name, call out "Guddi Diallo," for example, to a person named Diallo, to fool the spirits (*guddi* 'night').

4. A falling star announces the death of a great person or of coming disasters. When you see a falling star, you should make a whistling sound by sucking air into your lungs. This keeps misfortune away from you.

5. Three things that should not be done at night: sewing, borrowing a fire from a neighbor, and buying salt or even using its name. Instead of saying the word salt at night, you should say *saf cin* 'cooking flavor'.

6. When someone who is speaking near you sneezes, you should say *seede yàlla* 'testimony of God', as it is believed that a sneeze while talking indicates that God has confirmed as true what was being said.

7. If someone compliments you, especially about something concerning your body, you should say *kaar bu ma lekk* 'don't eat me', in case the person is a *dëmm* 'witch'. If the person is a witch, such compliments can harm you by *cat* 'the evil power of the tongue'. (As it is known that even a tree can be made to wither and die through the power of *cat*, so people need to be very wary of it being used against them, as they are weaker than trees.)

8. If you want to compliment a well-dressed person, you should take something you are wearing and throw it to the person and at the same time say *lalal naa la* 'I put what I have in front of you'. The person throws the object back saying *lalil naa la* 'I give it back'.

9. A woman *dëmm* 'witch' will never take shoes out from under a bed. (This can be used, e.g., to test your wife.)

10. Burning some of the hair of a *dëmm* will make him or her have a crisis and admit guilt. (Note that this puts responsibility on barbers, who must have the confidence of their clients, and carefully dispose of hair clippings.)

11. Drums and pans must not be beaten during the rainy season, and salt must not be buried in the ground, as either will adversely affect the rains. (Dakar and other Senegalese cities have city ordinances prohibiting the beating of drums during this season.)

12. When you eat, you must collect any fallen grains of rice and eat them, or you will run the risk of poverty. Everyone should give honor to food.

13. It is especially dangerous to remain outdoors on Monday and Friday nights as these are nights when souls and spirits roam about.

14. If you fear evil spirits, you should sleep on a mat on the floor; the closer to the ground you are the more protected you will be. (Note: there is fear of an evil spirit attacking you from under your bed.)

Selected Senegambian Taboos 263

15. The third and fortieth days after someone's death are important. On the third day you make the *sarax* 'offering of the third day', because often the soul doesn't know his or her body is dead until that day. Offerings are in the form of cake, cookies, or such that are given to relatives and friends. On the fortieth day, the soul of the dead goes to heaven, and on that day passages of the Qur'an are read and prayers are said on behalf of the dead.

16. Always give back touch for touch, slap for slap, and like actions even in joking, in case the other person is a witch to avoid any possible danger.

17. If you want to get someone to be angry at another person, whether husband or wife, or any other two people—turn over one of his or her shoes and leave the other right side up.

18. Always be careful of what you say because marabouts can hear you even if they are not anywhere near. They have special powers to hear what people say, called *xam-xamu yëg* 'the power of being present everywhere'.

References

Adams, Charles J. 1976. Islamic faith. In R. M. Savory (ed.), Introduction to Islamic civilisation, 33–45. Cambridge: Cambridge University Press.

Adams, Juanita, ed. 1984. Background notes: Senegal. Washington: U.S. Department of State.

Africa Confidential. 1989. Mauritania: War on black citizens. July 7, 30(14):2–3.

Ahmed, Akbar S. and David M. Hart, eds. 1984. Islam in tribal societies: From the Atlas to the Indus. London: Routledge and Kegan Paul.

Ali, A. Yusuf. 1983 [1934]. The holy Qur'an: Text, translation and commentary. Brentwood, MD: Amana.

Ames, David W. 1953. Marriage among the Wolof in the Gambia with a consideration of problems of marital adjustment and patterned ways of resolving tensions. Ph.D. dissertation. Northwestern University.

———. 1959a. Belief in 'witches' among the rural Wolof of the Gambia. Africa 29(3):263–73.

———. 1959b. Wolof co-operative work groups. In William R. Bascom and M. J. Herskovits (eds.), Continuity and change in African cultures, 224–37. Chicago: University of Chicago Press.

Ane, Mohamed Moustapha. 1961. La vie de Cheikh Ahmadou Bamba. (Translated from the Arabic by A. Samb.) Dakar: Dar-Senegalia.

Appia, Béatrice. 1940. Superstitions guinéennes et sénégalaises. Bulletin de l'IFAN, B 2(3–4):358–95.

Arberry, Arthur J. 1950. Sufism. London: Allen and Unwin.

———. 1955. The Koran interpreted. New York: Collier.

Arensberg, Conrad M. and A. H. Niehoff. 1971. Social change: A manual for community development. New York: Aldine.

Austin, Ralph. 1980. Sufism and its world view. Ultimate Reality and Meaning 3:50–69.

Bâ, A. Hampaté. 1972. Aspects de la civilisation africaine. Paris: Présence Africaine.

———. 1980. Vie et enseignement de Tierno Bokar. Paris: Editions du Seuil.

Barrett, David B., ed. 1982. World Christian encyclopedia. Nairobi: Oxford University Press.

Beals, Ralph L. and H. Hoijer. 1965. An introduction to anthropology. 3rd ed. New York: Macmillan.

Behrman, Lucy C. 1970. Muslim brotherhoods and politics in Senegal. Cambridge: Harvard University Press.

Benedict, Ruth. 1932. Configurations of culture in North America. American Anthropologist 34:1–27.

Berger, Monroe. 1970. Islam in Egypt today: Social and political aspects of popular religion. Cambridge: Cambridge University Press.

Berreman, Gerald D. 1972. Is ethnoscience relevant? In James P. Spradley (ed.), Culture and cognition, 223–32. New York: Chandler.

Bidney, David. 1953. Theoretical anthropology. New York: Columbia University Press.

Bock, Philip K., ed. 1970. Culture shock: A reader in modern cultural anthropology. New York: Alfred A. Knopf.

Bodiel, Thiam. 1949. Quelques superstitions ouoloves. Notes Africaines (Dakar), 41:13.

Boilat, David. 1984 [1853]. Esquisses Sénégalaises. Paris: Editions Karthala.

Boly, Pierre. 1990. Personal communication. Dakar.

Boudin, Philippe. 1985. Un Toubab à Touba, la mecque noir. Africa International 168.

Bourlon, A. 1962. Mourides et Mouridisme 1953. In M. Chailley, et al., Notes et Etudes sur l'Islam en Afrique noire, 53–74. Paris: Centre de Hautes Etudes Administratives sur l'Afrique et l'Asie modernes.

Bowen, Dorothy N. 1981. Cognitive styles of African theological students and the implications of those styles for bibliographic instruction. Ph.D. dissertation, Florida State University.

Bowen, Earle A., Jr. 1981. The learning styles of African college students. Ph.D. dissertation, Florida State University.

Bravmann, René A. 1983. African Islam. Washington: The Smithsonian Institution Press.

Brenner, Louis. 1984. West African Sufi: The religious heritage and spiritual search of Cerno Bokar Saalif Taal. Berkeley: University of California Press.

Bruner, Jerome S., Jacqueline J. Goodnow, and George A. Austin. 1972. Categories and cognition. In James P. Spradley (ed.), Culture and cognition, 168–90. New York: Chandler.

Budge, Wallis. 1961. Amulets and talismans. New Hyde Park, NY: University Books.

Bugnicourt, Jacques, S. E. Ndiane, and M. Sagna. 1987. Pauvreté ambiguë: enfants et jeunes au Sénégal. Dakar: Environment et Développement du Tiers Monde (ENDA) and Unicef.

Burling, Robbins. 1969. Cognition and componential analysis: God's truth or hocus pocus? In Stephen A. Tyler (ed.), Cognitive anthropology, 419–32. New York: Holt, Rinehart and Winston.

Buswell, James O. III. 1989. Toward a Christian metaanthropology. Journal of Interdisciplinary Studies 1(1–2):24–44.

Cardaire, Marcel. 1954. Etudes Soudaniennes. Koulouba (Mali): Institut Français d'Afrique Noire.

Cartey, Wilfred. 1970. Contemporary African literature. In John N. Paden and Edward W. Soja (eds.), The African experience, Vol. I: Essays, 582–91. Evanston: Northwestern University Press.

Cesaire, Aimé. 1939. Cahier d'un Retour au Pays natal. Paris: Editions Présence Africaine.

Chi-Bonnardel, Régine Nguyen Van. 1978. Vie de relations au Sénégal: la circulation de biens. Dakar: Institut Fondamental de l'Afrique Noir.

CLAD. 1977. Lexique Wolof-Français. 4 vol. Dakar: Centre de Linguistique Appliquée de Dakar.

Clarke, Peter B. 1982. West Africa and Islam. London: Edward Arnold.

Colloque de Dakar 19–24 janvier 1976. 1978. Afrique noire et monde méditerranéen dans l'antiquité. Dakar and Abidjan: Nouvelles Editions Africaines.

Colvin, Lucile G. 1972. Kajoor and its diplomatic relations with Saint-Louis du Sénégal, 1763–1861. Ph.D. dissertation, Columbia University.

———. 1974. Islam and the state of Kajoor: A case of successful resistance to Jihad. Journal of African History 15(4):587–606.

Conklin, Harold C. 1969. Lexicographical treatment of folk taxonomies. In Stephen A. Tyler (ed.), Cognitive anthropology, 41–59. New York: Holt, Rinehart and Winston.
Cosminsky, Sheila. 1976. The evil eye in a Quiché community. In Clarence Maloney (ed.), The evil eye, 163–74. New York: Columbia University Press.
Cottingham, Clement, Jr. 1969. Clan politics and rural modernization: A study of local political change in Senegambia. Ph.D. dissertation, University of California, Berkeley.
Coulon, Christian. 1981. Le Marabout et le Prince: Islam et pouvoir au Sénégal. Paris: Editions A. Pedone.
Coulson, Noel J. 1964. A history of Islamic law. Edinburgh: Edinburgh University Press.
Crick, Malcolm R. 1982. Anthropology of knowledge. In Bernard J. Siegel (ed.), Annual review of anthropology, 287–313. Palo Alto, CA: Annual Reviews.
Crowder, Michael. 1962. Senegal: A study in French assimilation policy. Oxford: Oxford University Press.
Cruise O'Brien, Donal B. 1971. The Mourides of Senegal: The political and economic organization of an Islamic brotherhood. Oxford: Clarendon Press.
———. 1975. Saints and politicians: Essays in the organisation of a Senegalese peasant society. London: Cambridge University Press.
Cruise O'Brien, Rita, ed. 1979. The political economy of underdevelopment: Dependence in Senegal. Beverly Hills: Sage Publications.
Cuoq, Joseph M. 1984. Histoire de l'islamisation de l'Afrique de l'Ouest: des origines à la fin du XVIe siècle. Paris: Librarie Orientaliste Paul Geuthner.
Curran, Brian D. and Joann Schrock. 1972. Area handbook for Mauritania. Washington: U.S. Government Printing Office.
Curtin, Philip D. 1975. Economic change in precolonial Africa: Senegambia in the era of the slave trade. Madison: University of Wisconsin Press.
Davidson, Basil. 1968. Africa in history: Themes and outlines. New York: Macmillan.
Dia, Oumar B. K. 1982. La fonction éducative du conte chez les Wolofs. Demb ak Tey (Dakar) 7:60–61.
———, et al. 1977. Lexique Wolof-Français. 4 vol. Dakar: Centre de linguistique appliquée de Dakar (CLAD) and Institut fondamental d'Afrique Noire (IFAN).

Diack, Mass. 1990. Sorcellerie: Les protagonistes de nouveau à la barre. Le Soleil (Dakar), June 6.

Diagne, Charles. 1984a. La sorcellerie, j'y crois! Famille et Développement (Dakar) 38:38–43.

———. 1984b. Profession: chasseuse de sorciers. Famille et Développement (Dakar) 38:44–46.

———. 1984c. Une suite de questions. Famille et Développement (Dakar) 38:54–55.

Diallo, Oumar. 1987. Interview, Wolof culture. Dakar.

Diédhiou, Djib. 1984a. La Dette. Famille et Développement (Dakar) 38:47–52.

———. 1984b. Vous avez dit sorcier? Famille et Développement (Dakar) 38:34–37.

Dilley, Roy M. 1984. Weavers among the Tukolor of the Senegal river basin: A study of their social position and economic organisation. Ph.D. dissertation, Oxford University.

Dione, Aliou. 1990. Personal communication. Dakar.

Diop, Abdoulaye-Bara. 1965. Société Toucouleur et Migration (enquête sur l'immigration toucouleur à Dakar). Dakar: Institut Français d'Afrique Noire.

———. 1981. Société Wolof: Tradition et changement. Les systèmes d'inégalité et de domination. Paris: Editions Karthala.

Diop, B. 1985. Les Marabouts à leur place. Promotion 2 (Dakar) 19:2–4.

Diop, M.-C. 1981. Les affaires mourides à Dakar. Politique Africaine (Paris) 1(4):90–100.

Diop, Sëriñ Mbaye. 1987. Interview, Dakar.

DuBois, Cora. 1955. The dominant value profile of American culture. American Anthropologist 57(6):1232–39.

Dupire, Marguerite. 1970. Organisation sociale des Peul: Etude d'ethnographie comparée. Paris: Librarie Plon.

Eickelman, Dale F. 1976. Moroccan Islam: Tradition and society in a pilgrimage center. Austin: University of Texas Press.

Elworthy, Frederic T. 1958 [1895]. The evil eye. New York: Julian Press.

Fakhouri, Hani. 1972. Kafr El-Elow: An Egyptian village in transition. New York: Holt, Rinehart and Winston.

Fal, Arame, R. Santos, and J. L. Doneux. 1990. Dictionnaire Wolof-français suivi d'un index français-wolof. Paris: Editions Karthala.

Faye, Louis D. 1983. Mort et Naissance: Le Monde Sereer. Dakar: Les Nouvelles Editions Africaines.

Faye, Mouhamed. 1987. Les Marchands d'illusion. Magazine ORTS (Dakar) 13:17.
Firth, Raymond. 1973. Symbols: Public and private. Ithaca, NY: Cornell University Press.
Fisher, Humphrey J. 1973. Conversion reconsidered: Some historical aspects of religious conversion in Black Africa. Africa 43(1):27–40.
Foltz, William J. 1969. Social structure and political behavior of Senegalese elites. Behavior Science Notes 2:145–63.
Foster, George M. 1965. Peasant society and the image of limited good. American Anthropologist 67(2):293–315.
———. 1972. A second look at limited good. Anthropology Quarterly 45:57–64.
Frake, Charles O. 1972. The ethnographic study of cognitive systems. In James P. Spradley (ed.), Culture and cognition, 191–205. New York: Chandler.
Friend, Joseph H. and D. Guralnik, gen. eds. 1956. Webster's new world dictionary of the American language. Cleveland: World.
Froelich, Jean-Claude. 1962. Les Musulmans d'Afrique noir. Paris: Editions de l'Orante.
Fürer-Haimendorf, Christoph Von. 1985. Priests. In Arthur C. Lehman and James E. Myers (eds.), Magic, witchcraft, and religion, 89–93. Palo Alto: Mayfield.
Gamble, David P. 1957. The Wolof of Senegambia, together with notes on the Lebu and the Serer. London: International African Institute.
Gardet, Louis and M. M. Anawati. 1948. Introduction à la théologie musulmane, essai de théologie comparée. Paris: Vrin.
Garrison, Vivian and Conrad M. Arensberg. 1976. The evil eye: Envy or risk of seizure? paranoia or patronal dependency? In Clarence Maloney (ed.), The evil eye, 287–328. New York: Columbia University Press.
Gassama, Makhily. 1978. Kuma: Interrogation sur la littérature nègre de langue française. Dakar and Abidjan: Les Nouvelles Editions Africaines.
Geertz, Clifford. 1968. Islam observed: Religious development in Morocco and Indonesia. New Haven: Yale University Press.
———. 1973. The interpretation of cultures. New York: Basic Books.
———. 1976. Art as a cultural system. Modern Language Notes 91:1489–90.
Gero, Glenn. 1990. Personal communication. Dakar.
Gibb, H. A. R. 1969. Islam: A historical survey. 2nd ed. rev. Oxford: Oxford University Press.
———. 1975. Islam. 3rd ed. Oxford: Oxford University Press.

———, et al. 1960 and 1965. The encyclopaedia of Islam. Vol. I, II, new edition. Leiden: E. J. Brill
——— and J. H. Kramers, eds. 1965 and 1974. Shorter encyclopaedia of Islam. Leiden: E. J. Brill.
Gibbs, James L., Jr. 1965. The Kpelle of Liberia. In James L. Gibbs, Jr. (ed.), Peoples of Africa, 199–240. New York: Holt, Rinehart and Winston.
Gilliland, Dean. 1986. African religion meets Islam: Religious change in northern Nigeria. Lanham, MD: University Press of America.
Gilmore, David D., ed. 1987. Honor and shame and the unity of the Mediterranean. Washington: American Anthropological Association.
Gilsenan, Michael. 1973. Saint and Sufi in modern Egypt: An essay in the sociology of religion. Oxford: Clarendon Press.
Girard, Jean. 1984. Les Bassari du Sénégal, fils du caméléon: Dynamique d'une culture troglodytique. Paris: Editions l'Harmattan.
Glélé, Maurice Ahanhonzo. 1981. Religion, culture et politique en Afrique Noir. Paris: Editeur Economica and Présence Africaine.
Gnignue, T. 1990. Grande mosquée de Dakar: un super grand imam. Sud Hebdo (Dakar) 103, May 3.
Gning, Birane. 1986. Touba passe l'éponge. Wal Fadjri (Dakar) 64:7–9.
Goldziher, Ignaz. 1981 [1910]. Introduction to Islamic theology and law. Princeton: Princeton University Press.
Goodenough, Ward H. 1957. Cultural anthropology and linguistics. Georgetown University Monograph Series on Language and Linguistics, 9:167–73.
———. 1967. Componential analysis. Science 156(3779):1203–9.
Gorer, Geoffrey. 1935. Africa dances. London: Faber and Faber.
Grant, Earl E. 1987. Folk religion in Islam: Its historical emergence and missiological significance. Ph.D. dissertation. Pasadena, CA: Fuller Theological Seminary.
Gravrand, Henri. 1961. Visage africain de l'Eglise: une expérience au Sénégal. Paris: Editions de l'Orante.
———. 1983. La Civilisation Sereer: Cosaan (les origines). Dakar: Les Nouvelles Editions Africaines.
———. 1990. La Civilisation Sereer: Pangool, le génie religieux Sereer. Dakar: Les Nouvelles Editions Africaines du Sénégal.
Greenberg, Joseph H. 1946. The influence of Islam on a Sudanese religion. Seattle: University of Washington Press.

———. 1970. The languages of Africa. 3rd ed. Bloomington: Indiana University Press.
Grimes, Barbara F., ed. 1988. Ethnologue: Languages of the World. 11th ed. Dallas: Summer Institute of Linguistics.
Guillaume, Alfred. 1956. Islam. 2nd ed. Middlesex: Penguin Books.
Guiteras-Holmes, Calixta. 1961. Perils of the soul: The world view of a Tzotzil Indian. New York: The Free Press.
Guralnik, David B., editor in chief. 1984. Webster's new world dictionary of the American language. New York: Simon and Schuster.
Gutherie, Donald. 1981. New Testament theology. Downers Grove, IL: Inter-Varsity Press.
Hall, Edward T. 1973. The silent language. Garden City, NY: Anchor Books.
———. 1976. Beyond culture. Garden City, NY: Doubleday.
Hamer, John H. 1973. Sidamo generational class cycles: A political gerontocracy. In Elliot P. Skinner (ed.), Peoples and cultures of Africa, 335–61. Garden City, NY: American Museum of Natural History.
Harris, Marvin. 1979. Cultural materialism: The struggle for a science of culture. New York: Vintage Books.
Hiebert, Paul G. 1982. The flaw of the excluded middle. Missiology 1:35–47.
———. 1985. The concept of culture and world view. In Anthropological insights for missionaries, 30–48. Grand Rapids, MI: Baker.
Hitti, Philip K. 1970. Islam: A way of life. South Bend: Gateway.
Hodges, H. A. 1968. Dilthey, Wilhelm. In David L. Sills (ed.), International encyclopedia of the social sciences, vol. 4, 185–87. New York: Macmillan.
Hodgson, Marshall. 1974. The venture of Islam. 3 vol. Chicago: University of Chicago Press.
Honigmann, John J. 1959. The world of man. New York: Harper and Row.
Horton, Robin. 1971. African conversion. Africa 41(2):84–108.
———. 1975a. On the rationality of conversion. Part I. Africa 45(3):219–35.
———. 1975b. On the rationality of conversion. Part II. Africa 45(4):373–99.
Houtsma, M. Th., et al. 1987. E. J. Brill's first encyclopaedia of Islam 1913–1936. 6 vol. Leiden: E. J. Brill.
Hughes, Thomas P. 1895. A dictionary of Islam. London: W. H. Allen (reprinted by Wm. C. Brown, Dubuque, IA).
IBS (International Bible Society). 1978. The Holy Bible, New International Version. Grand Rapids, MI: Zondervan.
Idowu, E. Bolaji. 1973. African traditional religion: A definition. London: SCM Press.

IGN 1977. Atlas National du Sénégal. Dakar: Institut Géographique Nationale.
Irvine, Judith T. 1973. Caste and communication in a Wolof village. Ph.D. dissertation, University of Pennsylvania.
Jahn, Janheinz. 1961. Muntu—an outline of African culture. New York: Grove Press.
Johnstone, Patrick. 1986. Operation world. 4th ed. Bromley, Kent: STL Books.
Jomier, Jacques. 1989. How to understand Islam. New York: Crossroad.
Joseph, Suad. 1978. Muslim-Christian conflict in Lebanon: A perspective on the evolution of sectarianism. In S. Joseph and B. Pillsbury (eds.), Muslim-Christian conflicts: Economic, political, and social origins, 63–97. Boulder, CO: Westview Press.
Kane, Mohamadou. 1981. Essai sur les contes d'Amadou Coumba. Abidjan: Les Nouvelles Editions Africaines.
Kane, Oumar. 1978. 'Intervention' after Woronoff. In Afrique noire et monde méditerranéen dans l'antiquité, Colloque de Dakar: 19–24 janvier 1976, 259–61. Dakar and Abidjan: Nouvelles Editions Africaines.
Kearney, Michael. 1972. The winds of Ixtepeji: World view and society in a Zapotec town. New York: Holt, Rinehart and Winston.
———. 1975. World view theory and study. In Bernard J. Siegel, et al., (eds.), Annual review of anthropology, 247–70. Palo Alto: Annual Reviews, Inc.
———. 1984. World view. Novato, CA: Chandler and Sharp.
Kesteloot, Lilyan. 1987. Anthologie négro-africaine. Alleur (Belgium): Editions Marabout.
———. 1988. Négritude et situation coloniale. Paris: Editions Silex.
——— and Cherif Mbodj. 1983. Contes et mythes Wolof. Dakar: Les Nouvelles Editions Africaines.
———, Christian Barbey, and Siré Mamedou Ndongo. 1985. Tyamaba, Mythe Peul, et ses rapports avec le rite, l'histoire et la géographie. Notes Africaines (Dakar) 185–86:1–72.
Khadduri, Majid and Herbert J. Liebesny, eds. 1955. Law in the Middle East. 2 vol. Washington: Middle East Institute.
Kirtley, Michael and Aubine Kirtley. 1985. Senegambia—A new and future nation. National Geographic Magazine 8:224–51.
Klein, Martin A. 1968. Islam and imperialism in Senegal: Sine-Saloum, 1847–1914. Stanford: Stanford University Press.

———. 1972. The Mourides. Review of The Mourides of Senegal by D. Cruise O'Brien. Journal of African History 13(1):157–58.

Kluckhohn, Clyde. 1944. Mirror for man: A survey of human behavior and social attitudes. Greenwich, CT: Fawcett Publications.

———. 1947. Covert culture and administrative problems. American Anthropologist 45:213–29.

——— and William H. Kelly. 1945. The concept of culture. In Ralph Linton (ed.), The science of man in the world crisis, 78–106. New York: Columbia University Press.

Kroeber, Alfred. 1948. Anthropology. Rev. ed. New York: Harcourt, Brace.

Kuhn, Thomas S. 1970. The structure of scientific revolutions. 2nd ed. Chicago: University of Chicago Press.

Lake, René. 1985. Il n'y avait pas que des musulmans au Magal de Touba. Le Soleil (Dakar), November 27.

Lambeck, Michael. 1990. Certain knowledge, contestable authority: Power and practice on the Islamic periphery. American Ethnologist 17(1):23–40.

Laye, Camara. 1954. The African child. Trans. by James Kirkup. Isle of Man, UK: Fontana/Collins.

Leary, Francis Anne. 1970. Islam, politics and colonialism: A political history of Islam in the Casamance region of Senegal, 1850–1914. Ph.D. dissertation, Northwestern University.

Lee, Dorothy. 1959. The conception of the self among the Wintu Indians. In Freedom and Culture, 131–40. Englewood Cliffs, NJ: Prentice-Hall, Inc.

LeRoy, E. 1982. Mythes, violences et pouvoirs. Le Sénégal dans la traite négrière. Politique Africaine (Paris) 2(7):52–72.

Le Soleil (Dakar). 1986. La Fièvre du Magal, October 22.

Lett, James. 1987. The human enterprise: A critical introduction to anthropological theory. Boulder, CO: Westview Press.

LeVine, Robert A. 1970. Personality and change. In John N. Paden and Edward W. Soja (eds.), The African experience. Vol. I: Essays, 276–303. Evanston: Northwestern University Press.

Lewis, B., et al. 1971. The encylopaedia of Islam. Vol. III. New ed. Leiden: E. J. Brill.

Lewis, I. M., ed. 1980. Islam in tropical Africa. 2nd ed. Bloomington, IN.: Indiana University Press.

Linares, Olga F. 1986. Islamic 'conversion' reconsidered. Cambridge Anthropology 11(1):4–19.
Lings, Martin. 1971. A Sufi saint of the twentieth century. London: Allen and Unwin.
Linton, Ralph. 1936. The study of man. New York: Appleton-Century-Crofts.
Lippman, Thomas W. 1982. Understanding Islam: An introduction to the Moslem world. New York: New American Library.
Loeffler, Reinhold. 1988. Islam in practice: Religious beliefs in a Persian village. Albany: State University of New York Press.
Magassouba, Moriba. 1985. L'islam au Sénégal: Demain les mollahs? Paris: Editions Karthala.
Malinowski, Bronislaw. 1961 [1922]. Argonauts of the western Pacific. New York: E. P. Dutton.
Maloney, Clarence, ed. 1976a. Don't say "pretty baby" lest you zap it with your eye—The evil eye in India. In Clarence Maloney (ed.), The evil eye, 102–48. New York: Columbia University Press.
———. 1976b. Introduction. In Clarence Maloney (ed.), The evil eye, v-xvi. New York: Columbia University Press.
———. 1976c. The evil eye. New York: Columbia University Press.
Maranz, David E. 1989. Des Interdits au Sénégal, recueillis à Dakar par Oumar Diallo. ms.
Mark, Peter. 1985. A cultural, economic, and religious history of the Basse Casamance since 1500. Stuttgart: Franz Steiner Verlag.
Marone, Ibrahima. 1970. Le tidjamisme au Sénégal. Bulletin de l'IFAN, sér. B 32(1):136–215.
Mbacké, Falilou. 1964. Le Xutba de Sërin Falilou, 2ème Xalif, le Magal à Touba. Transcription by Boubacar Fall. ms.
Mbacké, Serigne B. 1981. Les bienfaits de l'Eternal ou la biographie de Cheikh Amadou Bamba Mbacké. Part 2. Trans. from the Arabic by K. Mbacké. Bulletin de l'IFAN, sér. B vol. 43(1–2):47–108.
Mbiti, John S. 1969a. African religions and philosophy. Nairobi: Heinemann Kenya Ltd.
———. 1969b. Concepts of God in Africa. New York: Praeger.
McCarthy, Richard J. 1953. The theology of al-Ash'ari. Beirut: Imprimerie Catholique.
McKechnie, Jean L., gen. ed. 1975. Webster's new twentieth-century dictionary of the English language. Unabridged 2nd ed. Cleveland: Collins-World.

Mendelson, E. Michael. 1956. Religion and world-view in Santiago Atitlan. Ph.D. dissertation, University of Chicago.

———. 1968. World view. In David L. Sills (ed.), International encyclopedia of the social sciences, vol. 16, 576–79. New York: Macmillan.

Mercier, Paul. 1965. Evolution of Senegalese elites. In P. L. Van Den Berghe (ed.), Africa: Social problems of change and conflict, 163–78. San Francisco: Chandler.

——— and G. Balandier. 1952. Les Pêcheurs lebou du Sénégal. St.-Louis, Sénégal: Centre IFAN-Sénégal.

Mollien, G. 1820. Travels in the interior of Africa to the sources of the Senegal and Gambia . . . in the Year 1818. Ed., Bowdich.

Monteil, Vincent. 1966a. Une confrérie musulmane: les Mourides du Sénégal. In V. Monteil, Esquisses Sénégalais, 159–202. Dakar: Institut Fondamental de l'Afrique Noir.

———. 1966b. Esquisses Sénégalaises. Initiations et Etudes Africaines 21. Dakar: Institut Fondamental d'Afrique Noir.

———. 1980. L'Islam noir: une religion à la conquête de l'Afrique. 3rd ed. Paris: Editions du Seuil.

Moreau, René Luc. 1982. Africains musulmans: des communautés en mouvement. Paris and Abidjan: Inadès Edition and Présence Africaine.

Murdock, George P. 1959. Senegambians. In Africa: Its peoples and their culture history, 265–70. New York: McGraw-Hill.

———, et al. 1987. Outline of cultural materials. 5th rev. ed. New Haven: Human Relations Area Files.

Musk, Bill A. 1984. Popular Islam: An investigation into the phenomenology and ethnotheological bases of popular Islamic belief and practice. Ph.D. dissertation, University of South Africa.

———. 1989. The unseen face of Islam. Eastbourne, E. Sussex: MARC, Monarch Publications.

Nadel, Siegfried F. 1954. Nupe religion. London: Routledge and Kegan Paul.

Nasr, Seyyed Hossein. 1975. Ideals and realities of Islam. 2nd ed. London: George Allen and Unwin.

Ndaw, Alassane. 1983. La Pensée Africaine. Dakar: Les Nouvelles Editions Africaines.

Ndiaye, Mademba. 1990. Nous Sommes 7 Millions. Le Soleil (Dakar), July 13.

Ndiaye, Mbaye. 1990. Interview. Dakar, July 22.

New Encyclopedia Britannica. 1977. Senegal. Vol. 16:531–40. Chicago: Encyclopaedia Britannica.
Newbigin, J. E. Lesslie. 1966. Honest religion for secular man. London: SCM Press.
Niane, Djibril T. 1978. Introduction. Démb ak Tey (Dakar) 4–5:1–2.
Niang, Mody. 1984. Les "dëmms" au Sénégal. Famille et Développement (Dakar) 38:53–4.
Niasse, S. L. 1986. Etat-marabouts: Chaudes retrouvailles. Wal Fadjri (Dakar) 64:6–7.
Nicolas, Guy. 1980. Islam et Etat au Sénégal. Pouvoirs (Paris) 12:141–47.
Nida, Eugene A. 1975. Componential analysis of meaning. The Hague: Mouton.
Nolan, Riall W. 1986. Bassari migrations: The quiet revolution. Boulder: Westview Press.
Nyang, Sulayman S. 1984. Islam, Christianity, and African identity. Brattleboro, VT: Amana Books.
O'Brien. see Cruise O'Brien
Okoumba-Nkoghe. 1984. Le châtiment. Famille et Développement (Dakar) 38:56–9.
Ong, Walter J. 1969. World as view and world as event. American Anthropologist 71(4):634–47.
Opler, Morris E. 1945. Themes as dynamic forces in culture. American Journal of Sociology 51(3):198–206.
———. 1959. Component, assemblage, and theme in cultural integration and differentiation. American Anthropologist 61(6):955–64.
———. 1968. The themal approach to cultural anthropology and its applications to north Indian data. Southwestern Journal of Anthropology 24:215–27.
Ortigues, Marie-Celile and Edmund Ortigues. 1984. Oedipe africaine. 3rd ed. Paris: Editions l'Harmattan.
Ousmane, Sembène. 1960. God's bits of wood. Trans. by Francis Price. London: Heinemann Educational Books.
———. 1973. Xala. Paris: Présence Africaine.
Parrinder, E. Geoffrey. 1954. African traditional religion. London: Hutchinson's University Library.
———. 1976. Africa's three religions. 2nd ed. London: Sheldon Press.
Parsons, Talcott and Edward A. Shils, eds. 1951. Toward a general theory of action. New York: Harper and Row.

Paton, Alan. 1948. Cry, the beloved country. New York: Charles Scribner's Sons.
Peel, J. D. Y. 1968. Aladura: A religious movement among the Yoruba. London: Oxford University Press for International African Institute.
Pélissier, Paul. 1966. Les Paysans du Sénégal: les civilisations agraires du Cayor à la Casamance. Saint-Yrieix: Imprimerie Fabrèque.
Pike, Kenneth L. 1967. Language in relation to a unified theory of the structures of human behavior. 2nd ed. The Hague: Mouton.
Pollet, Eric and Grace Winter. 1971. La Société Soninké (Dyahunu, Mali). Brussels: Editions de l'Université de Bruxelles.
Quinn, Charlotte A. 1972. Mandingo kingdoms of the Senegambia: Traditionalism, Islam, and European expansion. Evanston: Northwestern University Press.
Radin, Paul. 1957 [1927]. Primitive man as philosopher. New York: Dover Publications.
Rahman, Fazlur. 1979. Islam. 2nd ed. Chicago: University of Chicago Press.
Ranger, Terence. 1983. The invention of tradition in colonial Africa. In Eric Hobsbawm and T. Ranger (eds.), The invention of tradition, 211–62. Cambridge: Cambridge University Press.
Ray, Benjamin C. 1976. African religions: Symbol, ritual, and community. Englewood Cliffs, NJ: Prentice-Hall.
Redfield, Margaret P., ed. 1962 [1952]. Human nature and the study of society: The papers of Robert Redfield. Vol. I. Chicago: University of Chicago Press.
Redfield, Robert. 1941. The folk culture of Yucatan. Chicago: University of Chicago Press.
———. 1952a. Letter to Mendelson. Reprinted in Margaret P. Redfield (ed.), Human nature and the study of society: The papers of Robert Redfield. Vol. I, 105–07. Chicago: University of Chicago Press.
———. 1952b. The primitive world view. Proceedings of the American Philosophical Society 96:30–36. Reprinted in Margaret P. Redfield (ed.), Human nature and the study of society: The papers of Robert Redfield. Vol. I, 98–105. Chicago: University of Chicago Press.
———. 1953. Primitive world view and civilization. In The primitive world and its transformations, 84–110. Ithaca, NY: Cornell University Press.
———. 1969. The little community and peasant society and culture. Chicago: University of Chicago Press.
Reminick, Ronald A. 1985. The evil eye belief among the Amhara of Ethiopia. In Arthur C. Lehmann and James E. Myers (eds.), Magic,

witchcraft, and religion: An anthropological study of the supernatural, 175–83. Palo Alto: Mayfield.

Reverdy, Jean-Claude. 1967. Une Société rurale au Sénégal: les structures foncières familiales et villageoises des Serer. Aix-en-Provence: Centre Africaine des Sciences Humaines Appliquées.

Rey, A. and J. Rey-Debove, gen. eds. 1988. Le Petit Robert 1 Dictionnaire. Paris: Le Robert.

Rickman, H. P. 1979. Wilhelm Dilthey: Pioneer of the human studies. Berkeley: University of California Press.

———, ed. and translator. 1976. W. Dilthey selected writings. Cambridge: Cambridge University Press.

Rogers, Everett M. 1983. Diffusion of innovations. 3rd ed. New York: Free Press.

Rokeach, Milton. 1979. Change and stability in American value systems, 1968–1971. In Milton Rokeach (ed.), Understanding human values, individual and societal, 129–47. New York: Free Press.

Ruthven, Malise. 1984. Islam in the world. Harmondsworth, Middlesex: Penguin Books.

Saglio, Christian. 1980. Senegal. Paris: Editions du Seuil.

Samb, Amar. 1969. Touba et son 'Magal'. Bulletin de l'Institut Fondamental de l'Afrique Noir (Dakar), sér. B 31(3):733–53.

———. 1972. Essai sur la contribution de Sénégal à la littérature d'expression arabe. Dakar: Institut Fondamental d'Afrique Noir.

Samb, El-Hadji Assane M. 1981. 'Cadior Demb': Essai sur l'histoire du Cayor. 3rd ed. Dakar: Edition GIA.

Sangree, Walter H. 1965. The Bantu Tiriki of western Kenya. In James L. Gibbs, Jr. (ed.), Peoples of Africa, 43–79. New York: Holt, Rinehart and Winston.

Sanneh, Lamin. 1979. The Jakhanke: The history of an Islamic clerical people of the Senegambia. London: International African Institute.

———. 1983. Christianity, Islam and African traditional religions. In West African Christianity, 210–41. Maryknoll, NY: Orbis Books.

Sapir, Edward. 1968 [1924]. The unconscious patterning of behavior in society. In David G. Mandelbaum (ed.), Selected writings of Edward Sapir in language, culture and personality, 544–59. Berkeley: University of California Press.

Sarr, El Hadji Malik. 1980. Les Lébous Parlent d'eux-mêmes. Dakar: Les Nouvelles Editions Africaines.

Scarcia, Biancamaria. 1981. Le Monde de l'Islam. Paris: Editions Sociales.

Schaffer, Matt and Christine Cooper. 1980. Mandinko: The ethnography of a West African holy land. New York: Holt, Rinehart and Winston.

Sène, Papa Massène. 1978. Xooy et fonction sociale du Saltigui. Démb ak Tey, Cahiers du mythe (Dakar) 4–5:3–6.

Senghor, Léopold Sédar. 1964. Liberté I: Négritude et Humanisme. Paris: Editions du Seuil.

Shenk, David W. 1981. The (Sufi) mystical orders in popular Islam. ms.

―――. 1983. The Tariqa: A meeting place for Christians and Muslims. Bulletin on Islam and Christian-Muslim Relations in Africa 1(3):1–31.

Simmons, William S. 1971. Eyes of the night: Witchcraft among a Senegalese people. Boston: Little, Brown.

Sissouma, Seydou. 1990. Pactée diplomatique à la Mauritanie. Le Soleil (Dakar), July 12.

Spradley, James P. 1972. Editor's Note to Ethnoscience and ethnomethodology, by George Psathas. In James P. Spradley (ed.), Culture and cognition, 206. New York: Chandler Publishing Co.

Stanton, H. U. Weitbrecht. 1969. The teaching of the Qur'an. New York: Biblo and Tannen.

Stenning, Derrick J. 1959. Savannah nomads. Oxford: Oxford University Press.

Stewart, Edward C. 1972. American cultural values. Chicago: Intercultural Press.

Strong, James. 1984. A concise dictionary of the words in the Hebrew Bible. In New Strong's exhaustive concordance of the Bible, 1–127. Nashville: Thomas Nelson.

Sturtevant, William C. 1974. Studies in ethnoscience. In Ben G. Blount (ed.), Language, culture and society, 153–76. Cambridge, MA: Winthrop Publishers.

Sy, Cheikh Tidiane. 1969. La Confrérie Sénégalaise des Mourides: un Essai sur l'Islam au Sénégal. Paris: Présence Africaine.

―――. 1970. Ahmadou Bamba et l'islamisation des Wolof. Bulletin de l'Institut Fondamental de l'Afrique Noire, sér. B vol. 32(2):412–33.

Sylla, Assane. 1978. La philosophie morale des Wolof. Dakar: Sankore.

Tax, Sol. 1941. World view and social relations in Guatemala. American Anthropologist 43:27–42.

Tedlock, Barbara. 1983. A phenomenological approach to religious change in highland Guatemala. In Carl Kendall, J. Hawkins, L. Bossen (eds.), Heritage of conquest thirty years later, 235–46. Albuquerque: University of New Mexico Press.

Thiam, Chérif. 1987. Fausses illusions et superstitions dérangent. ORTS Magazine (Dakar) 13:3,7.
Thomas, Louis-Vincent. 1959. Les Diola: Essai d'analyse fonctionnelle sur une population de Basse-Casamance. 2 vol. Dakar: Institut Français d'Afrique Noir.
────── and R. Luneau. 1975. La Terre africaine et ses religions. Paris: Editions L'Harmattan.
Titiev, Mischa. 1965. A fresh approach to the problem of magic and religion. In William Lessa and E. Vogt (eds.), Reader in comparative religion, 316–19. 2nd ed. New York: Harper and Row.
Traoré, Abdoulaye M. 1984. La sorcellerie aujourd'hui. Famille et Développement (Dakar) 38:33–59.
Triaud, Jean-Luis. 1988. Khalwa and the career of sainthood: An interpretative essay. In Donal B. Cruise O'Brien and Christian Coulon (eds.), Charisma and brotherhood in African Islam, 53–66. Oxford: Clarendon Press.
Trimingham, J. Spencer. 1959a. The influence of Islam upon social structure. In J. S. Trimingham, Islam in West Africa, 124–53. Oxford: Clarendon Press.
──────. 1959b. Islam in West Africa. Oxford: Clarendon Press.
──────. 1971. The Sufi orders in Islam. Oxford: Clarendon Press.
──────. 1980. The influences of Islam upon Africa. 2nd ed. London: Longman.
Trincaz, Jacqueline. 1981. Colonisation et Religions en Afrique Noire: L'exemple de Ziguinchor. Paris: Editions l'Harmattan.
Turner, Victor W. 1985. Religious specialists. In Arthur C. Lehmann and J. E. Myers (eds.), Magic, witchcraft, and religion, 81–88. Palo Alto: Mayfield.
Tyler, Stephen A., ed. 1969. Introduction. In Cognitive anthropology, 1–23. New York: Holt, Rinehart and Winston.
Vansina, J. 1973. Initiation rituals of the Bushong. In Elliot P. Skinner (ed.), Peoples and cultures of Africa, 304–25. Garden City, NY: American Museum of Natural History.
Voll, John O. 1986. Revivalism and social transformations in Islamic history. The Muslim World 76(3–4):168–80.
Von Grunebaum, Gustav E. 1988. Muhammadan festivals. New York: Olive Branch Press.

Wade, Amadou. 1964. Chronique du Wâlo sénégalais (1186?–1855), translated from the Wolof by Bassirou Cissé. Bulletin de l'IFAN, sér. B 26(3–4):440–98.
Wade, Mamadou. 1986. Régénération de l'Islam: 2ème declaration du veneré Cheikh Soumbounou. Le Politicien (Dakar) 148:2,7.
Wane, Yaya. 1969. Les Toucouleurs du Fouta Toro (Sénégal): Stratification sociale et structure familiale. Dakar: Institut Fondamental d'Afrique Noire.
Watkins, Mark Hanna. 1943. The West Africa 'bush' school. American Journal of Sociology 48:666–75.
Watt, W. Montgomery. 1962. Islamic philosophy and theology. Edinburgh: Edinburgh University Press.
Wauthier, Claude. 1967. The literature and thought of modern Africa. New York: Praeger.
Weber, Max. 1947. The theory of social and economic organization. Oxford: Oxford University Press.
———. 1958. The protestant ethic and the spirit of capitalism. New York: Charles Scribner's Sons.
Weekes, Richard V., ed. 1984. Muslim peoples: A world ethnographic survey. 2 vol. 2nd ed. Westport, CT.: Greenwood Press.
Westermarck, Edward. 1973 [1933]. Pagan survivals in Mohammedan civilisation. Amsterdam: Philo Press.
World Book Encyclopedia. 1986. Senegal. Chicago: World Book.
Woronoff, Michael. 1978. Structures parallèles de l'initiation des jeunes gens en Afrique noire et dans la tradition grecque. In Afrique noire et monde méditerranéen dans l'antiquité, Colloque de Dakar: 19–24 janvier 1976, pp. 237–54. Dakar and Abidjan: Nouvelles Editions Africaines.
Zahan, Dominique. 1970. Religion, spiritualité et pensée africaines. Paris: Payot.
el-Zein, Abdul H. 1974. The sacred meadows: A structural analysis of religious symbolism in an east African town. Evanston: Northwestern University Press.
———. 1977. Beyond ideology and theology: The search for the anthropology of Islam. In Bernard J. Siegel (ed.), Annual review of anthropology. Palo Alto: Annual Reviews.
Zempléni, András. 1966. La dimension thérapeutique du culte des Rab, Ndop, Touru et Samp, rites de possession chez les Lebous et les Wolof. Psychopathologie Africaine (Dakar) 2(3):295–439.

———. 1968. L'interpretation et la thérapie traditionnelle du désordre mental chez les Wolof et les Lebou (Sénégal). Thèse de Doctorat de 3º cycle, Université de Paris.

———. 1985. Du Dedans au Dehors: transformation de la possession-maladie en possession rituelle. International Journal of Psychology 20(4/5):663–79.

Zwemer, Samuel. 1917. Islam and animism. London: Victoria Institute Transactions.

———. 1920. The influence of animism on Islam: An account of popular superstitions. New York: Macmillan.

———. 1939. Studies in popular Islam: A collection of papers dealing with the superstitions and beliefs of the common people. New York: Macmillan.

Index

A

Abraham 84
abstract 4, 41, 45–46, 53, 90, 94, 101, 197
action 29, 62, 75, 78, 116, 139–40, 161, 174, 217, 223, 231
  prevenient action 156
adherent 24, 29, 68, 195–96, 224
affective 32, 35, 37
African traditional religion (ATR) 3, 30, 63, 65–66, 68, 86–87, 236–37
agricultural 16, 197, 204, 217, 223, 231
alcohol 111
Allah 44, 63, 68, 71, 74, 77, 79, 81, 84, 91–93, 97, 106, 108, 155–57, 161, 169, 180, 187–88, 230, 232, 236
allegiance 47, 65, 69, 71, 75, 78, 157, 196, 201, 212, 214, 223–24, 231
alliance 62, 68, 70, 72–74, 91–92, 100, 106–7, 152, 208, 222

alms 79–81, 160, 198
altar 11, 70, 73, 82, 88, 102, 125, 181, 229
amulet 20, 41–42, 44, 47–48, 57, 67, 69, 92, 116, 163–66, 170, 181, 185, 234
ancestor 14, 43, 61, 63–64, 78–79, 85–86, 100, 106, 122, 184, 197, 200–1, 227, 229–31
anecdotal 26–27
angel 63, 65, 93, 95, 100, 112, 183, 197, 214, 229–30, 232
animal 83–84, 107, 116, 164–66, 173, 177, 185, 202–3, 227, 234
apostasy 111
appearance 130, 132, 209, 214, 230
Arabic 2, 9, 17, 20, 25–27, 42, 63, 79–80, 92, 98, 100, 106, 108, 114, 154, 156–57, 160–61, 164–65, 183, 213–14, 216, 219–21, 230, 232–34
assemblage 51–53, 57
assertion 90, 232
assumptions, basic 2–3, 7–8, 12, 15, 17, 19, 26, 34–38, 40, 49, 51,

54, 59, 86–87, 90–93, 95, 133, 140, 142–43, 145, 148, 163, 168, 176–79, 189, 193–94, 206, 222
existential assumptions 7, 41–44, 59, 93
Islamic assumptions 90
ontological assumptions 41, 43–44, 93
augur 16, 147, 149, 158, 166, 183–84
autopractitioner 189

B

balance 101, 114, 134–35, 137, 152, 159, 163, 188, 223
counterbalance 99, 105
imbalance 17, 48, 140, 148, 209
Bamba, Amadou 71, 91, 96–97, 133, 161, 170–71, 197, 203–4, 206–19, 221–24, 226, 229–33, 235–36
banishment 162
banner 216, 219, 224
baobab 202, 229
baptism 75
baraka
See blessing
barke
See blessing
bath, ritual 85, 151
behavior 7, 12, 37–41, 45–47, 49, 51–54, 56, 59, 61, 91–92, 114, 156–57, 162, 194, 211, 238
being 17, 31, 44–45, 47–48, 54–55, 61–65, 72–74, 76–78, 82, 86, 91–92, 94–95, 99–100, 104–6, 108–9, 113–15, 134–36, 139–41, 143–44, 146, 153–54, 159, 166–

68, 179–80, 182–86, 189, 199, 222–23, 227, 231, 233, 238
belief 1–3, 5–6, 8, 21, 25–31, 35, 41–43, 47–48, 51, 57, 59, 61, 63–65, 67–68, 70, 76, 80, 83, 85, 87–90, 92–93, 105, 111–12, 116, 118, 124, 134, 140, 145, 148, 153, 157, 162, 167–70, 173–78, 188–89, 197–99, 201, 209, 211, 218–20, 222, 228, 231, 233–37
belief system 30, 89, 176, 188, 193
benediction 66, 81, 89, 131, 149, 157, 160–61, 234
Black-African 55, 113, 231–32
blessing 64, 69, 79, 102, 113, 133, 143, 160, 170, 183–84, 204, 212–13
baraka *(barke)* 42, 69, 77, 81, 112, 130–33, 183–84, 197–98, 213, 220, 223
material blessing 66, 77–78, 96, 125–26, 130–31, 134
spiritual blessing 69, 77, 89, 96–97, 116, 125, 131, 134, 223
body 114–18, 120–22, 124, 162
born 76, 78, 118, 132, 150, 200
breach 47, 99, 106, 108, 155
breath 31–32, 114, 173, 233
brotherhood 1, 25, 131–32, 171, 210–11, 217–19

C

cabalistic 69, 107, 165–66
caliph 97, 132, 204, 212–13, 215–17, 235–36

Index

caste 19–21, 96, 113, 124, 130, 170, 208–9
cat
  See evil tongue
causality 50
century 15, 17, 71, 109, 113, 152, 164, 203, 210
chant 78, 81, 85, 102, 122–24, 180, 199, 201–2, 212–14, 216, 221, 235–36
charms 63–64, 164–66
Christian 2, 21, 23, 62, 93, 111, 114, 122, 131, 164, 180, 219, 221
Christianity 29, 93–95, 111, 121–23, 125, 145, 180
circumcision 85, 89, 117, 199–200, 230
clairvoyance 69, 82, 107, 136
clairvoyant 70, 102, 121, 181
Clarke, P. 6, 9, 21–24, 71, 96, 190, 204
classification 7, 32–33, 43, 49–51, 57, 63, 80, 210
closure, fear of 40, 42
co-wife 171
cognition 37, 39, 48, 62, 65, 81, 87, 109, 135–36, 186, 191, 229
cognitive 7, 12, 30, 32–33, 35, 37
colonial 9, 15, 17–18, 20, 22, 24, 64, 142, 154, 190, 205–9, 217–19
commemoration 65, 84–85, 196, 211, 221
comparison 8, 35, 49, 58, 186, 196, 219
competition 22, 130, 143, 171–72, 177
complementary 76
  complementary distribution 179, 189
compliment 61, 175, 177

component 34, 37, 49, 51–53, 57–58, 142, 184, 186, 215, 217
componential 57–58
conceptual system 11, 15, 23, 34, 46, 68, 90, 98, 104, 228
conclusion 14, 53, 93, 147, 173, 222, 236
conquest 18–19, 21–23, 96, 100, 203, 205
conscience 55, 61, 120–21, 137, 222
constructs 8, 43, 46, 49, 54, 210
control 22–24, 27, 40, 51, 86, 114, 117–18, 120–21, 128, 139, 145–48, 152, 156, 159–60, 163, 167–70, 172, 179, 182, 186, 204–5, 212, 216
conversion 145, 229
converted 20, 67, 111, 218
cosmic 37, 48, 55, 65, 70, 82, 94, 99–100, 134–35, 137, 139–40, 144, 163, 179–80, 182–83, 186, 188, 202–3, 222–23, 228, 230
  cosmic node 79, 82
  cosmic order 62, 65, 76, 114, 134–35, 137, 202, 222, 228
  cosmic spectrum 180, 183
cosmology 77
cosmos 36, 42, 153
cowrie 148, 165, 181
cross-cultural 4, 7–8, 34, 43, 45, 76, 121, 168
culture 2–9, 11–17, 19, 26–28, 30–47, 49–59, 65, 70, 75–76, 85, 90, 93, 98, 102, 121–22, 125, 134, 137, 141–43, 153, 157, 164, 168, 178, 186, 188, 191, 193–94, 197–99, 204, 206, 208–9, 211, 217–23, 227, 231, 233–35, 237–38

implicit culture 40
cultus 64, 78–79, 85, 100, 123, 186, 225–27
curse 89, 102, 108, 133, 162–63, 174, 183–84, 192

D

deep-level 7–8, 19, 37, 39–41, 44, 46, 49, 87, 90, 102, 168, 193–94, 237
defense 103, 163, 175, 177–78
deity 43, 65, 68, 115, 136
dependence 24, 48, 112, 142, 205, 217, 219, 225, 229
destiny 76, 94, 115, 139, 146, 148, 156, 162, 184
devil 63, 181, 183, 185
dialog 62, 153
dimension 33, 37, 57, 77, 100, 113, 130, 166, 178, 209–10
disciple 65–66, 71, 75, 77, 81–82, 91, 96–97, 113, 130–32, 157, 161, 169–71, 181, 203–4, 212–14, 223–24, 226, 236
divination 82, 88, 104, 147–48, 150, 173, 183–84, 187, 189
diviner 95, 104, 147–48, 155, 181–82, 185, 188, 190
divinity 63, 69, 72, 82, 86, 88, 100, 156, 184, 200–1, 236
doctor 68, 73–75, 180, 182
domain 7, 45, 55–57, 65, 90, 94, 156, 176, 185, 194
  domain cluster 57
domination 21, 160, 205
double vision 95
drought 16

E

economic 17, 19, 22, 125, 128, 142, 172, 217, 220–21, 223, 235
economy 128, 142
eight-level 3–4, 30, 34–35, 37–38, 49–54, 56, 90, 238
elite 26, 95, 124, 206, 211
emic 36, 55–56, 85, 109, 186, 229, 238
emotion 55–56, 67, 80, 101–3, 115, 118–23, 194, 219, 223, 231
employment 128–29
enemy 96, 100, 139, 143, 154, 160, 163, 178, 208
equilibrium 77, 85, 99, 114, 119, 122, 153, 163, 199, 201–3
esoteric 4, 6, 26, 66, 69, 81–85, 89, 105–8, 113, 136, 139–40, 142–43, 152–53, 155, 163, 165–66, 169–70, 175, 178, 180–81, 188, 190, 201, 207, 214, 223
essential 29, 33, 36, 49, 89, 91, 112, 118, 134, 141, 145, 153, 158, 168, 179, 186, 188, 196, 203, 207, 209, 217, 221, 226, 235–36, 238
ethnic 5–7, 12–15, 19–21, 63–64, 66, 72, 85, 116, 152, 157–58, 160, 173, 189–92, 199, 201, 205, 218, 227–29, 234
ethnic group 6–7, 12–15, 19–21, 63–64, 66, 72, 116, 152, 158, 160, 173, 189–92, 199, 218, 227, 229, 234
  Cangin 4
  Diola 6, 13–14, 42, 63, 102, 108, 160–61, 190, 228
  Fulani 13, 21

Lebou 6, 12–13, 42, 72, 152, 189, 200–1
Palor 4
Saafi 6, 12, 42, 83, 229
Soninké 13
Tukolor 6, 12–13, 20–22
Wolof 4–6, 12–15, 18–22, 30, 41–42, 61–63, 67, 72, 76, 80–82, 87, 89, 95–96, 98–100, 102, 108, 114, 124, 126, 129–31, 136, 157, 160–61, 165–66, 171–75, 187–93, 197, 199, 201–7, 209, 217–18, 227–28, 232–33
ethnoscience 50, 55–58
ethos 35
etic 65, 76, 79, 82, 112, 133, 144, 156, 228
event 51–53, 56
evil 42, 46, 48, 71, 83, 89, 94, 107, 111, 132, 150, 157, 166, 173–74, 176–78, 181, 183–85, 187, 205, 224, 233–34
  evil eye 84, 89, 108, 164, 173, 176, 233–34
  evil mouth 166, 173
  evil tongue *(cat)* 42, 83, 89, 108, 125, 156, 173–74, 176–78, 184, 233–34
  evil touch 89, 173, 233
existential 7, 41–44, 59, 93, 119
explanation 11, 37–38, 41–44, 46, 48, 83, 91–93, 103, 108, 132, 135, 145, 147–48, 152, 154–56, 159, 163, 167–68
explanatory power 12, 47, 51, 187, 222, 237–38
exterior 45, 76–77, 79, 94–95, 97–99, 101–4, 110–12, 117, 122–23, 130, 133, 137

F

fasting 79–80, 82, 148, 154, 156
feast 84, 88, 126–27, 158, 200
fertility 15, 85, 92
folk 7, 11, 28–29, 32, 41–42, 44, 86, 93, 98, 136, 157, 164, 174, 188, 201, 211, 237
  folk explanation 41–42, 44, 93
  folk Islam 2, 237
  folk religion 1, 188
forbidden 74, 88–89
forces 17, 44, 48, 54–55, 61–62, 66, 68, 72–74, 78, 82, 86, 91–92, 94–95, 99–106, 109, 113, 119, 124, 134–36, 139, 141, 143–46, 153–54, 159, 163, 170, 172, 177, 180, 182–87, 189, 199, 201–2, 208, 222–23, 227
  cosmic force 139, 163
Foster, G. 12, 45, 238
France 219
French 5, 13, 19, 22–24, 66, 102, 164, 170, 203–5, 207, 216–17, 219, 223
fundamental 13, 28, 33, 35–36, 43–44, 77, 98–99, 110, 117, 145, 147, 161, 193, 205, 208, 210, 215, 221, 228
fundamentalism 75
future 66, 89, 102, 106, 115, 127, 129, 139, 146, 152, 187–88, 199

G

Gambia, The 9, 14, 16, 18, 126, 203
genealogy 77
generality 41, 46

generalization 41, 44, 46–47, 49, 58, 238
genie
 See jinn
global 7
goal 8, 11–12, 20, 23, 32–33, 46, 49, 57–58, 66, 86, 99, 104, 116–17, 121, 123, 137, 140–41, 147–48, 159, 163, 211, 236–38
God 21, 27, 32, 45, 47–48, 63, 68–69, 71, 75–77, 79, 82, 86, 91, 94–96, 102, 110, 112, 116, 122, 131, 146, 155–57, 160–61, 175, 183, 187, 197–98, 204, 208, 216, 219, 232–33, 236
good 12, 31, 36, 45–46, 63, 65–66, 72, 82, 91, 94, 115–16, 118, 131, 135, 140, 143–44, 148, 152, 158, 161, 163, 177–78, 190, 200, 238
gossip 172, 174
government 4, 15–16, 24–25, 99, 127–28, 130, 141, 158, 170, 175, 209, 220, 223, 227
great tradition 191, 218
Guinea-Bissau 9, 16, 160–61

H

hadith 89, 155, 188
hagiography 97, 161, 235
harmony 45, 47–48, 77, 79, 94, 99, 101, 109, 112–13, 116, 137, 139, 144, 148, 153, 209
heal, healer 6, 12, 42, 66, 72–74, 83–84, 92, 97, 102, 107, 114, 116, 118, 147, 167, 169, 178, 181–82
herb 23, 70, 181

hidden world 82, 95, 97–98, 146, 155
Hiebert, P. 37, 186
hierarchy 48, 51, 53, 65, 68–69, 75–76, 113, 125, 154, 161, 196, 226
historical 9, 14, 19–20, 22, 25, 29, 65, 74, 90, 114, 136, 153, 175, 188, 206, 211, 219, 231
history 3, 17, 19–20, 22, 25, 27, 71, 142, 164, 188, 198–99, 202, 206, 219, 228–29
holistic 28, 33–36
holy war
 See jihad
holy work 149, 157
Horton, R. 145, 167
hospitality 62, 127, 218, 225
human 28, 30–33, 37, 39, 48, 56, 59, 61–65, 73–74, 76–77, 81–83, 86, 94, 97, 99–101, 103–4, 109, 113–16, 118–19, 121, 129, 134–37, 139, 141–43, 148, 152–53, 159, 161–62, 167, 174, 176, 178, 182–83, 185, 187, 190, 197, 200, 202–3, 223, 227, 233–34
hypothesis 3, 193–94, 236, 238

I

idealism 31
identity 3, 15, 64, 87, 136–37, 173, 192, 205, 219, 230–31
idol 81–82, 111, 124, 227
illness 16, 43, 72–73, 92, 98, 108, 118, 147, 159, 177, 182, 192, 194, 225
image 12, 35, 45, 105, 123
implantation 3, 20, 67, 90, 217, 230

Index

implicit 40, 47–48, 59, 86, 123, 141, 143, 159, 179, 191, 223, 232, 236–37
imposition 171
impotence 108, 142
impotency 192
impurity 48, 85, 210
incense 11, 107, 122–23, 154–55
inductive 42–43, 45, 47, 57–58, 238
initiate 15, 48, 62, 67, 69, 71–72, 78, 81–82, 91–92, 95, 103, 105, 108–9, 119, 124, 148, 188, 200, 204, 223, 225
initiation 77, 85, 103, 105, 109, 116–17, 119–20, 124, 135, 180, 199–200, 209, 226, 230
insult 78, 131
integration 45, 51, 94, 101, 137, 200, 203, 209, 230
intent 11, 13, 46, 89, 94, 157, 234, 237
intercession 75, 77, 149, 157, 198, 220, 230
interdependence 45, 77, 94, 191
interior 44–45, 76–77, 80, 94, 97–99, 101–6, 110–13, 116–17, 122–24, 130–31, 133, 137, 141, 146–47, 153, 156, 168, 181, 192, 207, 213, 222
  interior vision 48, 95, 101–2, 105–6, 124, 146–47, 153, 156, 181
  interior world 102, 168, 222
intermediary 66–71, 73–77, 86, 91, 100, 106, 124, 135, 146–47, 154, 156–57, 169, 180
internal 103, 111–12, 117–18, 144, 178
interpretation 36, 147, 157, 167, 209, 218

invisible 45–48, 78, 94, 115, 124, 143, 146, 162, 183–85
Islam 1, 3, 11, 13, 17–18, 20–30, 63–72, 74–75, 78–90, 92–93, 95, 98, 100, 106, 108, 110–13, 118, 121, 124, 145, 148, 153–54, 159–63, 165, 169, 176, 178–81, 183–91, 195–99, 201, 203–6, 208–11, 215, 218–21, 225–27, 229, 232–33, 235–37
  mystical Islam 105
  orthodox Islam 1, 3, 65, 74–75, 80, 90, 93, 122, 161, 186, 188, 199, 211, 230, 236–37
  popular Islam 26, 68, 80, 86–87, 90, 93, 169, 178
  Sufi Islam 1, 3, 24, 66, 69, 78–80, 84, 122, 179, 183, 195, 197, 211, 220, 230, 236
Islamic 2–3, 6, 9, 11, 20–21, 23–30, 63–67, 69–70, 74–77, 80, 83–84, 87–90, 93, 97–98, 100, 105–6, 111, 113, 118, 145, 153–60, 163, 165–66, 180–82, 188–91, 195–98, 200–1, 203, 208–9, 214, 216, 219–20, 225–26, 228, 230, 232, 235–38
Islamization 13, 17–18, 20, 22–24, 162, 165, 196

J

jihad 6, 18, 20–24, 96, 100, 203, 206
jinn 63–64, 82, 88, 97, 100, 107–8, 112, 152, 155, 166, 181, 183–85, 197
judgment 31, 47, 68, 90, 140, 143, 216
justice 21, 134, 137, 198, 226

K

Kearney, M. 12, 30, 33–37, 43, 49–50
king 17, 22, 72, 97, 204–5
kingdom 18, 20, 22, 64, 96, 201–5, 208
knowledge 5–6, 37, 56, 58, 70, 75, 88, 92, 95, 97–98, 101–5, 117, 135–36, 139, 141, 146, 154–55, 161, 180, 186, 205, 210, 232, 236

L

law 20–21, 25, 45, 48, 62, 68–69, 75–77, 80, 95, 99, 109–11, 118, 129, 134, 137, 180, 197, 216, 223, 229, 233
Layenne
 See Sufi order
layman 69, 74, 101
Lee, D. 34
level 42–43, 45, 55, 65–66, 68–70, 76, 89–94, 99–101, 113, 127, 135, 139, 141, 145, 159–60, 163, 169, 172, 177, 185–86, 188, 190, 195, 203, 205, 216, 223, 226
 See also deep-level, eight-level, surface-level
linear 7, 50
litany 16, 81, 106, 155–56

M

Maba 18, 23, 203
Magal 91, 194, 198, 210–11, 214–16, 218–27, 230–33, 235–36, 238
magic 65–66, 70, 82–84, 86, 88–89, 107–8, 111–12, 141, 143, 149, 151, 154, 159–60, 164, 166, 170–71, 177, 181–84, 187–90, 201, 214, 233–35
 black magic 65, 70, 83, 88–89, 108, 112, 141, 159–60, 171, 181, 183
 magic potion 82, 88, 107, 170
 personal magic 84, 151
magical 23, 27, 41, 43–44, 159, 162, 164, 169, 171, 174–75, 201, 233–35
magnet 112, 121, 133, 144
malediction 131, 149, 160, 162, 184
Mali 20, 165
man 15, 31, 40, 42–43, 45, 48, 54–56, 61–62, 65, 67–68, 71–72, 75–77, 84, 87, 94, 99, 101–3, 105–6, 110, 112, 114, 122, 124, 127, 131, 133, 134–36, 144–45, 147, 169, 172, 188, 193, 199–200, 211, 218, 223, 227, 229–32, 236
man-nature 15, 228
marabout 20, 23–24, 42, 44, 64–73, 75, 81, 84, 91, 95, 102, 108, 130, 157, 160–62, 165, 169–70, 172, 175, 180–81, 183, 203–4, 206, 208, 212–14, 217, 231
mastery 103–5, 117, 120, 179, 182
matrix 210–11, 215, 220, 222
Mauretania 16, 170, 204, 207
Mecca 80, 219–20, 223
medicine 40, 70, 86, 154, 169, 184, 225
medium 101, 182, 185, 188–90
metaphysical focus 179–80, 183, 186, 189

Index

metatheme
  See theme
middle zone 186–87, 189
milieu 20, 59
mineral 165, 185, 202–3
miracle 76, 88, 97, 109, 113, 119, 122, 149–50, 160–61, 183–84, 221
misfortune 108, 139, 141, 146, 154, 162–63, 173–78, 183–84, 233–34
model 3, 12, 33–34, 37, 43, 50, 52, 97, 133, 238
  eight-level model 3–4, 30, 34–35, 37, 49–54, 56, 90, 238
modern 19, 32, 58, 75, 97, 111, 114, 118, 137, 148, 157, 164, 209
moral 23, 51, 54, 61, 65, 69, 106, 110–12, 115, 121, 131–32, 141, 194, 199, 201, 204–5, 207, 218, 222, 230
mosque 24, 64, 69, 82, 158–59, 180, 201, 212–14, 216, 219, 229–30, 234
mother 77–78, 131, 172, 202–3
Muhammad 69, 75, 79, 81, 84, 92, 96, 108, 131, 157, 214, 230
  Prophet 65, 96–97, 157, 180, 196, 219
Muslim 1–4, 11–14, 20–30, 42, 45, 47, 63–69, 74–75, 80, 85, 87, 90, 92, 100, 107–9, 111–13, 118, 131, 154–59, 161–65, 169, 175, 180–81, 183, 187–92, 195–96, 201, 203–5, 207–8, 216, 218–19, 223, 226, 230, 232, 236–38
mystical 80–82, 92, 95, 100, 102–3, 105, 107, 110, 121, 140, 143, 148, 155, 161–62, 169, 188, 213, 221
mysticism 1, 25, 95, 110

N

naming 85
nationalistic 211
naturalistic 37, 54
nature 15, 19, 31–32, 34–35, 40, 43, 47–48, 50–51, 53–55, 67, 101, 106, 110, 112, 114, 127–28, 130, 134, 137, 141, 144, 152, 188, 194, 199, 218, 226–31, 237
Navajo 42
network 15, 20–21, 91, 208, 226–27
neutral 2, 70, 116, 175, 181–82
Niger-Congo 12–13
normative 35, 37

O

occult 66, 88–89, 143
offering 71, 79–81, 83–84, 88, 91, 107, 152, 157, 186, 208, 223, 225
  Islamic offering 83
ontological absolute 7–8, 41, 44–47, 49–50, 58, 90, 93, 95, 259–60
Opler, M. 12, 51–52
oratory 81, 97, 174, 235
order
  See Sufi
organizing principle 12, 37, 49, 51, 56–57, 61, 70, 168, 237
orthodox 3, 25, 29, 65–66, 68–69, 74–75, 80–81, 90, 93, 107, 112, 155, 161, 163–64, 180, 186, 188–89, 191, 195, 198–99, 211, 223, 230, 236–37
  orthodox Islam, *see* Islam
  orthodox practice 1, 112

ostentation 174
other-decreasing 154, 159

P

pagan 11, 18, 74, 111, 181, 183, 191
pain 83, 117, 202
paradigm 34, 238
paradise 71, 79–80, 89, 93, 115, 160–61, 188, 218–19
parallel 3, 44, 67, 80, 83, 114, 153, 162, 165, 179, 236
pardon 88, 156
pattern 7, 12, 14, 32, 39–40, 42, 47, 49, 55, 59, 98, 128, 148, 196–97, 229, 231
peace 4, 16, 30, 47–48, 54–55, 61–62, 68, 70, 73, 76, 78, 85, 91–92, 94, 99–105, 109–10, 113, 118, 122–23, 125, 129, 132, 134–35, 137, 139–44, 160, 166, 178, 187–88, 204, 207, 222, 225–26, 237–38
   personal peace 55, 61, 109, 113, 119–20, 122–24, 142, 144, 178, 222
   social peace 55, 61, 99–100, 222
   transcendent peace 4, 30, 48, 55, 61, 68, 70, 91–92, 99, 104, 129, 134–35, 137, 139–40, 144, 178, 188, 222, 237–38
peaceful 20–21, 83, 137
peasant 12, 33, 36, 45, 49, 228
pedigree 77
peer 109, 171–72
personality 69, 96, 114, 133, 203
phenomena 2, 7, 19, 26, 33, 35, 37, 40–41, 43, 78, 86–87, 93, 98, 135, 148, 167, 178, 187, 194, 215
philosophy 61, 148, 188
pilgrimage 4, 30, 79–80, 82, 90–91, 97, 131–32, 161, 193, 195–98, 201, 210–12, 214, 220, 223, 226, 231, 238
poem 71, 81, 96, 136, 213–14, 235–36
poison 70, 83, 178
polarization 121
pole of attraction 133
political 13, 15, 17–19, 21–25, 51, 170, 195, 205, 207–9, 216–18, 220, 223, 228, 235
popular 26, 68, 80, 86–87, 90, 93, 169, 178–79, 198, 207, 210, 220
pork 111
potion 82, 88, 92, 107, 151, 170, 201
power 12, 22, 24–25, 27, 42, 44–45, 47–48, 51, 55, 62, 64, 66, 73–77, 82, 86, 92, 94–95, 97–98, 101–2, 105–8, 112, 114, 117, 135–37, 139–41, 143–44, 146, 148, 152–53, 155–56, 158–59, 161–62, 164–66, 168–76, 182, 184, 186–92, 204–9, 211, 213–14, 218, 222–24, 229, 233–35, 237–38
   esoteric power 4, 83, 85, 139, 143, 152–53, 163, 165, 180, 207
   hypnotic power 171, 184
   spiritual power 42, 89, 133, 140, 154, 165, 191, 207, 222
practice 6, 11, 19–22, 25–27, 29–30, 47, 63–65, 67–70, 72–74, 76, 78, 80–82, 86–89, 91–93, 96, 99, 102, 104–5, 108–12, 140, 147–

48, 153, 155, 159–60, 165, 169, 173, 176–82, 186–91, 206, 214, 219, 222, 226–27, 230–32, 237
practitioner 23, 26, 41, 58, 66, 70, 73–74, 87, 107, 147, 154, 169, 175, 179–83, 186, 188–92, 226
praxis 26, 79, 141, 211, 222, 237
prayer 64, 69, 75, 79–81, 83, 88, 102, 105–7, 111–12, 116, 119, 146, 149–50, 155–58, 160, 180, 186, 201, 207–8, 212, 236
pre-Islamic 29, 63, 65, 74, 89, 111, 163, 165, 190, 195, 200
precondition 155–56
prediction 135, 145–46, 167
prescription 47–48, 99, 135, 139, 145–48, 152–54, 156, 159, 163
presumption 17
priest 179–80, 182, 188–89, 207–9
primitive 27–28, 32, 189, 207
principle 12, 31, 37–38, 40, 44, 46–47, 49–51, 53–57, 61, 70, 76, 81, 83, 89, 94, 102, 115–16, 128, 139, 141, 146, 161, 168–69, 176–77, 194, 209, 216, 218, 233, 237
problem 5, 7, 11, 15, 17, 19, 47, 53, 68, 72–74, 82, 111, 115, 117, 142, 147, 168, 176–77, 182, 192, 222, 227
prohibition 111
prominence 130, 133–34
prophet 69, 75, 91, 95–96, 152, 180, 182, 188–89, 230, 232, 236
See also Muhammad, Prophet
proposition 7–8, 37, 44, 46, 51, 53–54, 57, 73, 87, 90–93, 144–45, 155, 193–94, 221, 227
prosperity 70, 79, 86, 91, 97, 131–32, 139, 167, 185

protection 41–42, 47, 70, 82–83, 113, 139, 156, 160, 163–64, 166, 178, 201, 212, 223–24, 229, 234
proverb 61, 76, 95–96, 99, 102, 129, 131, 133, 136, 171–72, 174, 187
purpose 3, 13, 16–17, 24–25, 27, 29–30, 36, 41–42, 46, 57, 67–68, 71, 79, 82, 86–87, 92, 94, 107, 110, 134, 136, 140–41, 144–45, 154–56, 159, 163, 165–66, 191, 198, 201–2, 237

Q

Qadri 24, 69, 180, 204
quest 4, 140, 144, 178
Qur'an 25, 27, 42, 44, 48, 63, 68–69, 75, 90, 92, 159, 169–70, 174, 186–87, 201, 204, 208, 232, 234–36
Qur'anic 66, 69, 86, 92, 149, 159, 162, 164, 166, 183, 235

R

radiance 76, 99, 101, 105
reality 7, 15, 19, 28, 31–32, 43, 45, 47–48, 53, 94–95, 98, 103–5, 109, 119, 124, 153, 155, 167, 179, 187, 189, 193, 237
reciprocal 61
recitation 27, 69, 92, 198, 234, 236
Redfield, R. 12, 32–33, 191
reincarnation 64, 115–16, 119
relational system 56
relationship 2, 7, 15, 31, 33, 43, 45, 49–51, 53–54, 57, 61, 65, 67, 73,

77, 80, 93–94, 99–100, 106, 110–11, 116–17, 119, 142, 144, 157, 168, 179, 190–92, 198–99, 205, 208, 218, 222, 225–28, 236, 238
religion 1–3, 11, 23, 27, 29–30, 43, 46, 48, 63–68, 70, 72, 74, 78–81, 86–87, 89–90, 93, 98, 106, 111, 114, 122, 124–25, 145, 148–49, 153–54, 156, 159–61, 163, 167, 178–80, 186, 188, 196, 198–99, 202, 206, 211, 215–17, 220–21, 223, 225, 232–33, 236–37
religious 2–3, 6–7, 11, 14, 18–19, 21–22, 25–26, 30–31, 64, 66, 78, 84, 86–88, 92–93, 96, 100, 102, 105–6, 109, 121–24, 126, 134, 148, 153–56, 167, 169, 178–82, 187, 190–92, 195–99, 201, 203, 207–8, 211, 214–18, 220–22, 224, 233, 235–36
  religious change 225
  religious practitioner 41, 179–80, 191, 226
  religious purpose 82
  religious system 2–3, 68, 77, 84, 86–87, 145, 169, 178–79, 186, 207, 236
replicability 8, 58
research 1, 4–6, 8, 12, 14, 29, 53, 58, 115, 142, 147, 173, 190, 234
retreat 65, 88, 105, 107–8, 148, 155, 229, 233
revelation 47–48, 66, 95–98, 109, 119, 135, 148, 153–55, 223, 230, 232
risk 106, 109, 129, 158–59
rite 23, 72, 82, 84–85, 89, 105–9, 120, 147, 150–51, 153–56, 179–82, 195–96, 199–202, 206, 221, 226, 230–31
ritual 11, 27, 48, 67, 69, 78–80, 83–85, 87–88, 90, 93, 106, 110, 112, 122, 124, 139, 151, 154–56, 158–59, 165, 167, 173, 175, 178–80, 182, 186, 188–92, 198, 200–1, 205, 207, 211–12, 220–21, 235, 238
rural 4–5, 15, 24, 67, 112, 137, 190, 204, 209, 228, 231

S

sacred forest 185, 199–200
sacred grove 230
sacrifice 62, 73, 78–79, 84–85, 107, 122, 143, 147, 201, 205, 225
  animal sacrifice 84
  blood sacrifice 73–74, 84, 89, 226
Sahara 67, 198
saint 11, 65, 70, 75–77, 79, 81, 91–92, 96–97, 100, 108, 111, 131–33, 157, 161, 180–81, 183, 195–98, 210–14, 216, 220–21, 224, 230, 235–36
Satan 63, 72, 224
scope 8, 31, 34, 53–54, 74, 142, 165, 168, 189, 211, 238
self 32–34, 36, 43, 50–51, 76, 88, 110, 113, 115–18, 130, 136–37, 140, 148–54, 158–60, 162, 164, 168–69, 182, 204, 228, 231–33
Senegal 4–7, 9, 13–14, 16, 18–24, 30, 62, 64, 71, 74, 96, 108, 115, 118, 120, 127–28, 130–31, 136, 148, 152, 158–60, 162, 165, 169–73, 175, 186, 190, 192–93,

Index

201–4, 207–10, 212, 215, 217–21, 223, 225, 228–30, 232–34
Senegal River 21, 96, 203
Senegambia 9, 11–12, 15, 17–20, 22, 46, 65–66, 72, 82, 95, 99–100, 106, 114, 116, 121, 123, 140–41, 143, 156, 173, 191, 195–99, 227, 233–34, 237
Senegambian 3–9, 11–22, 29–32, 36, 41–49, 54–55, 57, 59, 61, 63, 65, 67–68, 70–71, 74–76, 80, 84, 87, 89–94, 96–104, 106, 108, 111–15, 117–18, 120–22, 124–29, 131, 133–34, 139–40, 142–45, 147–48, 152, 157, 159, 161, 163, 165, 167–68, 170–71, 174, 178–79, 186, 193, 196–97, 201–3, 205–7, 209–10, 218, 221–22, 225–29, 231–38
sentiment 32, 119–23, 177
shadow 63–65, 162
shaman 70, 85, 162, 179–80, 182, 185, 188, 190, 201
slave 17–19, 21–22, 25, 61, 72, 100, 142, 204–5, 208, 232
slavery 75, 170
social supremacy 125, 129
solidarity 197, 221
sorcerer 118
sorcery 108, 118, 168
soul 61, 64–65, 71, 84, 99, 104, 109–10, 113–25, 128, 136, 157–58, 167, 175, 181, 185, 187, 197–98, 223
  soul attachment 110, 119, 124, 223
  soul awakening 109, 119, 124, 223
  soul memory 109, 119–23, 223

soul restoration 109, 119, 122–24, 223
space 32–33, 43, 50–51, 54, 73, 120, 123, 145, 167–68, 199
speech 25, 98, 103, 114, 117, 136, 216, 218, 232–33, 235–36
spell 83, 108, 170–71, 212
spirit 43, 47–48, 55, 61, 63–66, 70, 77, 79, 81–86, 88, 91, 94, 99–100, 102, 106–7, 114, 122, 124, 129, 137, 147, 149–50, 154, 159, 161–62, 167, 171, 181, 183–85, 188, 199–201, 222–25, 229–30
  ancestral spirit 72–73, 82
  malefic spirit 83–84
  protecting 82, 166, 229
  protector spirit 63, 88, 149–50, 162, 201
  rab 63–72, 82, 84, 88, 185
  spirit possession 70, 72, 85, 147
spiritual 42–43, 46–47, 61, 64–65, 67, 69, 71–75, 77, 81, 84–85, 89, 94–96, 103, 107, 109, 112–14, 119–20, 124–25, 129–34, 139–40, 143, 147, 154, 156, 162, 165, 167–68, 180, 191–92, 197–98, 201, 207–8, 213, 215, 222–24, 227
status 31, 115, 133, 135, 142, 170, 208, 224
structure 2, 18, 31, 43, 51, 58–59, 65, 86, 101, 168, 197, 213, 228
submission 65, 71, 78, 80–81, 141, 161
submit 45, 71, 75, 135, 157, 219, 228
subtheme
  See theme
success 20, 55, 73, 92, 96, 98–99, 116, 125, 132, 139–41, 143–44,

146–48, 159–60, 170, 187, 201, 203, 207–9, 212–13, 217, 222–24, 231, 233, 236
Sufi 1–3, 6, 24, 45, 65–67, 69, 71, 75, 78–82, 84, 95, 102, 108–9, 111–13, 121, 124, 131–32, 152, 161, 179–80, 183, 195, 197–98, 207, 210–11, 213, 220, 230, 236
See also Islam, Sufi
Sufi order 6, 24, 66–67, 69, 71, 81–82, 102, 111, 124, 152, 180, 195, 197, 207
  Layenne 24, 152
  Mouride 24, 65, 69, 71–72, 82, 91, 96, 102, 157, 170, 197, 207–11, 214–19, 221–26, 228, 230–33, 235–36
  Qadri 24, 69, 180, 204
  Tijani 6, 24, 69, 82, 102, 156, 171, 180, 196, 201, 203, 224
Sufism 71, 82, 198, 210, 220
Sunna 92
superior 51, 54, 62, 65, 76, 99, 102–5, 107, 134–37, 172, 180, 205–7, 232
supernatural 17, 28, 43, 48, 54–55, 62–64, 81–82, 86, 88, 105, 122–24, 135, 139, 144, 148, 153, 162, 167–70, 172, 176, 179, 182–86, 188, 199, 222–23
supramundane 66, 82, 85, 100, 103, 106, 115
surface 11, 31, 37, 39–42, 91–93, 96, 98, 159, 167, 203, 237
  surface-level 91–92, 159
suzerainty 62, 64–65, 135
symbiosis 55, 191, 227, 229
symbol 26, 52, 59, 77, 87, 101, 110, 119, 121–25, 136, 154, 165–67, 173, 208, 210–11, 215, 220–21, 223, 227, 230, 236
symbolic 4, 26, 110, 122–23, 135, 160, 198, 200, 210, 214, 238
syncretism 87, 199
syncretistic 11, 26, 189, 209
synthesis 53, 67, 125, 198

T

taboos 112, 261–62
Takrur 20
talisman 23, 69, 82, 88, 150–51, 154, 163–66, 181, 185, 214, 224, 235
tension 4, 9, 16, 22, 117, 129, 143, 171, 219, 223
thematic range 36–37, 43, 54, 238
theme 3–4, 7–8, 12, 30, 36–38, 40, 44, 49–55, 61–62, 67, 76–78, 82, 90–93, 95, 99–101, 109–10, 113, 125, 134, 145, 159, 163, 177–78, 194, 203, 222, 225–27, 230–31, 233, 237–38, 249–56
  metatheme 4, 44, 49–50, 53–58, 90, 93, 113, 139–41, 144, 155, 174, 193–94, 222–23, 230–31, 238, 249–56
  subtheme 53–54, 76, 82, 90, 104–106, 113, 119, 124, 155, 222, 249–56
theology 122, 188, 208, 211
theory 28, 33, 53, 230
thesis 3, 19, 53, 93, 109, 125, 193–94, 198, 211, 216, 221, 238
thinker 6, 43
Tijani
  See Sufi order

Index

tithe 71, 228
tolerance 61, 101, 154
tomb 91, 132, 161, 195, 198, 212–14, 230
tongue 42, 76, 83, 89, 108, 125, 156, 173–78, 184, 233–34
totem 63, 82, 85, 151, 185–86, 202, 229
Touba 4, 30, 82, 90–91, 97, 131, 170, 193, 195, 198, 210–14, 217–19, 224–25, 229–30, 238
traditional 2–3, 6, 13–14, 18, 22, 25, 29–30, 63–68, 70, 72–74, 77, 82, 85–87, 89, 100–2, 110, 113, 117, 118, 124, 136–37, 145, 148, 151, 153–56, 158–61, 163, 165–67, 169, 176, 178, 181, 190, 192, 196–97, 199–202, 204–9, 218, 225–31, 234–37
traditionalist 23, 63, 67, 118, 237
transcendent 45, 47–48, 99, 101, 105, 110, 121–23, 137, 140–41, 144, 153–54, 163, 222
  transcendent peace 4, 30, 48, 55, 61, 68, 70, 91–92, 99–100, 104, 125, 129, 134–35, 137, 139–40, 144, 178, 188, 222, 237–38
transempirical 17, 43, 50, 55, 62, 65, 68, 76, 85, 95, 99, 109, 119, 123–24, 134, 139, 141, 144, 148, 172, 182–85, 223
transempirical beings 44, 54, 61, 64, 72–74, 76, 78, 99, 104, 106, 109, 114, 135, 144, 146, 159, 199, 223, 227
transfer 46, 48, 83, 89, 94, 104, 150, 160, 176–77, 185, 198, 209, 233–34

Trimingham, J. S. 2, 11, 66–67, 106, 113, 195–98, 206, 225–27
Tukolor
  See ethnic group
typology 31

U

universal 11, 26–27, 32–34, 43–44, 49–50, 63, 74, 77, 84–85, 91–92, 95, 152, 158, 164, 171–72, 196, 218, 220–21, 227, 229, 232
universe 12, 31, 35–36, 43, 45–46, 50, 70, 77–78, 86, 94, 99, 110, 135, 137, 180, 184, 186, 194, 198, 202, 223
upper zone 183, 185–86, 188–89
urban 5, 15–16, 85, 100, 112, 118, 128–29, 137, 172, 176, 197, 209, 216–17, 223, 227, 231
uttered word 55, 174, 176, 233–35

V

validity 8, 29, 168, 179
value 5, 8, 26, 32, 34–35, 45, 61, 92, 94, 101–3, 112, 117–18, 123–24, 126, 128–29, 131, 134, 137, 140–43, 164, 167–68, 171, 173, 177, 198, 204, 206, 208, 213, 216, 226–27, 230, 234
variable 7, 37, 50, 210
vehicle 71, 164, 175, 177, 182, 210, 224
veneration 64, 75, 78–79, 81, 86, 124, 135, 157, 198, 201, 220, 226

visible 3, 39, 45–48, 66, 82, 93, 95, 97, 103, 109, 112, 119, 123–24, 131, 153, 175, 227
  visible world 78, 94–95, 97, 115, 124, 146, 183–85
vision 21, 31–32, 46, 48, 84, 95, 101–2, 105–6, 114, 124, 146–47, 153, 155–56, 160, 181, 183, 187, 191, 214–15, 223, 230, 234, 237
vital force 43, 104, 110
vital principle 115

W

well-being 91, 99, 106, 110, 131–32, 135, 141–43, 145, 189
Weltanschuung 30
Western 7, 15, 17, 25, 31, 34, 74, 102–3, 105, 113, 125, 148, 158, 180, 221, 225
wird 79, 81, 102, 106–7, 155
witchcraft 125
Wolof
  See ethnic group
world 26–27, 47, 55, 61–63, 66, 72, 78, 82, 84, 89, 104–5, 109, 115, 117, 119–20, 122, 124, 126, 135, 139–47, 154–55, 159, 170, 172–73, 176, 180, 183–88, 212–13, 216, 218, 230, 233, 235–36
world view 2–4, 7–8, 11–12, 15, 17, 19–20, 22, 30–40, 42–43, 45–46, 49–52, 54, 59, 67, 70, 75–76, 80, 86–87, 90–96, 102, 110, 129, 131, 134, 140, 142, 144, 157, 161, 168, 177–79, 188, 193–96, 198, 202–3, 206, 209, 221–22, 227–28, 231, 237–38, 257–58

X

xalwa 81–82, 84, 88, 105–9, 148, 153, 155, 185

Y

yoke 65

Z

zone 183, 185–89

Publications of the
International Museum of Cultures

1. **Sarayacu Quichua Pottery** by Patricia Kelley and Carolyn Orr, 1976. (Also available in Spanish as *Cerámica Quichua de Sarayacu*.) — $ 3.00
2. **A Look at Latin American Lifestyles** by Marvin Mayers, 1976. — $ 8.00
3. **Cognitive Studies of Southern Mesoamerica** by Helen Neuenswander and Dean Arnold, eds., 1977. (Also available in Spanish as *Estudios Cognitivos del sur de Mesoamérica*.) — $10.95
4. **The Drama of Life: Guambiano Life Cycle Customs** by Judith Branks and Juan Bautista Sánchez, 1978. — $ 5.00
5. **The Usarufas and Their Music** by Vida Chenoweth, 1979. — $14.95
6. **Notes from Indochina: on Ethnic Minority Cultures** by Marilyn Gregerson and Dorothy Thomas, eds., 1980. — $ 9.45
7. **The Dení of Western Brazil: A Study of Sociopolitical Organization and Community Development** by Gordon Koop and Sherwood G. Lingenfelter, 1980. (Also available in Portuguese as *Os Dení Do Brasil Ocidental—Um Estudo de Organização Sócio-política e Desenvolvimento Comunitário*.) — $ 6.00
8. **A Look at Filipino Lifestyles** by Marvin Mayers, 1980. — $ 8.45
9. **Nuevo Destino: The Life Story of a Shipibo Bilingual Educator** by Lucille Eakin, 1980. — $ 2.95
10. **A Mixtec Lime Oven** by Kenneth L. Pike, 1980. — $ 1.50
11. **Proto Otomanguean Kinship** by William R. Merrifield, 1981. — $12.00
12. **People of the Ucayali: The Shipibo and Conibo of Peru** by Lucille Eakin, Erwin Lauriault, and Harry Boonstra, 1986. — $ 9.00
13. **Sticks and Straw: Comparative House Forms in Southern Sudan and Northern Kenya** by Jonathan E. Arensen, 1983. — $12.00
14. **Grafting Old Rootstock** by Philip A. Noss, ed. 1982. — $10.95
15. **A View from the Islands: The Samal of Tawi-Tawi** by Karen J. Allison, 1984. — $ 6.90
16. **Yagua Mythology: Epic Tendencies in a New World Mythology** by Paul Powlison, 1985. — $12.00
17. **Gods, Heroes, Kinsmen: Ethnographic Studies from Irian Jaya, Indonesia** by William R. Merrifield, Marilyn Gregerson, and Daniel C. Ajamiseba, eds. 1983. — $15.00
18. **South American Kinship: Eight Kinship Systems from Brazil and Colombia** by William R. Merrifield, ed. 1985. — $12.00
19. **Five Amazonian Studies on World View and Cultural Change** by William R. Merrifield, ed. 1985. — $11.00
20. **The Formal Content of Ethnography** by Philip K. Bóck, 1986. — $ 9.50
21. **Tales from Indochina** by Marilyn Gregerson, Dorothy Thomas, Doris Blood, and Carol Zylstra, eds. 1987 — $11.00

22. **Current Concerns of Anthropologists and Missionaries** by Karl Franklin, ed. 1987 — $14.00
23. **Nucleation in Papua New Guinea Cultures** by Marvin K. Mayers and Daniel D. Rath, eds. 1988. — $22.00
24. **Development Program Planning: A Process Approach** by David Spaeth, 1991. — $12.50
25. **El Arte Cofan en Tejido de Hamacas. The Cofan Art of Hammock Weaving** by M.B. Borman, 1992. — $ 2.00
26. **Language Choice in Rural Development** by Clinton D.W. Robinson, 1992. — $ 5.00
27. **Mice are Men: Language and Society among the Murle of Sudan** by Jonathan E. Arensen, 1992. — $27.00
28. **Peace is Everything** by David E. Maranz, 1993. — $32.00
30. **Rituals and Relationships in the Valley of the Sun: The Ketengban of Irian Jaya** by Andrew Sims and Anne Sims, 1992. — $12.00

These titles are available at:

International Museum of Cultures
7500 W. Camp Wisdom Road
Dallas, TX 75236